Teacher Education

Teacher Education
The Key To Effective School Reform

Delbert Long and Rodney Riegle

Bergin & Garvey
Westport, Connecticut • London

Library of Congress Cataloging-in-Publication Data

Long, Delbert
    Teacher education : the key to effective school reform / Delbert Long and Rodney Riegle.
       p. cm.
    Includes bibliographical references and index.
    ISBN 0–89789–729–3 (alk. paper)
    1. Teachers—Training of—United States   I. Riegle, Rodney P.   II. Title.
    LB1715.L59   2002
    370'.71'173—dc21   2001035636

British Library Cataloguing in Publication Data is available.

Library of Congress Catalog Card Number: 2001035636
ISBN: 0–89789–729–3

First published in 2002

Bergin & Garvey, 88 Post Road West, Westport, CT 06881
An imprint of Greenwood Publishing Group, Inc.
www.greenwood.com

Printed in the United States of America

The paper used in this book complies with the
Permanent Paper Standard issued by the National
Information Standards Organization (Z39.48–1984).

10 9 8 7 6 5 4 3 2 1

Copyright Acknowledgments

The authors and publisher gratefully acknowledge permission to use excerpts from the following material:

Albert Shanker, "Where We Stand: Improving Our Schools," *New York Times*, May 17, 1992. Copyright © American Federation of Teachers (AFT).

Delbert H. Long, "Arthur Bestor on Education of Teachers," *The Educational Forum* (Summer, 1984), vol. 48, no. 4. Copyright © 1984 by Kappa Delta Pi, International Honor Society in Education.

Delbert H. Long and Roberta A. Long, *Education of Teachers in Russia* (Westport, Conn.: Greenwood Press, 1999), pp. 169–175, 176–204. Copyright © 1999 by Long.

To Our Wives

Roberta Long
and
Patricia Van West

Contents

Prologue: Thinking with Perspective

I have yet to see any problem, however complicated, which, when you looked at it in the right way, did not become still more complicated.

Poul Anderson

HISTORICAL BACKGROUND

As Americans welcomed the twentieth century, they could rightfully boast, and being Americans many did, that no country in history had ever educated so many of its citizens for such a long period of time as did the United States. To cope with the avalanche of students flooding into public schools, educators developed an organizational model for schools that resembled, in cost effectiveness and efficiency, Henry Ford's assembly line production of Model T and Model A automobiles. Schools became graded, based on age, and in time had three levels: elementary school—grades one through six; junior high—grades seven through nine; and high school—grades ten through twelve. A prescribed amount of time was devoted to the study of each subject in the curriculum. Students proceeded in lock-step fashion from one grade to the next, with the same precision and inflexibility as a Model T Ford being put together on an assembly line.

Teachers had much in common with assembly line workers. They were not expected to be highly educated or creative. They were expected to accept and carry out without question the rules, regulations, and curriculum guidelines laid down for them by school administrators, school board members and other policy makers, and a host of curriculum and teacher education experts. The teaching method typically utilized in the higher grades was lecture, and the objective was to give children the information and skills they needed to become productive workers on the farm and in the sprawling new industries in urban areas.

Intellectual and social demands on schools in the early years of the century were not very demanding—simply give children basic reading, writing, and arithmetic skills and a disposition to work hard and conscientiously. Furthermore, at the elementary school level, it was widely believed that practically anybody with a high school education and acquaintance with a few "tricks" of the teaching trade could teach. High school teachers, it was believed, needed more knowledge of the subjects they were going to teach but could learn how to teach them, for the most part, on the job.

Urbanization, industrialization, and new international responsibilities thrust upon Americans during and after the First World War, however, did demand more highly educated citizens than thought necessary during the nineteenth century, and this in turn required better educated and better trained teachers. The American response to raising teacher education standards was gradually to eliminate specialized teacher training institutions and to require prospective elementary and secondary teachers to be prepared together in colleges and universities that did not specialize in pedagogy. Hence, during the first five or six decades of the twentieth century, we see a transformation of teacher training institutions from normal schools (devoted initially to training elementary school teachers) to teacher colleges and then finally to universities and colleges.

By 1920, most state universities had a department of education staffed by professors of education. Professors in the arts and sciences had little respect for this new breed of professor. There were several reasons for this. People hired for education positions in colleges and universities were often graduates of normal schools and teacher colleges, not of universities. Many were not scholars but practitioners, such as school superintendents. Many lacked a solid background in a recognized academic discipline. In their classes, they sought to give secondary school teachers the same kind of insight into child development as that of elementary teachers. They insisted that all teachers should have some knowledge of how to teach and of the foundations of education: the history, philosophy, sociology, and psychology of education. Then, and still today, many professors in the arts and sciences denied that pedagogy is a legitimate field of study at the university level. They insisted that requiring prospective high school teachers to take work offered by education professors, whom they considered poorly educated, was a waste of time.

In spite of the coolness, and sometimes hostility, between professors of education and their colleagues in the arts and sciences, departments of education continued to proliferate and expand in number of faculty, students, and curricular offerings. Whatever shortcomings the new professors of education may have had, it cannot be denied that it was they—not the arts and sciences professors who ignored problems of public school and teacher education—who led the battle to raise both the professional and the general education requirements for teachers. They had considerable success in this effort.

In 1870, most teachers had only a few years of elementary schooling. In 1900, not one state required high school graduation and professional training for certification of teachers. By 1925, both were required by twenty-one states. In 1950, only twenty-one states required elementary teachers to have a college degree, and six states did not require a degree for secondary teachers. Today, all elementary and secondary school teachers in public schools are required to have a bachelor's degree, and a number of states require a master's degree for teacher certification.

The move toward preparing teachers in colleges and universities explains in part the Lynds' observation in their classic sociological study of the 1920s that Middletown teachers had, in comparison with the previous generation of teachers, more formal book training and less work with school children.[1] Instructors in normal schools and the early teacher colleges were practically oriented and concentrated on preparing their students for work in public schools and provided them with practical experiences working with children in schools.

In contrast, education professors in departments, schools, and colleges of education in universities—as well as many professors in teacher colleges trying to become universities—sought status and prestige by emulating their colleagues in the arts and sciences—that is, by concentrating their energies and talents not on the preparation of public school teachers but on the production of scholarly research, most of which had little to do with schools or teacher training. As it turned out, this concentration did not gain the respect of their non-education colleagues, and it alienated public school teachers who rightly assumed that many of their education professors had little interest in their preparation or in the public school problems they would have to contend with. For example, even in their research, education professors were concerned more with investigating problems related to students and their learning rather than with teachers and their teaching effectiveness. Prospective teachers, understandably, wanted their professors to train them to become effective teachers in real classrooms with real students.

CURRENT STATE

For some years now, all teachers in America, elementary and secondary, have been trained in institutions of higher learning. These may be public or private, but the great majority of American teachers are prepared in large state universities. In compliance with state certification requirements for teachers, institutions of higher learning require teacher candidates to have a general education and to acquire a professional education that includes an area of specialization. While the number and kind of course requirements vary considerably from one university to another, most universities require teachers to devote roughly an equal amount of time to general and professional education.

General education consists of course work in mathematics; the humanities; the social, natural, and physical sciences; and, occasionally, foreign languages. In the professional education component, students in elementary and secondary curricula take courses in the foundations of education and in the techniques and methods of teaching. Both foundation and meth-

odology courses are often combined with a series of field experiences involving work with children in public schools and sometimes private
schools. The area of specialization for secondary teachers consists of ten to
fifteen courses in the academic discipline in which they plan to teach. The
area of specialization for elementary teachers consists of taking one or more
courses relevant to each of the subject areas typically taught in an elementary school: reading, language arts, mathematics, social studies, science,
music, art, and physical education.

As a rule, prospective teachers conclude their professional work with a
two- to four-month supervised teaching experience in a public school. In
the past decade or so, however, a number of teacher training institutions
have increased the length of their teacher preparation program from four to
five years, with the fifth year frequently stressing a year-long internship in
a public school formally affiliated with the university or college. At the
same time, there are also now a number of "alternative" teacher education
programs that typically reduce the length of training and the amount of
professional education requirements necessary for an entry-level teaching
license. There are a few alternative programs that do away entirely with the
involvement of colleges and universities in the pre-service training of prospective teachers.

In the traditional teacher education programs, the general education
courses for elementary and secondary teachers, as well as the area of specialization courses for secondary teachers, are taught by professors in the
arts and sciences. All other courses required for teachers are generally
taught by professors of education.

Most of the continuing education for public school teachers is provided
by the same colleges and universities that prepare undergraduate students
to become teachers. A large percentage of public school teachers, both elementary and secondary, either have received or are currently working on a
master's degree. Local school districts provide various kinds of in-service
workshops and seminars for teachers, but this work is typically organized
with little input from teachers and does not concentrate on helping teachers
to improve student learning. The good news, however, is that in the past
decade there is a growing recognition on the part of federal, state, and local
educational policy makers on the close link between lifelong professional
development and student learning. Furthermore, leaders of the National
Education Association (NEA) and the American Federation of Teachers
(AFT) and a small but increasing number of school districts now advocate
professional development programs that enable teachers to work together
on a continuing basis to enhance student learning. We discuss this significant development in chapter 12.

The new demands on schools during the nineteenth century—promotion of equality of opportunity, morality, democracy, the free enterprise system, to name but a few—remain in force today but many more have been

added. In some states, schools are expected to enhance their students' religious beliefs by teaching "scientific creationism" as an alternative theory to Darwin's evolutionary theory. In all states, schools have been expected to promote racial integration, primarily by busing. Schools are expected to teach young people how to drive carefully. Schools must provide scientific facts that presumably will encourage students to avoid liquor, cigarettes, drugs, and an imprudent sexual life. Schools are expected to discipline children of parental neglect and to teach in regular classrooms children who are handicapped physically or mentally. Schools are expected to serve a custodial function by keeping all young people in school until the age of eighteen, even though many have no desire to be there.

It seems that whatever societal problem exists, most Americans immediately look to the schools to solve it. This unrealistic view of the school has contributed to the present lack of clarity about what schools should do and has complicated the process of preparing teachers.

At present, the chief characteristic of American teacher education is precisely the same one as for American public school education in general, and that is its extreme diversity and decentralization. In the United States, education of every kind and at all levels is primarily a function not of the federal government but of the fifty states and of the over five thousand local school districts. Because of this decentralization and unequal educational funding patterns, it is possible to find every possible kind of school in every state ranging from the very best to the very worst school imaginable. And the same thing can be said about American colleges and universities and teacher education programs.

In most states, it is not the teaching profession but rather the state legislature that controls licensing of teachers and approval of teacher training programs in colleges and universities. In well-established professions, such as law, medicine, architecture, and engineering, it is the profession that determines training programs for prospective members and licensing of those who successfully complete the program and pass the national professional examinations. By and large, legislators, however, tell "schools of education who they can teach, what they can teach, how they can teach, and even, how long they can teach it,"[2] and they generally make most of the decisions about licensing of teachers.

Furthermore, while there is a national body that accredits teacher education institutions, the National Council for Accreditation of Teacher Education (NCATE), only three states in 1991 required NCATE accreditation in order for their teacher training institutions to stay in business, and that number crept forward only to five by the end of the decade (all Maryland education schools are required by the state legislature to be NCATE accredited by 2004). An additional fourteen states, however, use NCATE standards to evaluate their education schools.[3] NCATE, in spite of its considerable efforts and successes over the years in raising standards for teachers, is not always supported even by professional educators. For example, the National Board for Professional Teaching Standards (NBPTS)—founded in 1987 to establish a system of voluntary advanced certification on a national basis for outstanding teachers—has thus far refused to require candidates seeking their certification to have graduated from an NCATE accredited teacher education program (only 500 of the more than 1,300 teacher training institutions are accredited by NCATE). Furthermore, the American Association of Colleges of Teacher Education (AACTE) voted in 1995 *against* a resolution requiring institutions to be approved by NCATE by 2001 in order to be a full member of the association. Many educators believe these actions by NBPTS and AACTE are detrimental to the drive to make teaching a legitimate profession.

The diversity of American schools and teacher preparation programs is so great that it is difficult to generalize about either. One thing, however, can be said with confidence: Most schools beyond the primary level and teacher training institutions—in spite of great social, economic, and technological transformations—have changed remarkably little in the past fifty or more years.

In a 1988 study of "good" secondary schools preparing most of their students for college, Linda McNeil observed that teachers delivered lectures in which they did practically all the talking and questioning. History lessons "consisted mostly of teachers' writing lists on the board for students to copy and memorize." What appeared to be a press to get through basic facts in order "to lay the groundwork for deeper study was not preparation for study—it was the study itself."[4] McNeil could have observed secondary schools fifty or more years earlier and made similar observations.

The teacher education program in most universities and colleges is essentially the one described by James Conant in his study of American teacher education in 1963,[5] and that program was essentially the same as that provided by colleges and universities in the 1930s, except that then the overall education was probably better than now, since professors, unlike now, took teaching seriously. As Robert Nisbet observed in a chapter he contributed to a book on great university teachers:

At Berkeley in the early 1930s . . . undergraduate teaching was taken seriously. No matter how illustrious one might be as a scholar or scientist, the reputation for giving a good course, above all for being a stimulating lecturer, meant a good deal to the faculty and therefore to the students. The time hadn't yet come at Berkeley—or any other university in this country, so far as I know—when teaching below the graduate level would be regarded as demeaning, would be stigmatized by faculty efforts to escape it, and when freshmen and sophomores would be consigned to the ministrations of the immature or incompetent.[6]

Teachers, of course, teach as they are taught, and many of the professors observed by teacher trainees in undergraduate school are not professors of education but professors of the arts and sciences.

In the 1980s, a number of reports were published that focused national attention on the need for reform of schools. By far the most prominent of these reports was *A Nation at Risk,* the 1983 report of the National Commission on Excellence in Education, during the Reagan presidency. This report declared that the American educational system was so bad that had a foreign power thrust it upon its citizens it would have been cause for a declaration of war.[7] This highly controversial report provoked Americans to start thinking seriously about their schools and the teachers in them. In 1986, the Holmes Group and the Carnegie Corporation published reports that focused the nation's attention on training of teachers.[8]

The most widely publicized report on teacher education during the 1990s was *What Matters Most: Teaching for America's Future.* This report was the result of a two-year study by a twenty-six member panel, chaired by North Carolina governor James B. Hunt and financed by the Rockefeller Foundation and the Carnegie Corporation of New York. The report was published in late 1996 and urged policy makers, philanthropic foundations, and educational institutions to work together to ensure that every child has a competent, caring, and qualified teacher by the year 2006. This call to action is an important step in the right direction, since it is based on the assumption, supported by common sense and research studies, that *the most important strategy for achieving the nation's educational goals is to recruit, prepare, and support excellent teachers for every school.* According to the report, "what is required is a great national crusade united behind the proposition that competent teaching is a new student right."[9] Such a crusade is welcome and needed, but it will come about only as more Americans recognize the centrality of teacher training to any effort to improve public schools.

THE IMPORTANCE OF PERSPECTIVE

Public school education was once the pride of the fledgling American democracy that developed into the world's greatest superpower during the twentieth century. By the turn of the twenty-first century, however, public school education had fallen on hard times. Many Americans lost faith in the ability of public schools to provide children with a quality education. In some states, an increasing number of voters supported publicly financed educational vouchers that could be used by parents to send their children not only to public schools of their choice but to private schools as well. In some states, there are public schools being managed by private entrepreneurs.

Americans are quite rightly demanding good public schools. The problem is how to get them. The greatest and most persistent obstacle to good public schools is the historical indifference of the American public to teacher education. Few Americans know much about or have any sustained interest in how the teachers of children and young people are educated. This is unfortunate. Teacher education may be an unglamorous subject, but it is a "burning presence that lurks at the edge of all proposals to improve schools and cannot be ignored."[10]

The basic theme of this book is that the key to improving public schools is to improve the lifelong education of teachers. It will not be an easy job. Teacher education is a complex process that is made even more difficult by long-standing problems. The lament a half-century ago of a prominent teacher educator could still be made today:

The teacher education system of the United States, with the exception of a very few states, is a hodge-podge of programs which are in the main a travesty upon professional education. If our medical education system represented the same degree of chaos and inferiority, good doctors would be few and far between. If our engineering courses were no better, ours would be one of the backward nations, industrially and technologically. We even provide a better-planned and better-financed system of professional education for those who raise pigs than we do for those who teach children.[11]

The purpose of this book is to assist the reader to develop a broad perspective on schooling and preparation of teachers. Such perspective is desirable for all citizens but essential for those who propose educational reforms and for those who must evaluate and act on them. It is essential for two reasons.

First, with perspective, one is more apt to question the assumptions underlying various proposals for educational reform. Such questioning should act as an intellectual safeguard that discourages the hasty implementation of proposals that may be based on questionable assumptions—money and human resources are too scarce to squander on ill-conceived proposals.

Second, perspective also stimulates the imagination. This is critical to developing a concept of what education should be. By starting with an ideal (assuming that it is rational, coherent, and inspirational), it is possible to inject purpose and meaning into the educational process. Without such an ideal, education may not rise above the level of traditional practice. As the philosopher Alfred North Whitehead noted, "The result is stagnation."[12]

We begin the process of creating perspective in part one by summarizing the perspective of nine prominent educational critics on public schools and teacher education: John Dewey, Robert Hutchins, Arthur Bestor, James Conant, Theodore Brameld, Charles Silberman, Ivan Illich, Albert Shanker, and Chester Finn. Collectively, they represent a broad spectrum of educational thought in twentieth-century America. We have chosen these particular critics because they believe in quality teachers and because they tackle—each in a distinctive, provocative way—some of the perennial questions that should be considered in any effort to reform schools and teacher education. In part two, we analyze the present-day status of teacher education and suggest how it might be improved. In part three, we speculate on what the future holds and how that will impact teacher education. Our analysis and suggestions for improvement of teacher education reveal our indebtedness to the intellectual stimulation of our nine critics. Finally, we conclude with an epilogue directed especially toward policy makers.

The twenty-first century promises to be a "high-tech" century. The leading countries will be those that give highest priority to developing the brainpower of all its citizens. Sadly, in recent years, the United States has settled for second-class education of its children and their teachers. Of one thing we can be sure. Significant improvement of American education is a pipe dream without significant improvement of teacher education.

NOTES

1. Robert S. Lynd and Helen Merrell Lynd, *Middletown: A Study in American Culture* (New York: Harcourt, Brace and Co., 1929), pp. 206–207.

2. Lynn Olson, "Reformers Seek to Untangle Web of Rules, Regulations to Improve Quality, Spark Innovation in Teacher Training," *Education Week,* 13 March 1991, p. 31.

3. Ibid., p. 36; Ann Bradley, "NCATE Unveils Standards Based on Performance," *Education Week,* 24 May 2000, pp. 1, 14.

4. Linda McNeil, "Contradictions of Control, pt. 1: Administrators and Teachers," *Phi Delta Kappan* 69 (January 1988): 333–339.

5. James B. Conant, *The Education of American Teachers* (New York: McGraw-Hill, 1970).

6. Robert Nisbet, "Teggart of Berkeley," in *Masters: Portraits of Great Teachers,* ed. Joseph Epstein (New York: BasicBooks, 1981), pp. 69–70.

7. Interestingly, when the United States economy is bad, as in the early 1980s, public schools get the blame. When the economy is booming, such as in the late 1990s, public schools receive no credit. In fact, public schools should neither be blamed nor praised for the status of the economy. As with public health, there are many factors contributing to the status of the economy.

8. *Tomorrow's Teachers: A Report of the Holmes Group* (East Lansing, Mich.: Holmes Group, 1986); *A Nation Prepared: Teachers for the 21st Century* (New York: Carnegie Forum on Education and the Economy, 1986).

9. *What Matters Most: Teaching for America's Future* (New York: National Commission on Teaching & America's Future, 1996), p. 57.

10. Kevin Ryan, ed., *Teacher Education: The Seventy-fourth Yearbook of the National Society for the Study of Education, pt. 2* (Chicago: National Society for the Study of Education, 1975), p. ix.

11. Ralph W. McDonald, "Toward Professional Maturity," in *Journey to Now: 1946–1961* (Washington, D.C.: National Education Association of the United States, 1961), pp. 34–35.

12. Alfred North Whitehead, *The Aims of Education and Other Essays* (New York: Free Press, 1967), p. 29.

I

Past (1900–2000)

1

John Dewey (1859–1952):
The Progressivist

In 1894, John Dewey became chairman of the combined departments of philosophy, psychology, and pedagogy at the University of Chicago. There he pioneered in teaching methods, curricula, and theory and came to be identified as the foremost proponent of student-centered or progressive education. Progressive education was part of a broader social and political reform movement called the Progressive Movement, a movement that flourished in the quarter century before World War I. This was the time of "muckrakers" such as Lincoln Steffens who exposed corruption, waste, crime, and brutality in American life and encouraged citizens to do something about it. Whatever the cause, Progressivists typically looked to the schools as the best instrument for improving society, and Dewey urged schools to accept this new responsibility.

In addition to his work with schools, Dewey was at various times in his long life president of the American Psychological Association, president of the American Philosophical Association, founder and first president of the American Association of University Professors, and one of the original organizers of the American Civil Liberties Union. In addition, Dewey authored over 1,000 published books and articles. He is arguably the most influential educational theorist of the twentieth century and is one of the few Americans who is acknowledged on a world scale.[1]

EDUCATIONAL AIMS AND REFORM

The aim of education, according to Dewey, is to enable individuals to continue their education. In his words, "the object and reward of learning is the continued capacity for growth."[2] Dewey rejected any rigid, universal requirements as antithetical to the very essence of education. Curricular content and organization, as well as teaching techniques and methods, should vary with the interests and capacities of the student and the needs of his/her community. Dewey insisted that education deserves our most profound attention because it is the confluence of the three most powerful motives of human activity—affection, social growth, and scientific inquiry.[3]

Dewey emphasized the role of teachers and teacher training in educational reform. He argued that the important thing, the "controlling thing," in any educational movement is the personality and training of those who are to carry it on. Moreover, he maintained that the training of teachers is the strategic point in the educational campaign. Only from such a "fortress" can the battle be carried on economically and effectively. It is through the improvement of the standards, ideals, and working equipment of the teacher that the cause of education is to be advanced. Thus, the better training of teachers and the providing of a better school life for children are "Siamese twins" of educational reform.[4]

TEACHER EDUCATION

Dewey suggested the need for two different kinds of teacher training institutions. First, there should be some schools whose main task is to train rank and file teachers—schools whose function is to supply the "great army of teachers" with "the weapons of their calling." It should be the province of such schools to give instruction along lines already well established rather than to experiment along new lines. They should, indeed, be receptive to new ideas, but in undertaking the primary preparation of teachers for the classroom, it should not be their main function to generate new ideas or methods.[5]

Parallel to such training schools should be those which direct their energies to the education, not of the rank and file, but of the leaders of educational systems—teachers in normal and training schools, professors of pedagogy, superintendents, and principals of schools in large cities. Such persons, Dewey observed, are not in need of an introduction to the rudiments of their work. They have already served their apprenticeship in practice and learned the rudiments of the theory. Training schools of this type should devote themselves more directly to the work of pedagogical discovery and experimentation. The first kind of training (for the rank and file), Dewey believed, could be accomplished largely in normal schools, but the second kind of training should be the responsibility of the universities and done mainly at the graduate level.[6]

Shortly after assuming his position at the University of Chicago, Dewey commented in a memorandum to William Rainey Harper, the president of the university, that the work done in pedagogy in America was vague, mechanical, and useless. He urged Harper to exploit this situation and place the University of Chicago in the national forefront by expanding the department of pedagogy. The rest of the memo outlines the details of the necessary components of such a department.[7]

First on Dewey's list was an "educational museum," which would include collections of instructional apparatus, books illustrating teaching, architectural plans of schools, and so on. Second was a staff. Dewey suggested starting with two and building up to five or six full-time faculty members. They were to be specialists in various areas with personal knowledge of schools. Their duties would include visiting schools, reporting their observations, giving suggestions to schools, and lecturing in the university on methods of teaching in their respective branches. These kinds of activities would, according to Dewey, give the university a "hold" on the curriculum and teaching methods in the schools and also ensure real and practical teaching in the university. Moreover, advanced students could accompany the faculty on their visits and get a first-hand look at the schools while the university could at the same time improve its recommendations of teachers. The third and final item on Dewey's list was a practice or experimental school, extending ultimately from kindergarten all the way to college.[8]

In an 1897 memo to Harper, Dewey elaborated on the various "lines of work" in a "fully equipped" department of pedagogy. He reduces these to five major categories:

- Educational Physics and Physiology, which concerns the educational plant and the adaptation of the plant to the physical welfare of the students. Plans, drawings, photographs, and other relevant materials, should be collected. Courses such as school decoration aesthetics and the theory of physical exercise and health should be conducted.

- Educational Sociology, which deals with the organization and administration of the educational system, both in relation to other social conditions and institutions and in its own workings. In addition to a study of internal school organization and management, this entails examining systems of education in relation to political, economic, religious, and intellectual conditions of society, including a comparative study of the various European systems.

- Educational Psychology, which includes child study and psychology as applied to instruction. The adaptation of school resources and subject matter to the child, and the question of methods in relation to the learning process should receive attention here.

- General Pedagogy under which Dewey subsumed philosophy of education. This includes theoretical consideration regarding the nature, ends, and aims of educational work and the intellectual organization of curriculum and methods.

- Educational History, which has two subdivisions: first, the history of educational systems, for example, Chinese, Greek, Roman, Medieval; the history of the development of the curriculum, and second, the history of the theory of education, which includes the study of educational classics from Plato on; the study of the epochs of educational reform and the writings which influenced them; the relation of educational thought to philosophical, ethical, and religious thought; and a consideration of educational theories in relation to the general culture and intellectual atmosphere of the times.[9]

The work of professional education students at the University of Chicago was classified under three heads. First, they pursued courses in academic subjects calculated to increase and strengthen their scholarship and particularly put them "in command of the intellectual standpoint and method which are absolutely indispensable in genuine culture."[10]

Second, they discussed and tested principles of education. The work of the professional student was based upon instruction in psychology and had for its aim not the acquisition of technical distinctions but "insight into the conditions and modes of healthful growth, and of whatever impedes or arrests that growth." These principles were then tested by "the study of children with a view to making the theory concrete and definite through recognition of its particular applications; and the practice is enlightened, enlarged, and liberated through personal appreciation of its animating purposes and scientific base."[11]

Third, professional education students studied subject matter with reference to its use in secondary and elementary schools. This aspect of their study represented a union of the two previous factors. It entailed an adequate understanding of subject matter in a particular branch and required insight into general psychological and educational principles. Consequently, there was a considerable group of studies in geography, history, nature study, and so on, which future teachers studied in light of the selection and organization of subject matter and with reference to the first two phases of their professional program.[12]

It is significant that while Dewey did mention the importance of discussing and testing principles of education, students in education were not required to do any practice teaching, at least not in the way it is usually conducted today. Dewey elaborated on this distinction in a 1904 article entitled "The Relation of Theory to Practice in Education." He began by assuming that adequate professional instruction of teachers should not be exclusively theoretical; that it should involve a certain amount of practical work. The primary question, Dewey asserted, is not whether there should be any practical work at all. The real issue is the *aim* of the practical work. On the one hand, the object of practical work can be to give teachers in training working command of the necessary tools of their profession, control of the techniques of class instruction and management, and skill and proficiency in the work of teaching. This type of practice work is apprenticeship. On the other hand, practice work can attempt to make theoretical instruction real and vital and to impart a knowledge of subject matter and the principles of education. This is the laboratory point of view.[13]

Dewey granted that these two points of view are, of course, not mutually exclusive, but insisted that there is a fundamental difference in the conception and conduct of practice work depending upon which view is dominant. He argued that the laboratory idea is superior to the apprenticeship idea on several grounds. First, he pointed to precedents in the other professional schools (such as law and medicine), all of which have moved increasingly away from the apprenticeship toward the laboratory model. Dewey cited two reasons for this trend. First, professional schools have a limited amount of time at their disposal and thus must make as efficient use of it as possible. This does not mean, said Dewey, that apprenticeship is a bad thing, but only that laying a sound intellectual foundation is prior to acquiring and perfecting technical skills. Second, Dewey argued that professional schools cannot possibly furnish adequate, realistic conditions for acquiring technical skills. Moreover, these skills could be acquired in a much shorter time on the job. Thus, Dewey suggests that education should follow the lead of the other professional schools away from apprenticeship and toward the laboratory.[14]

Dewey's second major justification of the laboratory model asserts that apprenticeship places an emphasis on acquiring technical skills, and this in turn focuses the attention of the student in the wrong direction. According to Dewey, students have two major problems to solve—the mastery of subject matter and educational principles and the mastery of techniques of class management—and they cannot give equal attention to both at the same time. Moreover, when students are plunged prematurely into the classroom they will invariably concentrate on maintaining order instead of developing the kind of insight that will enable them to conduct their teaching based on sound educational principles.[15]

A third way that Dewey argued that the laboratory model is superior to the apprenticeship model is its ability to develop habits that are theoretical rather than empirical. Dewey observed that students trained in an apprenticeship manner tend to adjust their teaching according to haphazard observation of other teachers, blind experimentation, and random advice from others. Dewey admitted that students who master the technical skills of classroom management may at first appear to be superior in the classroom to students who obtain a thorough grounding in educational theory, but it is at the expense of their future growth as teachers. The latter will continue to improve by building on their theoretical foundations, but the former, lacking any theoretical foundations, will stagnate. Furthermore, according to Dewey, it is the lack of a sound grounding in educational principles that accounts for the dearth of intellectual independence among teachers. This characteristic manifests itself annually in the flocking of teachers to the latest educational fads.[16]

At this point, Dewey shifted to an attack of the critics of the laboratory model. First, he pointed out that their assumption that theory is abstract, remote, and useless unless the student is immediately set to work illustrating it in his/her practice teaching is faulty. This notion fails to take into account, said Dewey, the fact that beginning students possess a large amount of practical experience already in the form of prior social encounters with children who are relatives or acquaintances.[17] In an attempt to add to this kind of built-in store of experience, Dewey would then require prospective teachers to observe the teaching of others. However, this observation should be conducted from a theoretical rather than from a practical standpoint. Thus, students should not be observing in order to accumulate a store of methods but rather to develop the ability to "see what is going on in the minds of a group of people who are in intellectual contact with each other."[18]

Second, Dewey charged that critics of the laboratory model do not give sufficient credit to the fact that subject matter, properly presented, provides prospective teachers with excellent training in one kind of teaching method, namely scientific method. Indeed, it is this fact that accounts for the existence of good teachers at the collegiate level who have had no pedagogical training. Thus, Dewey argued that scholastic knowledge provides teachers with one important kind of pedagogical training—the ability to think scientifically. In this way, he rejected the absolute dichotomy between theory and method that permeates the thinking of the critics of the laboratory model. He adds that it is crucial for students to develop the habit of viewing the entire curriculum as reflecting the growth of the mind itself. This in turn demands consecutive and longitudinal consideration of the curriculum rather than the typical cross-sectional study. Thus, the student should be led to see that the same subject matter in geography, nature study, or art develops not merely day to day in a given grade, but from year to year throughout the entire movement of the school. Furthermore, students should realize this before they get much encouragement in trying to adapt subject matter in lesson plans for this or that isolated grade.[19]

After a period of observation, Dewey would have students gradually begin to assist the regular teacher with special students and in the selection and organization of subject matter (but again, always with an emphasis on theory). This stage would then blend into one in which students were given actual teaching to do. At this latter stage, however, Dewey would require that students not only be permitted to act upon their own intellectual initiative, but that they be required to do so. Thus, their ability to take hold of situations for themselves would be a more important factor in judging them than their following any particular set method or scheme. Dewey warned that students should not be supervised too closely and that supervision should be geared toward getting students to judge their own work critically and in light of educational principles. Dewey charged that the practice of allowing students to teach a few lessons while under constant inspection and then immediately criticizing their performance is nothing short of a travesty. Such methods, according to Dewey, may result in the mastery of certain tricks of the trade, but they will not develop thoughtful and independent teachers.[20]

Finally, if all the stages thus far outlined have been successfully completed, and there is sufficient time left in the program, then Dewey would permit some work of the apprenticeship type. Even at this stage, however, he suggested that the student be given as much responsibility as possible with a minimum of supervision. Moreover, the purpose of this period would be mostly to identify and exclude those students who are simply not fit for teaching. Dewey concluded with the observation that training schools for teachers do not perform their full duty by simply accepting and conforming to present educational standards. Educational leadership is an indispensable part of their office. Education must be improved "not simply by turning out teachers who can do better the things that are now necessary to do, but rather by changing the conception of what constitutes education."[21]

Of course, Dewey also recognized that a teacher training program, no matter how well conceived, cannot overcome certain innate characteristics of prospective teachers. He suggested the following prerequisites for would-be teachers:

- Good health: One special feature is emphasized in connection with teaching—those persons who are subject to "nervous strain and worry" should not go into teaching.

- A natural love of contact with the young: There are those, observed Dewey, who are bored by contact with children. They can be more useful in other professions.

- A natural love of communicating knowledge along with a love of knowledge itself: There are scholars, Dewey noted, who have the latter in a marked degree but who lack enthusiasm for imparting it. To the "natural-born" teacher, however, learning is incomplete unless it is shared.

- An active and keen interest in one branch of knowledge along with interest and skill in following the reactions of the minds of others: Dewey would not require a teacher to be a "high-class" scholar in all the subjects he or she has to teach, but he does say that a teacher ought to have an unusual love and aptitude in some one subject. The teacher will then have the "feel" for genuine information and insight in all subjects and will communicate by "unconscious contagion" love of learning to others. According to Dewey, the teacher can be distinguished from the scholar by interest in watching the movements of the minds of others and by being sensitive to their response, or lack of it, to the subject matter presented.

- A disinclination to view the young as inferior: Dewey warned those individuals who acquire a manner that is either tyrannical or patronizing to refrain from becoming teachers.

Dewey noted that there are communities in which politics plays an important role in education. He suggested that would-be teachers ask themselves whether they have the strength of character to sustain their integrity against such influences without becoming "timeservers, chairwarmers, (or) placeholders."[22]

In summary, Dewey believed in a theoretical, scientific approach (the "laboratory model") to teacher training. Moreover, just as his approach to the education of children emphasizes the needs of the individual child, his views on the education of teachers focus on the needs of individual teachers. Finally, Dewey was adamant about the importance of teacher education and its central role in the improvement of the educational system.

NOTES

1. George Dykhuizen, *The Life and Mind of John Dewey* (Carbondale, Ill.: Southern Illinois University Press, 1973), p. xv.

2. John Dewey, *Democracy and Education* (New York: Macmillan, 1916), p. 117.

3. Ibid., pp. 203–204.

4. John Dewey, "Significance of the School of Education," *Elementary School Teacher*, 4 (March 1904): 442.

5. John Dewey, "Pedagogy as a University Discipline," *University (of Chicago) Record*, 1 (September 1896): 353–354.

6. Ibid.

7. John Dewey, "Pedagogy Memorandum," unpublished memorandum to William R. Harper, Chicago, December, 1894. The memorandum is preserved in the Harper Collection in the archives at the University of Chicago.

8. Ibid.

9. John Dewey, "Plan for Organization of Work in a Fully Equipped Department of Pedagogy," typewritten enclosure in a letter to William R. Harper, Chicago, 8 January 1897, 7 pp. Published as Appendix in *American Educational Theory* by Charles J. Brauner (Englewood Cliffs, N.J.: Prentice-Hall, 1964).

10. John Dewey, "The University of Chicago School of Education," *Elementary School Teacher*, 3 (November 1902): 200–203.

11. Ibid.

12. Ibid.

13. John Dewey, "The Relation of Theory to Practice in Education," *Third Yearbook*, National Society for the Scientific Study of Education, pt. 1 (Bloomington, Ill.: Public School Publishing, 1904), p. 9.

14. Ibid., pp. 10–17.

15. Ibid.

16. Ibid.

17. Ibid.

18. Ibid., p. 16.

19. Ibid., pp. 10–17.

20. Ibid., p. 18.

21. Ibid., p. 30.

22. John Dewey, "To Those Who Aspire to the Profession of Teaching," in *My Vocation . . . or What Eminent Americans Think of Their Calling*, comp. Earl Granger Lockhart (New York: H. W. Wilson, 1938), pp. 325–334.

2

Robert Hutchins (1899–1977): The Medievalist

Robert Maynard Hutchins was one of the most controversial figures in American education in the twentieth century. He became president of the University of Chicago in 1929 at the tender age of thirty. He introduced study of the Great Books and abolished the football team. His career at Chicago was a stormy one, and his ideas for reforming American education typically elicited either very strong praise or equally strong denunciations. He subsequently served as associate director of the Ford Foundation and president of the Fund for the Republic, founded the Center for the Study of Democratic Institutions, and was chairman of the Board of Editors of Encyclopedia Britannica.[1]

In his book, *Teacher Education in America*, Merle Borrowman points out that from the very beginning the debate over how teachers should be educated has been characterized by the dichotomy between the proponents of what he calls the liberal view of teacher education and the proponents of what he labels the technical view of teacher education.[2] Advocates of the former would make professional preparation for teaching incidental to a liberal education while advocates of the latter stress the importance of specialized educational training. Robert Hutchins, of course, represents the paradigmatic example of the liberal view.

EDUCATIONAL AIMS AND REFORM

When asked his opinion as to the ideal education, Hutchins replied that it is one that develops the intellect. He arrived at this conclusion by the following process of elimination. First, he maintained that educational institutions are the only institutions that can develop intellectual powers. Second, the ideal education, according to Hutchins, is not an ad hoc education, not an education directed to immediate needs; it is not a specialized education, or a pre-professional education; it is not a utilitarian education. Thus, it is an education calculated to develop the mind. For Hutchins this meant the three Rs, the liberal arts, and "the greatest works that the human race has produced." He believed that these are the permanent necessities, the intellectual tools that are needed to understand the ideas and ideals of our world. He did not exclude later specialization or later professional education but insisted that without the intellectual techniques needed to understand ideas, and without at least an acquaintance with the major ideas that have "animated" mankind since the dawn of history, no one may call themselves educated.[3]

Hutchins placed a large part of the blame for what he saw as a miserable educational system directly on the teachers. He maintained that it is possible to come to only one conclusion—it is not the inadequacy of the students but the inadequacy of the environment and the "irresolution" of teachers that is responsible for the shortcomings of American education. This is due in part to the confusion that pervades teacher education. He lamented the fact that the students who were going to be teachers were being put through a procedure that was designed to produce investigators. Thus, the classes, the courses, the content, and the aims of teacher education were confused at best.[4]

Hutchins condemned accreditation, certification, and requiring degrees for teachers. He argued that these things have made the system less flexible, perpetuated vested interests and habits, and "bolstered" up occupational monopolies. Hutchins lamented the fact that it is impossible to become a teacher in the public schools of America without passing courses offered by departments or schools of education in colleges or universities. "The result of these requirements is a standard, in a manner of speaking, for the selection of teachers. But courses in education are not likely to be difficult or significant. Their positive effect seems to be to give the schools, colleges, and departments of education large enrollments."[5]

Hutchins contended that American education is characterized by a waste of money, time, and talent. He argued that Americans do not take education seriously. They do not value those who are charged with the responsibility for it as evidenced by the atrocious salaries paid to teachers. He noted that in other countries teachers may not get much money, but at least their prestige is high.[6] It is revealing, said Hutchins, that teachers in American elementary and secondary schools are not expected to belong to learned societies. This can only mean that they are not expected to know very much about their subjects. Thus, it was not surprising to Hutchins that school teaching has failed to attract a large population of the "abler" young people.[7]

TEACHER EDUCATION

As a solution to these problems, Hutchins outlined his views on the proper education of teachers. First, the prospective teacher's general education should be identical with that of the lawyer, doctor, and clergyman. With a good education in the liberal arts (which are grammar, rhetoric, logic, and mathematics) teachers will have learned the basic rules of pedagogy. "The liberal arts train the teacher in how to teach, that is, in how to organize, express, and communicate knowledge."[8]

After completing a general education, prospective teachers would, like all other university students, study metaphysics, the natural sciences, and the social sciences. Here content becomes important, for Hutchins maintained that this is when the prospective teacher should learn "what to teach." However, prospective teachers would study these three areas without any vocational aim. That is, the subject matter would be the same for those who were planning to enter a learned profession as those who were not.[9] According to Hutchins, the only thing that should be learned in a university is the general principles, the fundamental propositions, the theory of any discipline. This is in part because the practices of the profession change so rapidly that any attempt to inculcate them may merely succeed in teaching students habits that will be a disservice to them when they graduate.[10]

Hutchins maintained that the subject matter of any learned profession is intellectual. Thus, though the rules of the trade may be learned in the field, and indeed can only be learned there, the "intellectual content" of the profession can generally be mastered only in a university. Moreover, Hutchins argued that to the extent to which the attention of the student is directed to vocational interests and away from the intellectual content of the discipline, the university fails to do "the only thing it might do" and attempts something in which it is bound to fail. Furthermore, turning professional schools into vocational schools degrades the universities and does not elevate the professions. Hutchins also contended that it cannot accomplish the only purpose it can have, namely, the preparation of students for the practice of their life work. It is, in short, bad for the student as well as the universities and the professions. In an even stronger vein, Hutchins stated that to the extent to which universities and professional schools abandon creative thought and "degenerate" into trade schools, the profession must degenerate into a trade.[11]

It is clear then that Hutchins thought it bad to vocationalize the universities, but he did admit that the professional atmosphere had an "electrical" effect on some students. However, he insisted that this atmosphere is "ruinous" to attempts to lead students to understand the subject because it requires that the teacher make clear at every step that the questions being discussed have a direct bearing on the students' future experiences and on

their success in meeting them. According to Hutchins, every learned profession has a great intellectual heritage and that should be the prime object
of attention of professional schools.[12]

For certain learned professions (law, medicine, and theology), Hutchins
suggested that if the learned professions cannot be trusted to "communicate" the practices of the professions to the young, it may be desirable to at-
tach to the university "technical institutes" in which the student may
become familiar with these "routines." The relationship of these technical
institutes to the university would be like those of research institutes where
persons are engaged in collecting information in the social or natural sciences. These institutes, though they have no place in the university proper,
may find a "haven" in connection with universities. The members of these
institutes would not be members of the university faculties unless they
were also working on "fundamental" problems in metaphysics, social science, or natural science. Persons working on such fundamental problems,
and only these, would have a voice in matters affecting the conduct of the
university and the content of its work. Research institutes would train people to carry on research of the type that they carry on themselves but would
have no other educational function. Similarly, technical institutes would be
primarily practical or vocational in nature. Thus, lawyers, doctors, theolo-
gians, and empirical researchers would continue their training in post-uni-
versity institutes. However, prospective teachers would not be required to
undergo any such further training.[13]

In summary, Hutchins' plan for the education of teachers is composed of
three parts. First, they would master the "arts of pedagogy," which are, according to Hutchins, the abilities to organize, express, and communicate
knowledge, during their general education in the liberal arts. Second, they
would master their "intellectual subject matter" during their university education, taking care not to "vocationalize" their studies. Third, they would
learn "the rules of the trade" or the day-to-day practices of teaching on the
job. In addition, accreditation, certification, required courses in education,
schools and departments of education, and required degrees for teachers
would all be abolished while higher salaries, higher prestige, memberships
in learned societies for teachers, as well as a national plan for education
would all be encouraged.

NOTES

    1. Mary Ann Dzuback, *Robert M. Hutchins: Portrait of an Educator* (Chicago:
University of Chicago Press, 1991), pp. 1–10.

    2. Merle Borrowman, *Teacher Education in America* (New York: Teachers Col-
lege Press, 1965).

    3. Robert Hutchins, *The Higher Learning in America* (New Haven, Conn.: Yale
University Press, 1936).

    4. Ibid., pp. 2–3.

5. Ibid., pp. 84–86.

6. Robert Hutchins, "The Lesson of Krushchev's Little Red Schoolhouse," *The Education Digest* 23 (October 1958): 2.

7. Robert Hutchins, *Some Observations on American Education* (Cambridge: Cambridge University Press, 1956), p. 87.

8. Hutchins, *Higher Learning,* p. 114.

9. Ibid., p. 106.

10. Ibid., p. 48.

11. Ibid., pp. 44–52.

12. Ibid., pp. 37–57.

13. Ibid., pp. 110–111.

3

Arthur Bestor (1908–1994): The Academician

In spite of the protestations of critics such as Robert Hutchins, the progressive education movement continued to flourish and to receive widespread attention—positive and negative—during the 1930s and early 1940s. It was always a loosely coordinated, diverse movement that changed its emphasis over the years, ranging from understanding the child in the first two decades of the century to using the schools to transform society during the 1930s.[1]

Shortly after the Second World War, progressive education as a formal movement with a professional organization and journal collapsed. The reasons for the collapse are many, and Lawrence Cremin discusses them in his book, *The Transformation of the School*.[2] For our purposes here, it is sufficient to mention only two things. First, though many of the basic principles of progressive education remained to be implemented in public schools, they had become widely accepted in theory; in short, in Cremin's words, "the movement became a victim of its own success."[3] Second, after 1945, attacks on progressive education became increasingly more widespread and virulent.

The first wave of these attacks consisted of far-right extremists who sought and found a scapegoat responsible for the ills of society. The scapegoat was the American public school system. Professing that modern education, as influenced by John Dewey and his followers, had departed radically from the academic, moral, and religious standards inherent in traditional education, the extremists attacked the schools, blaming them for the spread of juvenile delinquency, socialism, atheism, and communism. Many irate voices demanded that the public schools be abolished.[4]

Stunned by the attacks, educators closed ranks and lashed back at the extremists, calling them enemies of the public schools. As the attacks on the schools began to subside with the demise of McCarthyism, yet another group of critics of education appeared on the national scene. Highly literate and polemic, this new group of critics wrote widely read books with flashy, exposé titles such as *Quackery in the Public Schools* and *Educational Wastelands*. School people, however, often made no distinction between this new group of critics and the earlier extremist group and frequently labeled the new critics enemies of the public schools. But the new critics, including people such as Arthur Bestor, Albert Lynd, Hyman Rickover, and Mortimer Smith, were not enemies of the public schools. They simply opposed the progressive educational philosophy and teaching methodology that had guided educational development for a number of years.

While apparent today, it was not readily evident in the early 1950s that public school education, as society in general, was beginning a process of national re-evaluation. The educational critic who received the most national attention during this period was a prominent historian, Arthur Bestor. Praised by the media and condemned, with a few exceptions, by the educational establishment, Bestor was a significant force in arousing a lethargic public to re-examine the public school system and in making education a topic of national debate during the 1950s.

EDUCATIONAL AIMS AND REFORMS

The *educational* needs of society, according to Bestor, should determine the purpose of education. The word "educational" has been emphasized because Bestor makes a careful distinction between the needs of society in general and its educational needs. The needs of society in general are manifold and diverse, and various institutions have been organized to meet many of these needs. Whatever particular major need a society has, an appropriate organization or profession has been established to fulfill the need. Since people need, for example, physical health, the medical profession has arisen to take care of this specific need. Just as every organization or profession is primarily concerned with meeting one particular need of society, the formal school has been charged by society to meet one of its most important, if not the most important need: to raise the intellectual level of the nation. "This is its great task in a democracy," Bestor believed.[5]

Bestor recognized that intellectual training is not the only important thing in life, but he argued that it is indispensable in modern society. Effective living in the modern world requires that each person develop his or her intellectual powers to the maximum. If a democracy is to safeguard its cultural values, all of its citizens must be able to think critically. To lack faith in the common person's intellectual ability is to lack faith in the very foundation upon which a democracy rests—an intelligent, enlightened population.

To understand Bestor's education perspective, it is necessary to understand what he meant when he used the terms "intellectual training" and "liberal education." Intellectual training, Bestor acknowledged, is a formidable phrase, but it means simply the "deliberate cultivation of the ability to think."[6] To teach students to think is the function of liberal education at all levels of education. Thus, Bestor made no distinction between intellectual training and liberal education. The question is, what constitutes liberal education and intellectual training? Bestor gave a succinct answer: "Liberal education is training in intellectual disciplines of general applicability."[7]

At the high school level, the disciplines of general applicability are science, mathematics, history, English, and foreign languages. These disciplines are fundamental in modern life and, for this reason, must also be fundamental in public schools. What an intellectual discipline can do for students is to provide them with a way of thinking peculiar to a particular discipline, that is, to provide them with a method of inquiry by which a discipline attains knowledge. In a complex world, Bestor maintained that it is essential that each person develop to some extent this power—the ability to reason logically, to weigh evidence, and to draw conclusions that can stand up to the most severe criticism of other well-informed people.

Since the turn of the twentieth century, Bestor claimed that public schools have progressively de-emphasized the importance of intellectual training in the disciplines, and in so doing have lost their sense of direction. Bestor attributed the lack of direction of the school system primarily to the faulty thinking of educationists: teacher educators, school administrators, and educational bureaucrats. Being culturally isolated from the real world of learning composed of scholars, scientists, and professionals, educationists are so intellectually unsophisticated they have permitted, if not actually sought, the disintegration of the intellectual studies.

Bestor acknowledged there are problems involved in giving a sound education to all children. The solution, however, is not to drain courses of intellectual content, but to so improve pedagogical techniques that virtually all students will profit from fundamental intellectual training. Bestor insisted that the goal of Americans should be to give to every one of its citizens the quality education that was once reserved for an aristocracy.

TEACHER EDUCATION

Bestor was particularly interested in teacher education because the thesis of his major book on public school education, *The Restoration of Learning*, is that schools exist to teach something, and that something is the power to think. To do this requires teachers who themselves know how to think. Thus teacher education in Bestor's perspective should be basically education in how to think; that is, it should be liberal education, training in those intellectual disciplines that have general applicability.

Teacher preparation programs should develop teachers who have the ability to consider evidence according to the reasoning processes and critical methods accepted by the discipline involved. Bestor was convinced that teachers who are well educated are not those who are masters of pedagogical jargon but who are so dedicated to gaining knowledge and intellectual power that their learning inspires learning in their students. The best way to develop such teachers is to give them a thorough knowledge of the fundamental disciplines, that is, a liberal education.[8] In Bestor's judgment, the ideal of liberal education "is to produce men and women with disciplined minds, cultivated interests, and a wide range of fundamental knowledge. Who in our society needs these qualities more than the teacher? . . . Whatever else a teacher may need, he must possess ready command of a variety of intellectual skills and a fund of accurate knowledge. Otherwise he can never make any significant or enduring impression upon the minds of his pupils."[9]

To understand the rationale for Bestor's recommendations for the reform of teacher education, it is helpful to understand the distinctions he made among the types of educational programs in colleges and universities.

According to Bestor, the introduction of the elective system at the college and university level, has led to the idea that all programs are of equal value as a means of liberal education. This idea has resulted in the college offering three distinct types of education: liberal, professional, and vocational. The most important distinction between liberal education and the other two types is that liberal education treats the student as a human being first, rather than as a potential doctor, lawyer, or teacher.

Furthermore, liberal education is based upon the general intellectual disciplines, that is, those disciplines with a universal applicability and not diluted by a vocational bias. Professional education, however, is based on a specific group of disciplines and addresses a particular group of problems. Much more emphasis is given to these problems than would be appropriate in a general program of liberal education. As distinct from liberal and professional education, which are based upon intellectual disciplines (the former, the general disciplines; the latter, the specialized), vocational education does not rest upon extensive training in either the general or specialized disciplines.

Although vocational education may be a legitimate supplement to liberal education, it is nevertheless narrow in its outlook, focused only on the practical skills, the mere know-how, that are needed in an occupation. Its concern is not with the theoretical knowledge that underlies an occupation and that advances it.

Bestor went on to say that real vocational training is an important part of the educational system, but then added that it should not be weakened by being confused with pseudo-vocational programs consisting of a smattering of courses designed for no higher purpose than to look good on a job application. He suggested that the study of pedagogy, study of the teaching-learning process, could be genuine vocational training but asserted that it is in fact the most blatantly anti-intellectual and vocational of all programs. Pedagogy has degenerated into nothing more than pseudo-vocational training.[10]

The greatest degradation in the field of American education, Bestor believed, has resulted from the development of pseudo-vocational programs in the field of pedagogy. These programs have been initiated and perpetuated by an "interlocking directorate." This directorate is composed primarily of college of education professors, with assistance from most state department of education officials, and many public school administrators. Being powerful politically outside the university, the ringleaders of this directorate, the college of education professors, have been permitted to educate prospective teachers in their own way. That is, rather than teach their students how to think, they prepare the students only for purely vocational proficiency.

Instead of trying to improve teacher education, pedagogues have been busy setting up an "iron curtain." Behind the iron curtain, "in slave-labor camps, are the classroom teachers, whose only hope of rescue is from without." That is, they can only be rescued by the "free world of science and learning" which is "menaced but not yet threatened . . . [by] a new breed of educator, who has no real place in—who does not respect and who is not respected by—the world of scientists, scholars, and professional men."[11]

Bestor's recommendations for the reform of teacher education rest on two basic assumptions. First, teacher education ought to be a function of the entire university. Second, for teaching to be a profession instead of an occupation, it must establish high standards of knowledge and scholarship.

Concerning the first assumption, Bestor proposed that a university establish a distinct Faculty of Teacher Training. Its members would be drawn from all departments that offer programs leading to a reorganized M.Ed. This faculty would have its own committees and administrative officers, would approve curricula, supervise teacher placement, and initiate school surveys and educational commissions.

In addition to the Faculty of Teacher Training, Bestor recommended establishing, under the jurisdiction of the graduate school, an autonomous Institute of Educational Research. This institute would not confer any degrees nor have a body of graduate students it could call its own. Rather, its facilities would be available for part of the training of Ph.D. candidates, for instance, in psychology or political science, who desire a specialty in educational psychology or school administration.

At the undergraduate level Bestor proposed, as previously noted, that the prospective teacher should have an education in the liberal arts and sciences—the general intellectual disciplines. The graduate training of teachers would be the same as their undergraduate training; more training in the fundamental intellectual disciplines. The graduate courses, however, would be structured to the peculiar needs of a teacher rather than to those of a research specialist.

Graduate students who pursue such a program for a full academic year would receive a master's degree if they pass a comprehensive written examination in two disciplines of their choosing. If, after the completion of three years of study, graduate students can pass oral and written examinations in five fields, they should be given a doctorate. Bestor did not require a thesis for either degree, although an essay of substantial quality and originality in each student's field would be required. The customary graduate foreign languages requirement would also be retained.

Once such a program is inaugurated, Bestor proposed a process of devolution of the importance and power of departments of education. Most of their present functions would devolve upon already existing departments. The end result would be a small undergraduate department of pedagogy engaging in supervision of practice teaching and perhaps providing an expanded extension program of on-the-job training for experienced classroom teachers. Graduate work for teachers would focus on the new M.Ed. and Ed.D. programs and would be under the auspices of the regular departments of liberal arts and sciences. Bestor cautioned that such a reorganized program would constitute a major surgical operation and that its implementation should be gradual.

Turning now to Bestor's second assumption—that in order to be a profession, teaching must establish high standards of knowledge and scholarship—it is obvious that Bestor did not consider public school teaching to be a profession but thought it should be and could be if educators first recognize what a genuine profession really is.

Although educationists are confused as to the nature of a profession, there is really no particular mystery about it, according to Bestor. Professional people are expected to have three distinctive qualifications. First, they must have a great body of knowledge and a command of specific intellectual processes, both of which are capable of being measured by examinations and similar means. Second, they must have the ability to apply their knowledge in carrying out the functions of their profession. Third, their character must be such that their clients will respect and admire them.

Bestor was adamant that teaching will never become a profession if the pedagogues have their way. All that the pedagogues provide teachers, he claimed, are courses in the mere know-how of teaching. To become a profession, teaching must do as other professions: (1) postpone until the very end the highly specialized training needed for actual practice of a profession; and (2) require as an absolute prerequisite a demanding education in the liberal arts and sciences, unsullied by vocational demands. If these two conditions are met, Bestor believed it was possible for teaching to establish high standards of knowledge and scholarship and, with the establishment of such standards, to convert the present vocation of teaching into a genuine profession.

NOTES

1. Lawrence A. Cremin, *The Transformation of the School: Progressivism in American Education, 1876–1957* (New York: Alfred A. Knopf, 1961).

2. Ibid., pp. 347–353.

3. Ibid., p. 349.

4. Mary Anne Raywid, *The Ax-grinders: Critics of Our Public Schools* (New York: Macmillan, 1962).

5. Arthur Bestor, *The Restoration of Learning: A Program for Redeeming the Unfulfilled Promise of American Education* (New York: Alfred A. Knopf, 1956), p. 96.

6. Ibid., p. 28.

7. Ibid., p. 80.

8. Ibid., pp. 69, 80. Our discussion of Bestor's ideas on teacher education relies on this book.

9. Ibid., pp. 242–243.

10. Ibid., pp. 68, 75, 79, 81.

11. Ibid., p. 178.

4

James Conant (1893–1978):
The Compromiser

The last book James Conant wrote was an autobiography, which he titled *My Several Lives: Memoirs of a Social Inventor.* The title was appropriate. He was in turn a professor, college president, U.S. ambassador, and public school reformer. President of Harvard University for twenty years and ambassador to the Federal Republic of Germany during the height of the cold war period, Conant was a well-known public figure when he embarked on the last of his four lives, the life of a full-time public school reformer.

In 1957, he resigned his position as ambassador, returned to the United States, and with the assistance of a foundation grant, recruited a small team of educators to assist him in conducting a national study of the American secondary school. The results of the study were published in 1959 in a book titled *The American High School Today.* Other than reducing the number of small high schools, Conant assured the American people that "no radical alteration in the basic pattern of American education was necessary to improve public high schools."[1] Other reports followed but this book and *The Education of American Teachers,* published in 1963, were the two books that received by far the most public attention.[2]

EDUCATIONAL AIMS AND REFORMS

Fundamental to Conant's ideas on education are his beliefs that a well-founded education philosophy should be part of a comprehensive social philosophy and that education is a social process. The social philosophy espoused by Conant encourages Americans to put into practice what he considered the highest ideas embodied in the American democratic way of life: a commitment to the laissez-faire economic system, a decentralized political system, a fluid social structure, a devotion to a belief in the dignity of the individual, the obligation of human beings to each other, personal liberty, and a willingness to work well with others to achieve worthwhile goals. What contributes most to perpetuation of this way of life is the commitment of Americans to the ideas of equality of opportunity and respect for all honest work. These two ideas, basic to Conant's social philosophy, are equally germane to his educational philosophy. So important are they that he considered them "the fundamental premises of American education." Whatever else the school does, it must instill in young people a commitment to these two ideas.[3]

Just as educational philosophy cannot be separated from social philosophy, the school cannot be separated from the society it serves. Education, Conant insisted, is a social process; that is, schools exist to serve particular communities in a particular society. Conant's commitment to the democratic way of life and to the idea that education is a social process led him to the conclusion that the ideal form of secondary school for Americans is the comprehensive high school, a school that attempts to meet the needs of all the young of a given community.[4]

TEACHER EDUCATION

The major obstacle to improvement of teacher education in Conant's judgment is the long-standing feud between professors in schools of education and professors in arts and sciences (the "academic" professors). Conant believed his recommendations in *The Education of American Teachers*, if implemented, would do much to resolve this feud.[5] According to Conant, what most divides these two camps is the teacher certification process. Basing certification on specified courses required by the state is "bankrupt" because there is no conclusive evidence that teaching ability is improved by any specific course, be it a professional course in a school of education or a general education course in one of the academic faculties. The fact is that education professors do not agree on what knowledge they should convey to future teachers, nor do academics agree on what academic courses should comprise a general education for prospective teachers. These two groups of professors agree only on two things: for prospective teachers, a bachelor's degree is necessary and practice teaching is very important if it is conducted well. Since no one seems to know for sure what college courses are essential for developing teaching skill, Conant concluded that neither state departments of education nor voluntary accrediting agencies should specify how much time should be given to either academic or education courses.

Conant, therefore, recommended that the National Council for Accreditation of Teacher Education (NCATE) and regional accrediting associations serve only as advisory bodies to local school boards and teacher education institutions and that the state, for certification purposes, require only that a teacher candidate hold a bachelor's degree and complete a state-approved student teaching program. Further, since nobody knows for sure what courses make a good teacher, he recommended that institutions of higher learning be permitted by the state to develop whatever teacher education program they consider best, subject only to two conditions. First, the president of the institution must certify on behalf of both the academic and education faculty that a candidate is prepared adequately to teach on a particular level or in certain fields. Second, the institution must establish in conjunction with a public school system a practice teaching arrangement that is approved by the state department of education. Thus, Conant advocated an all-college or university approach to teacher education and urged institutions of higher learning, state departments of education, and local school boards to form a three-fold partnership responsible for teacher education.

To each of the agents involved in the partnership, Conant gave clearly defined responsibilities: the university or college controls entrance to student teaching; the state—utilizing state department, university and public school personnel—certifies on the basis of successful student teaching; and the local board assumes final responsibility for deciding who teaches in its school district.

While Conant considered teacher education to be a partnership of three agents, there is no doubt that he considered the institution of higher learning to be the senior partner, for at the end of his book on teacher education, he summarized in two words the conclusion of his study. The two words are "freedom" and "responsibility" and both words refer specifically to institutions of higher learning. "The state," Conant said, "should allow each college and university the maximum degree of freedom to develop its own program. Each institution should assume the maximum degree of responsibility for those graduates it certifies as being competent to teach."[6] Such freedom and responsibility, presumably, will promote competition among institutions to provide quality teacher education programs, and this in turn should encourage education and academic professors "to join hands to enhance the reputation of their particular institution."[7] Conant concluded that "once the quarreling educators bury their hatchets, the layman may put his present worries [about teacher education] aside."[8]

Though Conant believed institutions should develop teacher education programs they consider best, he nevertheless discussed in some detail what he considered a worthwhile undergraduate general education and professional education program for future teachers. He acknowledged that there may be other programs as good or better than his. He outlined a program only to show that it is possible to prepare teachers adequately in four years for their first teaching post.

Conant suggested that the concentration for secondary school teacher trainees should be only in one teaching field and that the content of the field should correspond to the needs of high school teachers. To ensure that academic departments provide concentrations appropriate for secondary school teachers, Conant urged a close liaison between subject matter departments and public schools. Conant also proposed that elementary teachers have an area of concentration. The concentration for kindergarten through grade three teachers would consist of work in English, social studies, and mathematics, and the concentration for grade four through six teachers would be in either English, mathematics, social studies, or science.

Conant assumed that his proposed general education program would provide teachers with a "certain level of sophistication" that would enable them to talk intelligently on "difficult topics" outside their field with students, colleagues, and professional men and women, and by so doing, earn their respect as a learned member of the community. Further, if teachers in a school are to form a group of learned persons working together, they need to have much in common intellectually. To develop teachers with a certain degree of sophistication, Conant proposed that teacher training institutions provide teacher trainees with a two-year general education component consisting of a broad academic education: four years of English and foreign languages; three years of mathematics, natural science, and history and social studies; two years of art and music. To ensure a minimum level of intellectual ability for prospective teachers, Conant recommended the same demanding high school program for future teachers as he did for the academically talented students in his study of the American high school. He also proposed that students be accepted into the teacher education program only if they are scholastically in the upper third of their high school graduating class.

According to Conant, student teaching (with an accompanying methods course) is the one essential element in professional education that nobody disputes. He is confident that if the state provides a close examination of the student teacher in the actual process of teaching, it will possess the most reliable device to ensure the training of competent teachers. The success of a university's student teaching program, however, depends greatly on whether it implements Conant's recommendation that professors supervising student teachers should have practical experience and status comparable to that of clinical professors in medical schools. Such a person should be an outstanding public school teacher employed by a university on either a full-time basis or a part-time basis. He or she would have a salary and status equal to that of any other professor in the institution. Conant expected clinical professors to keep abreast of new developments in such pedagogical subjects as educational psychology and to work closely with academic professors in their university, making sure that they understand what future high school teachers need to know.

While Conant considered student teaching to be the only essential, as distinct from desirable, element in the professional preparation of a future teacher, he acknowledged that such courses as the philosophy, history, sociology, and psychology of education can enhance what an apprentice teacher can learn on the job from an outstanding teacher, with one important provision. The professors of education who teach these courses must be well-qualified philosophers, historians, sociologists, and psychologists who are committed to public schools and their improvement. These professors of education should serve as intermediaries between student teachers and their supervising teachers and the professors of the relevant scientific and philosophical fields, helping both groups to bridge the gap that separates theory and practice. With such professors, the disciplines of history, philosophy, political science, anthropology and sociology, and psychology can be applied effectively to the study of education. The professor of the philosophy of education, for example, can use the tools of the logical analysts and develop in his or her students an ability to think clearly and critically about important educational issues raised by psychologists, professional educators, and informed laymen.

According to Conant, educational disciplines such as educational psychology and educational philosophy bear the same relationship to the training of teachers as medical sciences such as biochemistry and microbiology bear to the training of doctors. The educational sciences, however, are not nearly as well developed as the medical sciences, as is evident by the inability of professors of education to agree on what common body of knowledge all future teachers should have prior to initial employment. For this reason, Conant assigned a small role to the educational sciences in the undergraduate preparation of teachers. He felt most prospective secondary school teachers should take only one three-hour course in educational psychology and one three-hour course in either the philosophy, history, or sociology of education. Such work he considered desirable but not essential. Student teaching and methods work, however, are essential. Thus, Conant recommended that *all* future secondary teachers be required to take nine hours of student teaching and methods work and suggested that *most* be encouraged to take six hours of work in two educational disciplines.

Concerning the professional preparation of elementary teachers, Conant believed that the program for kindergarten through grade three teachers should prepare them in the methodology and content of all the subjects taught in these early years, and the program for grade four through six teachers should provide them with a more in-depth study of content and methods of teaching a specific subject or cluster of subjects typically taught in these grades. They would receive only an introduction to the remaining subjects normally taught in an elementary school.

Conant's more important ideas on graduate and in-service education for teachers may be summarized briefly, for he gives little attention to these two areas. A master's degree, according to Conant, should increase a person's competence as a teacher and should be based on the teacher's undergraduate program. School boards should provide financial assistance and leaves of absence to enable teachers to study toward a master's degree during the summer or during a full-time semester residence at a university.

Assuming that a master's degree candidate in secondary education has a certificate in a single field, Conant made two suggestions. First, the degree program might include further work in psychology, history, and philosophy of education, and a seminar on methods. Second, a major portion of the program, perhaps two-thirds, might be devoted to preparing students to handle advanced placement work in their particular fields or to preparing them to teach in another field. If one teaches in a slum school, Conant urged him or her to spend some time on sociology and those aspects of political science and economics that relate specifically to school problems and urban conditions. Conant also suggested that the students spend about a third of their time broadening their knowledge in their undergraduate area of concentration.

Concerning in-service education, Conant proposed that such work not be tied to course credits and that it be directed as a "group attack" on a matter of mutual concern to a group of teachers in a particular school or school district. Both academic and education professors, at the taxpayer's expense, should assist teachers in coping with the mutual concerns they themselves identify.

In summary, Conant's basic recommendation for reform of teacher education is that the state require, for certification purposes, only a bachelor's degree and successful experience in a state-approved student teaching program. Conant proposed that the program be coordinated and supervised by a clinical professor. Such revamping of the certification program would encourage a team approach to teacher education involving institutions of higher learning, state departments of education, and local school systems, with each having clearly defined responsibilities. Furthermore, the new certification program would do much to end the feud between education professors and academic professors, a feud which in Conant's judgment has been the major obstacle to effective teacher education reform.

NOTES

1. James B. Conant, *The American High School Today: A First Report to Interested Citizens* (New York: McGraw-Hill, 1963), p. 12.

2. James B. Conant, *The Education of American Teachers* (New York: McGraw-Hill, 1963).

3. James B. Conant, *The Citadel of Learning* (New Haven, Conn.: Yale University Press, 1956), p. 47; James B. Conant, *Education in a Divided World: The Function of the Public Schools in Our Unique Society* (Cambridge: Harvard University Press, 1948), p. 230; James B. Conant, *Education and Liberty: The Role of the Schools in a Modern Democracy* (New York: Vintage Books, 1953), p. 1.

4. For Conant's view on education as a social process, see: Conant, *Education and Liberty*, pp. 1–2; and James B. Conant, *Slums and Suburbs* (New York: McGraw-Hill, 1961), pp. 1, 12, 43.

5. Our discussion of Conant's perspective on education of teachers relies solely on *The Education of American Teachers*.

6. Conant, *The Education of American Teachers*, p. 217.

7. Ibid.

8. Ibid., p. 21.

5

Theodore Brameld (1904–1987): The Utopian

James McClellan devoted the third chapter of his 1968 book, *Toward an Effective Critique of American Education,* to an analysis of the ideas of Theodore Brameld. He begins by asking the question, "Why bother with Theodore Brameld?" and comments that "one could well argue that Brameld's proposals for educational policy and his arguments in support of them are no more relevant to the present educational situation than are Horace Mann's arguments from phrenology." McClellan then adds that "an attempt to study the structure of Brameld's thought resembles nothing so much as B'rer Rabbit's encounter with Tar Baby." McClellan nevertheless justifies the inclusion of Brameld among the significant figures in American education because he has been in the forefront of every "forward-looking movement" of the past thirty years. McClellan concludes that "policy arguments would be far poorer than they are" without Brameld's contributions.[1]

Brameld was a former professor of philosophy at Boston University and a proponent of an educational philosophy that he referred to as "reconstructionism." Highly controversial and provocative, Brameld was a dedicated internationalist who firmly believed that education was the key to establishing a world community.

EDUCATIONAL AIMS AND REFORMS

Brameld called for a new system of universal, compulsory schooling, with a radically new secondary school as its cornerstone.[2] This four-year school would serve everyone between the ages of seventeen and twenty and would be organized around the study of great problems, such as the environment and population control. Preparation for the high school would require a three-level elementary system, beginning for some children at age two, for the rest at age three-and-a-half. Higher education would be concerned primarily with the pursuit of research on the social problems treated in the secondary school, but would also allow for liberal and/or technical education for all who seem capable of profiting from such study.

Brameld proposed that the school cultivate the student as the instrument of social change. Teachers must encourage their students to examine the evidence for and against such a role, presenting alternative proposals scrupulously, and allowing the children to argue their own views publicly. He charged teachers at all levels of the educational program with the responsibility for having and expressing convictions, but at the same time providing maximum opportunities for study of evidence and arguments opposed to as well as in favor of their convictions.

Brameld insisted that an ideal culture cannot be had without the cultivation of intelligent cooperation. Society, he claimed, has to be more than an aggregate of individuals pulling this way and that. Fundamentally, the school must teach and stress the social character of men and women and the obligation of mankind to replace narrow nationalistic biases with a worldwide community.

TEACHER EDUCATION

In his book, *Education as Power*, Brameld devotes a chapter to outlining his plan for the preparation of teachers and begins with a disclaimer about the practicality, or lack thereof, of the plan: "While the proposed design is not necessarily applicable today, it should not be dismissed for this reason. Too many of us in education seem peculiarly prone to short sighted planning in the name of practicality. Actually, if we are educators worthy of the name, we have to be 'impractical' also, impractical in the sense of holding strong commitments and strong objectives as targets toward which we can aim. In our perilous age, only a deliberately audacious design for education is worthy of our profession."[3]

Brameld's design for reform of teacher education was as audacious as his reform plan for education in general. According to Brameld, teacher trainees should complete a seven-year program of study, with phase 1 consisting of two years of general education; phase 2, two years of behavioral sciences; phase 3, a year of educational theory; phase 4, a year of more thorough study of the area or areas in which a teacher plans to major (since primary teachers have no major except the behavioral sciences, they would give more attention in phase 4 to subjects normally taught in a primary school); phase 5, a year of internship.

Brameld contended that any plan for teacher education should start with the premise that teaching is a "high profession." He argued that teachers deserve a preparation at least equivalent in quality to that available in the best schools of medicine. He believed that there is general agreement that physicians in training have the following four educational needs: (1) a well-rounded, challenging general education; (2) a solid knowledge in the subject area which is most necessary to all practitioners; (3) a thoughtful theory or philosophy of medicine that helps them understand the contributions of medicine to the growth of civilization; (4) an abundance of rich experiences in effective practice—that is, in the techniques of medicine. By analogy, Brameld applied these four basic educational needs for prospective physicians to his plan for the preparation of teachers.

General Education

Brameld argued that general education is of comparable importance to medicine and education because both teachers and physicians, as servants of the public, are in need of "broad acquaintance with the main currents of scientific, social, and other knowledge if they are to relate effectively their specialized roles to the wider whole of human experience." To Brameld, general education should consist of "large clusters of problem-centered fields of study" that would provide students with "an integrated, organized understanding of the great areas of life and reality."[4]

One such cluster would deal with problems of the physical and biological sciences and their significance to the problems of modern man (for example, the dangers and promises of atomic energy). While considering these problems, students would acquire an understanding of the most essential principles of atomic physics. Similarly, they would learn biological principles while studying problems of population control. To Brameld, the objective of the study of all of the major areas of general education (including science, arts, communications, economics, politics, and social relations) should be the solving of great problems that impede the establishment of a democratic world civilization. Brameld believed that the two-year general education program should be open to all citizens of average intelligence and eventually become universal for average citizens of about nineteen and twenty in all countries of the world.

Behavioral Sciences

Concerning the second part of the four major requirements for teacher education, Brameld held that just as physicians, regardless of specialty, are expected to know thoroughly the subject matter most necessary to their profession, the physiological sciences, so all teachers should know thoroughly the subject matter most necessary to their profession—the behavioral sciences. These sciences are those that have to do with the way men and women, individually and socially, behave. Prospective teachers should devote as much time to the study of behavioral sciences as future

doctors do to the study of the physiological sciences. For Brameld, the behavioral sciences comprise the universal subject matter of the average
teacher and all other subject matters are secondary. Finally, Brameld proposed that the behavioral sciences be organized so as to include many of the
kinds of problems that teachers constantly face in the classroom, such as
emotional conflicts during adolescent development.

Educational Theory

The third major requirement for Brameld's new teacher education program consisted of one year of the study of educational theory, particularly
the history and philosophy of education. Brameld asserted that, just as in
medicine, this requirement was very weak. He suggested that this was in
part due to the fact that many of the courses in educational theory are
taught by incompetent instructors, and are both sterile and divorced from
the rest of the professional curriculum. Moreover, they are rarely related to
the kind of practice that Brameld proposed. Yet, he maintained that philosophy of education should give the teaching profession its single most powerful reason for being—it provides the teacher with clear purpose and
dedication and "offers him the stamina to endure the hardships that accompany his duties."[5]

After admitting that the organization of the introductory course in educational philosophy would vary somewhat with the training, point of view,
and qualifications of the instructor, Brameld provided some general guidelines.[6] First, educational philosophy should be interpreted in its cultural
setting, rather than as an intellectual discipline studied for its own sake. It
should concern itself with how the conflicting and emerging elements of
culture are expressed through philosophic concepts and issues, and how
current beliefs should be concretely applied in formal and informal education. Second, while the instructor should always at some point indicate his
or her own convictions, the main emphasis in the first course should be
upon fair consideration of each of the major types of educational philosophy currently most influential. Finally, the introductory course should fa-
miliarize students with special philosophic problems helpful in achieving
clarity of beliefs about issues of education and culture. Thus, the philosophical tools of ontology, epistemology, and axiology, for example, should
be brought to bear upon educational and social problems.

In addition to the introductory course in educational philosophy,
Brameld proposes that those students sufficiently interested should be permitted to elect more intensive courses. First, a series of courses, presuppos-
ing an introductory course, should examine each of the major types of
educational philosophy. A course in perennialism, for example, would concentrate on the writings of Aristotle and St. Thomas Aquinas and their application to educational theory. Brameld also suggests that experiments

should be set up in associated laboratory schools to illustrate how each philosophy results in radically different types of educational practice. Second, there should be a group of courses in "problems and techniques," to encourage the use of the most important philosophical tools. A course in critical thinking for teachers, for example, would put epistemology into operation by applying such tools as semantics, logic, and propaganda analysis to educational materials such as textbooks, movies, and radio. Another course of this kind would stress axiology by examining problems of value in educational fields such as the social studies, arts and sciences.

Toward the end of their teacher education program, Brameld would require all students to take one final course in educational philosophy. It would be conducted by a group of instructors who would attempt to impart to graduating students a comprehensive outlook upon their profession by presenting the chief issues and values of the entire field.

Internship/Practice

Just as a medical education program concludes with a full-time internship, so should a teacher education program, according to Brameld. He did not, however, restrict practice to the last year. He believed that practice should be provided throughout the seven-year program. In addition, he suggested that every student, beginning in general education and continuing afterwards, should become active in community affairs. Every prospective teacher "needs to learn, not merely *about* action, but *through* action—scientific, economic, social, political, and esthetic action—under the leadership of experts who can interpret the significance of what is being experienced."[7]

As students advance through the various phases of their program in the behavioral sciences and other areas, practice would increasingly focus upon educational problems. Many of these problems would still be community oriented (family relations, for example), but others would be school oriented. Brameld envisioned the school becoming "a magnificent laboratory for an almost infinite range of research and involvement which behavioral scientists still largely ignore."[8]

Brameld concluded his plan for teacher education by posing a question—"How can we [teacher educators] carry to fruition a design for teacher education worthy of our high profession?"[9] His answer was that teacher educators should take the offensive by proposing a far stronger program than any in existence. They should concede that current programs in teacher education are appallingly weak; but instead of "cringing" before the pressures of liberal arts and sciences critics, they should construct a much better professional program than any that the critics could propose. Brameld warned that "only an audacious policy that places preparation for any kind of educational service on a level at least equal in standards to that of the medical profession will serve us now."[10]

NOTES

1. James E. McClellan, *Toward an Effective Critique of American Education* (Philadelphia: J. B. Lippincot, 1968), pp. 129–130.

2. Theodore Brameld, *Toward a Reconstructed Philosophy of Education* (New York: Holt, Rinehart and Winston, 1956). The discussion in this section draws on this book.

3. Theodore Brameld, *Education as Power* (New York: Holt, Rinehart and Winston, 1965), p. 64. Unless otherwise noted, the discussion in this section relies on this book.

4. Ibid., pp. 65–66.

5. Ibid., p. 72.

6. The rest of the section on educational philosophy draws upon Theodore Brameld, *Ends and Means in Education: A Mid-Century Appraisal* (New York: Harper and Row, 1950).

7. Brameld, *Education as Power*, p. 71.

8. Ibid.

9. Ibid., p. 72.

10. Ibid., p. 136.

6

Charles Silberman (1925–): The Neo-Progressivist

Charles Silberman is a man of many talents. Over the years he has been a journalist, magazine editor, college teacher, and best-selling author. One of his most widely read, provocative books is *Crisis in the Classroom*, published in 1970, in the midst of the civil rights movement and political activism on college campuses.[1] In this book, Silberman argued that the monumental challenge facing Americans is to create and to perpetuate a more humane society. Such a society is possible when masses of people are educated not only to think but to feel and to act. To do this, Silberman called for fundamental changes in public schools, colleges, and universities. In *Crisis in the Classroom*, Silberman discussed what these changes should be. He was concerned with the development of "educators," when that term is broadly defined to include not only teachers but all people—doctors, lawyers, architects, and journalists—who exert, for better or worse, an educational influence on the populace. He focused, however, on the reform of education of public school teachers and their mentors, college and university professors.

EDUCATIONAL AIMS AND REFORMS

Silberman argued that it does little good to reform university teacher education without at the same time reforming public school education, for the training of a teacher is not restricted to undergraduate or graduate university teacher education programs. On the contrary, the real education of teachers begins when they take over their first class and this education continues throughout their lives.

Thus, no matter how outstanding a teacher preparation program at a university might become as a result of reforms, the positive educational influence exerted on its graduates will be short-lived if they start teaching and continue teaching in schools characterized by docility, passivity, conformity, and lack of trust. The ethos of such schools subjects neophyte teachers to a powerful, continuous education in "mindlessness."

Educators are mindless when they fail "to ask *why* they are doing what they are doing" and to carefully consider the implications of their actions.[2] Silberman believed that many young teachers will succumb to a mindless environment and will begin in time to teach in the same mindless way as most of their colleagues. For this reason, Silberman insisted that reform of teacher preparation must be considered in conjunction with the reform of public school education.

How should schools be reformed? Silberman urged teachers and their administrators to adopt some attitudes and convictions enunciated over the years by John Dewey and his followers:

- The quality of a child's school experience should be cherished in its own right, not merely as preparation for more schooling or life as an adult.
- Learning is generally more effective if it is based on what interests the learner rather than what interests the teacher.
- Instruction should be individualized and be consistent with clearly articulated goals about what is most worth learning.
- Good teaching consists in finding the right balance between individual growth and fulfillment and transmission of definite skills, intellectual discipline, and bodies of knowledge.
- Education is more than the transmission of knowledge—it is the molding of men and women.

How teachers teach and how they act may be more important than what they teach because the real test of the value of one's formal education is whether a love of learning has developed and whether that love has fostered a desire to continue learning throughout life.

In schools where teachers, administrators, and parents share these and similar ideas, it is possible in Silberman's judgment to advance the education not only of children but of teachers. In such schools, where the focus is on inquiry rather than the one-way transmission of information, it is possible for teachers to become learners along with their students: in short, to become, in John Dewey's words, "students of teaching." Development of these schools on a wide scale, however, demands radical changes in the training of teachers in institutions of higher learning.

TEACHER EDUCATION

The most needed change in Silberman's view is that teacher education should become a university-wide function involving not only education professors but professors in the arts and sciences. He acknowledged that education professors have a greater responsibility for the professional component and liberal arts and sciences professors a greater responsibility for the liberal education component, but insists that both components must be closely interrelated.

Liberal Education

Silberman believed that the weakness of teacher education is in large part due to the weakness of liberal education as a whole. He believed liberal education should bring students to a point beyond which they can continue to educate themselves throughout life. In general, however, it does not do this, for preparing students for life-long learning is not the objective of most professors. The result is that in most universities liberal education is in a chaotic state, and teacher education suffers accordingly.

"To be educated to the point where one can educate himself, or others," meant to Silberman that a person must not only be able "to think seriously about the means and ends of education (one's own, and others'), but about the *consequences* of education as well—about the way education shapes and molds the people being educated."[3] This in turn means that to be educated is to know how to apply knowledge in such a way as to make it effective in one's own life and the society in which one lives.

The best way for people to find out what they know and the relevance of their knowledge is to teach what they have learned to someone else. In a society becoming more and more highly specialized, the capacity and desire to educate, to make one's knowledge understandable and available to others, is becoming increasingly important. Silberman cautioned, however, that the way to make knowledge relevant is not to require students to take some courses in communication skills. What is needed is to persuade students, and before them the faculty, that it is incumbent upon the person of knowledge to make himself or herself understood. Otherwise, what he or she knows runs the risk of being ineffective or irrelevant.

Having made these points, Silberman concluded that to develop educators should be a central purpose of the college or university. As a first step in this direction, Silberman would require all students, not just those who plan to teach, to engage in teaching as a regular part of the undergraduate experience. Such an experience would encompass teaching fellow students in the college classroom, public school youngsters, or people involved in such government programs as the Peace Corps. Implementation of such a program would help make knowledge relevant to college students, and this in turn would help them as future professionals to make their knowledge relevant to others. The second step in the reform of liberal education is to put the study of education where it should be, "at the heart of the liberal arts curriculum, not at its margins. For the study of education is the study of almost every question of importance in philosophy, history, and sociology.

Our concept of education reflects our concept of the good life, the good man, and the good society; and . . . there can be no concept of the good life or the good society apart from a concept of the kind of education needed to sustain it."[4]

With teaching and the study of education an integral part of liberal education, Silberman said it is possible for a university to bring students to a point where they can continue to educate themselves after graduation. It is possible but only if professors develop a clearer concept of what liberal education should be. If professors are to do this, a process must be established in universities that permits and encourages a continuing dialogue among professors about the purposes, content, and processes of liberal education. Such a continuing dialogue is necessary for there is no one route to a liberal education. Acccording to Silberman, there are many routes, but each must have coherence and purpose: "each must reflect some conviction about what is worth knowing and doing and being."[5]

Silberman questioned whether professors will feel a real need for the dialogue if their own education has been limited to the arts and sciences. A course in the techniques of teaching their subject or a course or two in the history and philosophy of education would not be of much help either because the weakness of graduate education is less in the curriculum than in its overall tone and purpose. As explained by Silberman, what happens is that the elite universities in the United States, fifty of which train 90 percent of the Ph.D. graduates who enter academic life, recruit research-minded professors and then reward them for doing what they were hired to do. The result is an overemphasis on research at the expense of good teaching.

To produce researchers dedicated to liberal education, Silberman recommended that universities train teaching assistants working on their doctorates not only to do research but to educate. For teaching assistants to develop into educators, Silberman said they should be required to engage in a systematic study of education, and their classroom teaching should be supervised by senior professors who are dedicated to excellence in teaching. Such professors can help the teaching assistants "understand why they are teaching what they are teaching, and how it relates to the larger discipline they are studying, as well as to knowledge in general."[6]

Professional Education

Silberman claimed schoolteachers are being trained to be technicians in public schools as they *are*. That is, they are being trained to work in schools that are characterized by mindlessness. To combat this problem, Silberman urged colleges and universities to provide prospective teachers with "alternative pictures" of what teaching and learning *can be*, along with the methodologies needed to implement them. If they are not to teach in the same mindless way they were taught, prospective teachers must be provided with a sense of purpose, or a philosophy of education.

To Silberman, giving teachers a strong sense of purpose should be the central task of teacher education. He urged education faculties to think seriously about educational purpose and to arrange a curriculum that reflects the purposes so established. If educationists are to produce teachers who not only know how to teach but who are also students of teaching, they must expose their students to a curriculum that reflects some carefully considered conceptions of education. To do this, faculty members must continually ask themselves what difference it makes, if any, whether their students are educated at their university or someplace else. Few education faculties have asked such a question, and that explains to Silberman why professional education in most universities is in a pitiful state.

Silberman was particularly adamant about one point: For teachers to grow professionally throughout life, colleges and universities must provide them with knowledge about knowledge, that is, knowledge "about the ramifications of the subject or subjects they teach, about how those subjects relate to other subjects and to knowledge—and life—in general."[7]

Silberman concluded that a central role in teacher education must be given to the history and philosophy of education, as well as to the psychology, sociology, and anthropology of education. Taught properly, such study combines liberal and professional education and raises questions that teachers must think carefully about if they are to do their part in shaping the purposes and processes of education. The most important of these questions are those concerning the ends and means of educational practice and their relationship to the achievement of societal goals in a democracy.

Agreeing with Israel Scheffler that "to link the preparation of teachers with such questions . . . is the special opportunity of the university,"[8] Silberman went a step further and stated that "it is its special responsibility as well," for it is the universities—not the public schools or some other special training institutions—that are best equipped "to enlarge the intellectual context within which the teacher views his work—to give him the intellectual tools with which to analyze and understand, and therefore ultimately to improve, the education of the young."[9]

In sum, Silberman:

- questioned the assumption that the liberal education and professional education of teachers at the undergraduate level should be sharply distinguished and that the former should be so emphasized as to almost exclude the latter;
- insisted that teacher education should be a cooperative effort of public schools, education professors, and arts and sciences professors;
- believed that the advancement of education of children begins not only with improving the education of public school teachers but with the improvement of the education of their teachers—professors in education and in the arts and sciences;

- reminded us to heed Lawrence Cremin's admonition that "it will do Americans little good to quicken their pace in education if they do not know where they are going,"[10] hence the necessity of developing educators with a philosophical habit of mind.

NOTES

1. Charles E. Silberman, *Crisis in the Classroom: The Remaking of American Education* (New York: Random House, 1970).

2. Ibid., p. 11.

3. Ibid., p. 381.

4. Ibid., p. 384.

5. Ibid., p. 402.

6. Ibid., p. 510.

7. Ibid., p. 489.

8. Quoted in Silberman, *Crisis,* p. 492.

9. Ibid., p. 492.

10. Lawrence Cremin, *The Genius of American Education* (New York: Vintage Books, 1965), p. 31.

7

Ivan Illich (1926–):
The Radical

Ivan Illich was born in Vienna and educated in Rome and Salzburg. He has been a parish priest in New York City, a vice-rector of the Catholic University of Puerto Rico, the founder of a famous center for cross-cultural studies in Cuernavaca, Mexico, and a worldwide lecturer. Illich is considered one of the most radical political and social thinkers of the twentieth century. His educational views first became widely known with the publication of his book *Deschooling Society* in 1971, a time that coincided with political activism in American life.

Illich's basic thesis is simple. By its very nature, formal schooling is an institution designed to maintain the status quo. In order to accomplish any meaningful reform, we must abolish compulsory attendance laws and eliminate all academic credentialing. Most of the traditional functions of the school can and should be eliminated or assigned to other agencies in society. According to Illich, we are witnessing the end of the "age of schooling."[1]

EDUCATIONAL AIMS AND REFORM

In Illich's view, an educational system should do three things: (1) provide people with access to learning resources, (2) place those who want to learn in contact with those who want to teach, and (3) present those who want to bring an issue before the public with an opportunity to do so. Thus, it clearly follows that schooling should be optional, not compulsory. In addition, discrimination in hiring, voting, or admission to centers of learning based on credentials or certificates allocated by formal schools should be prohibited by law.[2]

According to Illich, trying to improve schools is a hopeless activity. New curricula, improved pedagogical techniques, decentralization, alternative schools, electronic gadgetry, open classrooms, voucher plans, compensatory education, all miss the point. They are doomed to failure because they fail to address the "ritualistic" or "hidden" curriculum that permeates everything that goes on in school. Radical change will follow only from a change in the basic structure of education because obligatory public schools inevitably reproduce the consumer society no matter what is taught in them.[3]

TEACHER EDUCATION

Many people might assume that Illich's position would seem to logically preclude the very concept of teacher education; at the very most he could not have much to say about the subject. Interestingly enough, it is exactly this kind of thinking, confusing education with schooling, that prompted Illich to protest against the present educational system in the first place. Obviously, Illich did not have very much to say about teacher *schooling* except to criticize it and call for it, along with schooling in general, to be abolished. But just because Illich had no constructive plan for the reform of teacher schooling within our formal educational system, does not mean that he has nothing to contribute to a book on teacher *education.* In fact, he did develop a wide-ranging plan for teacher education in a deschooled society that combines the most ancient model of teacher education, apprenticeship, with the technology of a computer society.

To achieve this goal of a deschooled society, Illich recognized that the major obstacle that must be overcome is the resistance of the formalized teaching profession.[4] Moreover, according to Illich, this resistance will get worse before it is finally broken because educators who are aware of the impending breakdown of schools will engage in a frantic attempt to teach more people about more things. Illich cautioned that teachers, like doctors, tend to believe that at least some of the generally useful knowledge they hold cannot be expressed outside their hieratic code. Thus, it is useless to expect the American Medical Association or the National Education Association to explain in ordinary language the "professional gangsterism" of their members.[5]

Illich lamented that education, the one type of investment that could give long-range returns, is conceived mostly as training for bureaucrats who will maintain the existing apparatus.[6] According to Illich, this is possible because of one of the most evil devices ever foisted upon an unsuspecting public—the concept of teacher certification. He charged that neither learning nor justice is promoted by schooling because educators insist on packaging instruction with certification.[7] Furthermore, insisting on the certification of teachers is another way of keeping skills scarce.[8]

In order to counter this entrenched habit of requiring certification by law, Illich proposed that there should be no laws with respect to the establishment of education and that there should be no graded curriculum that is obligatory for all.[9] Illich would guarantee the right of each citizen to an equal share of public educational resources, the right to certify his share of these resources, and the right to sue for them if they are denied. A generalized GI bill, or an edu-credit card in the hand of every citizen would effectively implement this guarantee.

Illich maintained that abolition of compulsory schooling, abolition of job discrimination in favor of persons who have acquired their learning at a higher cost (i.e., in a formal school environment), plus establishment of edu-credit would permit the development of a free exchange for educational services. This exchange could be influenced by various devices: Premiums paid to those who acquire certain needed skills, interest-bearing edu-credit to increase the privilege of those who use it later in life, and advantages for industries that incorporate additional formal training into the work routine. Another guarantee to protect the consumer against the monopoly of the educational market would be analogous to anti-trust laws.[10] In his writing, Illich is aware that when the legitimacy of educational certification breaks down, other more primitive forms of discrimination are bound to assume renewed importance. However, he seems much less fearful of that evil than of the menace perpetrated by the present system.[11]

To take the place of formal schools and certified teachers, Illich suggested that we "plunge our imagination" into the construction of scenarios that would allow a bold reallocation of educational functions among industry, politics, short scholastic retreats, and intensive preparation of parents for providing early childhood education.[12] Moreover, various forms of in-service apprenticeship in factories and programmed math and language teaching could assume a large proportion of what we have previously called "instruction."[13]

For most widely shared skills, in Illich's view, a person who demonstrates the skill is the only human resource we ever need or get. Illich pointed out that in speaking, driving, cooking, and other common tasks we are often barely conscious of formal instruction and learning. He saw no reason why other complex skills, such as the mechanical aspects of surgery, playing musical instruments, reading, or using directories and catalogues, could not be learned in the same way.[14] Furthermore, skill centers, which would be judged by customers on their results, and not on the personnel they employ or the process they use, would open unsuspected working opportunities frequently even for those who are now considered unemployable. Indeed, Illich claimed that there is no reason why such skill centers should not be at the work place itself, with the employer and the work force supplying instruction as well as jobs to those who choose to use their educational credits this way. Thus, instruction at the skill level is based on trial and error, observation, and apprenticeship that is not limited to certified teachers.[15]

Illich did recognize, however, the need for three distinctly educational competencies: One to create and operate the kinds of educational exchanges or networks he outlines; another to guide students and parents in the use of these networks; and a third to act as an "initiator" or leader in undertaking difficult intellectual exploratory journeys. Illich suggested that only the former two, educational administrators and pedagogical counselors, can be conceived of as branches of an independent profession.

According to Illich, to design and operate the networks would not require many people, but it would require people who understand education and administration in a way quite different from and even opposed to that of schools.[16] Illich maintained that today's educational administrators are concerned with controlling teachers and students to the satisfaction of others—trustees, legislatures, and corporate executives. Network builders and administrators would have to demonstrate genius at keeping themselves, and others, out of people's way, at facilitating encounters among students, skill models, educational leaders, and educational objects.[17] Many persons now attracted to teaching are profoundly authoritarian and would not be able to assume this task.

Building educational exchanges would mean making it easy for people, especially the young, to pursue goals that might contradict the ideals of the "traffic manager" who makes the pursuit possible. Instead of the kind of authoritarian characteristics presently common in certified teachers, the operation of learning webs would require some of the skills and attitudes now expected from the staff of a museum, a library, an executive employment agency, or a maitre d'hotel. While network administrators would concentrate primarily on the building and maintenance of roads providing access to resources, the pedagogues would help students find the path that could lead fastest to their goals. If a student wanted to learn spoken Cantonese from a Chinese neighbor, the pedagogue would be available to judge their proficiency and to help them select the textbook and methods most suitable to their talents, character, and the time available for study. Pedagogues could counsel the would-be airplane mechanic on finding the best places for apprenticeship or recommend books to somebody who wanted to find challenging peers to discuss African history. Like network administrators, pedagogical counselors would conceive of themselves as professional educators.[18]

Illich admitted that the role of the educational initiator, the master or "true" leader, is somewhat more elusive than that of the professional administrator or pedagogue. The relationship of master and disciple is not restricted to intellectual disciplines. It has its counterpart in the arts, in physics, in religion, in psychoanalysis, and in pedagogy. It exists in such enterprises as mountain climbing, silver working, politics, cabinet making, and personnel administration. What is common to all "true" master-pupil relationships is the awareness both share that their relationship is literally priceless and in very different ways a privilege for both.[19]

Illich predicted that the most enterprising and gifted among these masters would probably find more congenial work, more independence, and even higher incomes by specializing as skill models, network administrators, or guidance specialists.[20] As far as financial compensation is concerned, Illich would have the "teacher" paid according to the number of pupils attracted for any full two-hour period. He visualized very young leaders and great educators as the two types most prominent in such a system.

The same approach would be taken toward higher education. Students could be furnished with educational vouchers that would entitle them to ten hours of yearly private consultation with the teacher of their choice and, for the rest of their learning they would depend on the library, the peer-matching network, and apprenticeships.[21] It should be noted that Illich's conception of a library is much broader than normal. At its best, the library is the prototype of what Illich designated as a "convivial tool." He recommended that "repositories for learning tools" should be organized and expanded so as to facilitate access to tapes, pictures, records, labs filled with the same scientific instruments with which most of the major breakthroughs of the last century were made.[22]

Finally, Illich envisioned a learning society in which only those who had taught others for an equivalent amount of time would have a claim on the time of more advanced teachers. In this way an entirely new elite would be promoted, an elite of those who earned their education by sharing it.[23]

In summary, there is much that appears new in Illich's vision of teacher education in a deschooled society—at least on the surface. Upon closer inspection, however, many of his proposals have their roots in the distant past. To be sure, his networks and the skills needed to create and implement them are novel ideas possible only in a technologically advanced society. However, suggestions such as having society and industry play a larger role in on-the-job training for most skills, placing the responsibility for early childhood education with parents, abolishing teacher certification, and requiring teachers to seek financial support from their students bring back memories of America before the turn of the century and, indeed, of the sophists in Ancient Greece. In fact, the road to becoming anything from a skill model to an educational administrator or pedagogical counselor and even a "master" seems to lie with that most ancient of teacher education models—apprenticeship.

NOTES

1. Ivan Illich, "After Deschooling, What?" in *After Deschooling, What?* eds. Alan Gartner and others (New York: Perennial Library, 1973), pp. 5–6.

2. Ivan Illich, *Deschooling Society* (New York: Harper and Row, 1972), p. 108.

3. Ibid., p. 38.

4. Ivan Illich, *Celebration of Awareness: A Call for Institutional Revolution* (Garden City, N.Y.: Doubleday, 1970), p. 121.

5. Ivan Illich, *Tools for Conviviality* (New York: Harper and Row, 1973), p. 16.

6. Illich, *Celebration of Awareness*, p. 146.

7. Illich, *Deschooling Society*, p. 16.

8. Ibid., p. 129.

9. Illich, *Celebration of Awareness*, p. 179.

10. Ibid., p. 180.

11. Illich, *Tools for Conviviality*, p. 71.

12. Illich, *Celebration of Awareness*, p. 110.

13. Ibid., p. 108.

14. Illich, *Deschooling Society*, p. 126.

15. Ibid., p. 21.

16. Ibid., p. 141.

17. Ibid., p. 142.

18. Ibid., pp. 142–143.

19. Ibid., pp. 144–145.

20. Ibid., p. 148.

21. Ibid., p. 136.

22. Illich, *Tools for Conviviality*, p. 65.

23. Illich, *Deschooling Society*, p. 130.

8

Albert Shanker (1928–1997): The Unionist

Albert Shanker was perhaps most famous as the president of the 907,000 member American Federation of Teachers from 1974–1997. He was an advisor to several presidents and held memberships on the AFL-CIO Executive Council, the U.S. Council on Competitiveness, the Joint Council on Economic Education, the National Endowment for Democracy, and the Trilateral Commission, among others. He was born and raised in New York City and earned a bachelor's degree in philosophy from the University of Illinois. Although his early reputation as a union militant stuck with him, he never hesitated to speak his mind about what was wrong with schools. His most lasting contribution to American education was his crusade to establish collective bargaining for teachers.[1]

EDUCATIONAL AIMS AND REFORM

According to Shanker, the aim of education is to teach students problem-solving skills so that they in turn can seek solutions to problems that plague human civilization.[2] Children of all backgrounds must master a demanding core curriculum that will prepare them to live in a democratic society, compete in the global economy, and benefit from postseconday education.[3] To do this, schools must focus on teaching students language, mathematics, history, geography, and science.[4] Moreover, a public education system that educates students in such a manner is a critical linchpin in the preservation of a democratic form of government.

Shanker argued that the educational system in the United States needs reform because so many students are not getting anything out of it. He espoused several reforms including raising standards for both students and teachers and giving teachers the ability (through collective bargaining) to control their own profession. He also insisted that unless the country is willing to significantly improve the working conditions of teaching (e.g., salaries, pension, benefits, and site-based decision-making authority), it will be impossible to attract a sufficient number of high quality teachers into the profession.[5] Until there is a public commitment to enhancing the quality and professionalism of teachers, school reform is unlikely.[6]

TEACHER EDUCATION

Improving standards in schools and colleges for all students was Shanker's first step toward improving teacher education. For Shanker, the only way to get really competent teachers is to insist that all students become proficient at their subjects before they are allowed to graduate. This would increase the number of competent students entering and graduating from college and eventually produce more teachers who are proficient in their subject.[7]

Shanker had three recommendations regarding preparation programs for prospective teachers. First, eliminate generic instructional methods courses.[8] Second, place more emphasis on teaching prospective teachers content. Shanker granted that good teachers should be skilled in techniques of classroom management and that they should also be sensitive to who their students are and know what kinds of approaches will help them learn. But, according to Shanker, these things are worth very little unless a teacher knows the subject.[9] Third, strengthen the clinical component by involving exemplary teachers both at field sites and as clinical faculty members of education departments.[10]

Before being licensed, Shanker recommended that graduates of teacher education programs pass a bar exam like doctors and lawyers currently do. This would result in a higher qualified teaching force and have the added advantage of increasing public respect for teachers' qualifications. Shanker granted that this kind of paper-and-pencil test will not show who can actually teach. However, he believed that assessments requiring performance skills should be postponed until the end of a probationary period and be used as a prerequisite for attaining tenure. He insisted that a paper-and-pencil test can sort out those teachers who are literate from those who are not as well as separate those teachers who know their subject from those who do not.[11]

According to Shanker, a teacher's education is only beginning when he or she takes a first job. Teachers, especially new ones, need to get out of their self-contained classrooms so they can interact with their colleagues. Without a chance to reflect on their teaching and discuss it with more experienced colleagues, new teachers may flounder and fall back on techniques they saw their own teachers use, whether or not these techniques worked. According to Shanker, almost every other profession has a better system of induction for new members than teaching. He specifically praised intern-ships that provide help from experienced colleagues and allow beginners to ease into accepting full responsibilities.[12]

Shanker also thought it was important to devote a sufficient amount of time and money for teacher in-service. He pointed out that the automobile industry devoted ninety-two hours of training and thousands of dollars a year per employee and suggested that it would take at least that much time and money for professional development to keep teachers up to date.[13]

Beyond in-service programs, Shanker championed the concept of a na-tional teacher certification program for truly outstanding teachers and sup-ported the establishment of the National Board for Professional Teaching Standards. The first stage of this program involved submitting a portfolio of work that included videotapes of classroom lessons along with extensive written material describing and analyzing how the teachers would help their students learn. Then they must travel to an assessment center where they would undergo two days of oral and written assessments.[14]

Finally, Shanker advocated a system of peer review developed by teacher unions in collaboration with their school districts. In this system master (i.e., experienced and excellent) teachers would observe probation-ary teachers and offer them help when they need it. At the conclusion of the probationary period, these master teachers would make recommendations about who should be offered tenure and who should be let go. Peer review would also include assistance to tenured teachers who need help with their teaching.[15]

In summary, for Shanker, teacher education was just one part of a more general campaign to improve education through the vehicle of teacher unionization. But Shanker's views are not just traditional union rhetoric. He advocated that teacher unions work cooperatively with legislators, state departments of education, local policy makers, universities, licensing bodies, and professional standards boards.[16] *The Wall Street Journal* charac-terized Shanker as "a respected educational leader whose vision of Ameri-can school reform has shaken up the status quo."[17]

NOTES

1. Dickson A. Mungazi, *Where He Stands: Albert Shanker of the American Federa-tion of Teachers* (Westport, Conn.: Praeger, 1990).

2. Ibid., p. 109.

3. Albert Shanker, "Quality Assurance: What Must Be Done to Strengthen the Teaching Profession," *Phi Delta Kappan*, 78 (November 1996): 220.

4. Albert Shanker, "Reforming the Academic Mission of School," (keynote ad-dress to the Annual Conference of the AFT, held in Washington, D.C., July 8–11, 1993) AFT Files, Washington, D.C.

5. Mungazi, *Where He Stands*, pp. 110–111.

6. Shanker, "Quality Assurance," p. 220.

7. Albert Shanker, "Where We Stand: Opportunity to Learn Standards," *New York Times,* 30 May 1993, sec. E, p. 7.

8. Albert Shanker, "Where We Stand: A Landmark Revisited," *New York Times,* 9 May 1993, sec. E, p. 7.

9. Albert Shanker, "Where We Stand: Remembering Teachers," *New York Times,* 29 December 1996, sec. E, p. 7.

10. Shanker, "Quality Assurance," p. 224.

11. Albert Shanker, "Where We Stand: Testing Teachers," *New York Times,* 8 January 1995, sec. E, p. 7.

12. Albert Shanker, "Where We Stand: Sink or Swim," *New York Times,* 22 January 1995, sec. E, p. 7.

13. Albert Shanker, "Where We Stand: Ninety-two Hours," *New York Times,* 24 January 1993, sec. E, p. 7.

14. Albert Shanker, "Where We Stand: Beyond Merit Pay," *New York Times,* 15 January 1995, sec. E, p. 7.

15. Albert Shanker, "Where We Stand: The Wrong Target." *New York Times,* 15 September 1996, sec. E, p. 7.

16. Shanker, "Quality Assurance," pp. 223–24.

17. "Albert Shanker's Vision of America," *Wall Street Journal,* 24 November 1987, p.7.

9

Chester Finn (1944–):
The Conservative

Chester Finn is a media favorite. When print or television reporters desire a
reaction to some educational issue, more often than not, they turn to him.
Finn is a former professor and was assistant secretary at the U.S. Department of Education under the Reagan administration. Currently, he is Senior Fellow at the Manhattan Institute and president of the Thomas B.
Fordham Foundation. Articulate, outspoken, and polemical, Finn wants to
wake up the American people to a "secret killer"—the diseased state of the
American public school system.[1]

EDUCATIONAL AIMS AND REFORMS

When it comes to educational reform, Finn is no incrementalist. He demands a complete overhaul of wrongheaded practices, ideas, and customs
in the schools and society. The most important of these needed changes are
the following:

- The American people must wake up to the painful reality that their local schools,
  which in Gallop polls they express satisfaction with, are just as bad as they believe other schools to be.

- Schools must concentrate on what they can do best: promote the cognitive learning of young people. Schools cannot do this job well if energy and resources are
  diverted to things that other institutions should be doing.

- Schools must provide every student with a liberal education, with a common
  core of learning. Finn does not believe the core should occupy the entire curriculum or that students should learn the core at the same rate. He stresses that different pedagogical and organizational modes are essential if everyone is to learn the
  core curriculum.

- Schools must be accountable for their actions. The essence of accountability, Finn says, is the same for schools as for other institutions: accurate information and clear goals, feedback on how well the goals have been achieved, and insistence that consequences be tied to success or failure.

- Schools must replace standardized multiple-choice tests with comprehensive, mostly essay examinations comparable to those in European countries and elsewhere. These exams should test what teachers are supposed to teach, and teachers should teach to the test. Furthermore, the testing program should be linked, equated, and amalgamated so as to make it easier to compare educational achievement at the local, state, national, and international levels.

- Parents must have the right to choose the schools best for their children. Parental choice, Finn believes, will force schools to be more competitive, and hence, more efficient and productive.[2]

- Colleges and employers and the community at large must help the schools provide rewards for those students who excel academically and sanctions for those who do poorly.

- The education bureaucracy must be pruned vigorously. Local school boards and superintendencies have outlived their usefulness. Their huge bureaucracies make needed changes difficult to implement and their non-teaching personnel drain money away from the classrooms. For school reform to be effective, Finn believes a number of key decisions should be moved up to the states and practically all other decisions should be made by individual schools and parents.[3]

- The importance of teaching facts must be restored to the schools.

- Revolutionary educational reform must, on the whole, be initiated and sustained not by educators but by political leaders, business leaders, and the general public. Since the education profession is rife with such dubious notions as facts are unimportant, it cannot be trusted to reform the school system.

TEACHER EDUCATION

What should a teacher be able to do, according to Finn? He expects teachers not only to "vary their pedagogy to suit the abilities, backgrounds, and interests of their students,"[4] but also to be able to do the following:

- develop a "school community" in which teachers "share a belief structure, a value system, a consensual rather than hierarchical governance system, and a set of common goals that blur the boundaries between their private and organizational lives";[5]

- "work collegially to establish curricula for their subjects from kindergarten through twelfth grade";[6]

- "tailor instructional strategies to the capabilities and preferences of the staff as well as the values of parents";[7]

- "engage parents and community";[8]

- "link the school's efforts with those of other agencies, from police to child-welfare authorities";[9]

- "decide what their school will specialize in" and how it will "distinguish itself from others."[10]

To do all these things well obviously requires highly sophisticated skills and a broad intellectual and professional perspective, but Finn does not expect prospective teachers to gain any of this in a traditional university or college teacher preparation program. In fact, he does not believe that a teacher should be required to have any professional training in a teacher training institution.

Finn believes that perhaps the best way to recruit and keep able, well-qualified people in school teaching is to redefine the pool of prospective instructors. Admission into teaching should not be confined to recent graduates of traditional preparation programs. Rather, entry to teaching should be opened up to mid-career people and to young college graduates with degrees in academic fields who want to try teaching. To give them a reasonable chance of succeeding as teachers, Finn urges schools to provide neophyte teachers with sufficient on-the-job supervision, mentoring, and pointers on classroom management. Those who do well should be retained, and those who do not should be encouraged to enter another line of work.

Finn supports the movement to raise the quality of the teaching force, but he opposes the "conventional wisdom" that "holds that tighter regulation of entry is the only way to ensure that all children have qualified teachers." In his judgment, "the hoops and hurdles that we make prospective teachers clear have failed to assure their subject matter knowledge, classroom prowess, or success in raising pupil achievement. Why, then, suppose that more hoops and hurdles will yield a different result?" He calls for a different approach, one based on "common sense." This approach proposes to boost teacher quality by "simplifying entry and hiring, welcoming diversity, allowing principals to employ the teachers they need, and gauging quality chiefly by student achievement."[11]

When it comes to education of teachers, Finn's "rule of thumb is simple: Any well-educated adult of sound character, who knows a subject and is willing to try teaching it to children, should be a candidate for entry into the classroom."[12]

NOTES

1. Unless otherwise indicated, the discussion on Finn in this chapter draws on Chester E. Finn, Jr., *We Must Take Charge: Our Schools and Our Future* (New York: Free Press, 1991).

2. For more information, from Finn's perspective, on this controversial topic, see Bruno V. Manno, Chester E. Finn, Jr., Louann A. Bierlin, and Gregg Vanorek,

"How Charter Schools Are Different: Lessons and Implications from a National Study," *Phi Delta Kappan* 79 (March 1998): 488–498.

3. In a recent article, Finn complained that parents take a "minimal interest in their children's studies, fail to meet with teachers, and do not participate in school events." Finn concluded on a pessimistic note, at odds with his frequently expressed faith in the good sense of parents. Until such time, he said, as the "minds and hearts of American parents" are transformed, there is "no good reason to hope that their children will become much better educated or much better behaved than they are right now—and plenty of reason to fear that many of them will be worse." Chester E. Finn, Jr., "Can Parents Be Trusted?" *Commentary* 108 (September 1999): 237.

4. Chester E. Finn, Jr., "A Fresh Option for the Non-College Bound," *Phi Delta Kappan* 68 (November 1986): 237.

5. Chester E. Finn, Jr., "Toward Strategic Independence: Nine Commandments for Enhancing School Effectiveness," *Phi Delta Kappan* 65 (April 1984): 519.

6. Diane Ravitch and Chester E. Finn, Jr., *What Do Our 17-Year-Olds Know* (New York: Harper and Row, 1987), p. 229.

7. Finn, *We Must Take Charge*, p. 267.

8. Ibid.

9. Ibid.

10. Ibid., p. 266.

11. Chester E. Finn, Jr., foreword to *Better Teachers, Better Schools*, ed. Marci Kanstoroom and Chester E. Finn, Jr. (Washington, D.C.: Thomas B. Fordham Foundation, 1999), p. v.

12. Finn, *We Must Take Charge*, p. 268.

II

Present (2000)

10

Recruitment and Retention of Teachers

Public education rests precariously on the skill and virtue of the people at the bottom of the instructional pyramid.

Tracy Kidder, author and Pulitzer recipient for nonfiction literature

CRITICS ON RECRUITING AND RETENTION OF QUALITY TEACHERS

With the exception of Chester Finn and the late Albert Shanker, the critics examined in this book were active professionally in periods not particularly afflicted with a teacher shortage "crisis"; hence, they have few specific suggestions relevant to recruitment and retention. They do, however, have something important to say about the kind of teachers that should be hired and retained. By and large, they insist that teachers be *learned* people.

In China, it is widely believed that a teacher needs "ten barrels of water to give the students one cup of water." Our critics agree, though they differ on the various kinds of knowledge a teacher should have. As Conant noted, schoolteaching requires a certain level of scholarly sophistication if teachers are to earn respect as learned members of the community. Further, Conant argued that if teachers are to work together as a group of learned persons, they need much in common intellectually, hence, the great importance of a solid liberal education. In industrialized countries in Asia and Europe, people have long believed and acted upon the belief that a teacher must first of all be a learned person. In Europe and Asia, such a person is not only broadly educated in many subjects but also knows well his or her subject matter and how to teach it effectively.

LACK OF RESPECT FOR AMERICAN TEACHERS

The popular comedian, Rodney Dangerfield, is fond of lamenting that "I get no respect." He must come from a long line of public school teachers. In the colonial period and some decades thereafter, the stereotype of the teacher was Washington Irving's bumbling Ichabod Crane. James Carter, the "father" of American teacher education, observed that "if a young man be moral enough to keep out of the State-Prison, he will find no difficulty in getting approbation for a school-master."[1] In the nineteenth century, women gradually replaced men as teachers in the lower schools and, like their male predecessors, were paid a pittance and "boarded 'round" in the homes of the parents of their students. As the historian David Tyack noted, "Most Americans took more care in selecting blacksmiths to shoe their horses—and paid them better—than teachers to instruct their children."[2]

In 1901, William T. Harris, a school superintendent and the president of the National Education Association—controlled at the time by school administrators—disdainfully dismissed a challenge from the convention floor by Margaret Haley to his assertion that public education was flourishing under capitalism. Haley, who later organized the Chicago Teachers Federation, had the temerity to bitterly complain that teachers were grossly underpaid. Harris, no doubt with a sniff or two, replied that the assembly should "pay no attention to what the teacher down there has said . . . for I take it she is a grade teacher, just out of her schoolroom at the end of school year, worn out, tired, and hysterical."[3]

To be sure, teachers are better paid now than in 1901, but they are still underpaid, and they still get little respect, as a National Teacher of the Year Award winner found out. The winner of this prestigious award in 2000 is a kindergarten teacher in Georgia. When invited to speak at a meeting of the Georgia Senate, he spoke out on needed educational reform in his state. For this presumably brazen behavior, his invitation to speak at the House of Representatives was withdrawn, and the governor refused to attend a photo session for him and twenty other nationally recognized Georgia educators.[4]

In spite of the frenetic efforts to reform education since the early 1980s, teachers have by and large been excluded from participating in these efforts. Not a single active classroom teacher signed either of the two major teacher education reform reports during the 1980s, the reports by the Holmes Group and the Carnegie Foundation. In the 1990s, teachers continued to be virtually excluded from the numerous panels and commissions devoted to education reform. Only one or two teachers, for example, were invited to participate in the 1996 Governor's Open Education Summit with big business; and of the sixty-six people on the Georgia Commission on School Reform, only three or four were practicing teachers.[5]

Furthermore, one of the most critical characteristics of a learned profession is the right to control entrance into the profession. In the great majority of states, teachers have no say in the development or grading of examinations for teacher licensure. In contrast, engineers, architects, lawyers, and doctors are the seminal players in any effort to reform their professions and develop the licensure examinations for prospective members of their professions.

Lack of respect for teachers accounts in large part for their inadequate pre-service and in-service education and their low salaries, dead-end careers, and often pathetic working conditions. These defects make recruitment and retention of quality teachers a problem that has garnered national attention.

RECRUITMENT OF TEACHERS

Toward the end of 2000, *Newsweek* magazine devoted a cover story to the shortage of teachers, and a report released by the National Commission on Mathematics and Science Teaching for the 21st Century, better known as the John Glenn Commission, also gave considerable attention to recruitment and retention of quality teachers.[6]

We should note here that there is *not* at present a shortage of teachers in general, that is, in all the different areas of specialization—elementary school teacher, English teacher, physics teacher, special education teacher, and so on. According to the American Association of Employment in Education, in 1997 there were more teachers than needed in most fields in the Northeast, Middle Atlantic, Rocky Mountain, and Northwest states and a shortage of teachers in most fields in Alaska and an appreciable number of fields in the West and South. Nationally, for some time there has been a surplus of elementary school teachers and teachers of English, social studies, physical education, health education, and business education. Shortages of teachers typically occur in different regions of the country in such fields as bilingual education, special education, and, especially, in mathematics and physical science, the two fields in which teachers can make much more money in private industry than in schools.[7]

There have indeed been periodic teacher shortages over the years in various fields in different regions of the country, but not for long at any one time. Educational policy makers solve the recurring "crisis" with a simple expedient—rather than raising teacher standards when there is a teacher shortage, they violate the standards for teacher licensure and hire people with substandard professional qualifications, and they pressure principals to assign licensed teachers in, for example, English to teach a class in history or biology, two subjects in which the English teacher probably does not have even a minor, let alone a major. This endemic practice is called "teaching out-of-field."

- Nationwide, more than a fourth of new teachers start teaching without being fully qualified (that is, meeting all the requirements for a standard teaching license issued by a state); 12 percent are hired with no license, and another 15 percent hold temporary, provisional, or emergency licenses.[8]
- More than fifty thousand people start teaching each year with only an emergency or substandard license.[9]
- Forty-one percent of all 12th grade students enrolled in physical science classes (chemistry, physics, earth science or space science) are taught by teachers without at least a minor in any of these physical sciences.[10]
- Fifty-three percent of secondary history students are taught by teachers who do not have a major or minor in history.[11]
- Twenty-eight percent of secondary math teachers and 18 percent of science teachers do not have a major or minor in mathematics.[12]
- In English and history, over four million secondary school students are taught every year by teachers without a major or minor in the field.[13]
- Only New Jersey and Colorado require middle school teachers to have majors in subjects they teach.[14]
- In Los Angeles, around 60 percent of newly hired teachers have emergency licenses, and most teachers in California with these licenses have the daunting task of trying to teach children how to read in grades 1, 2, and 3.[15]

If one believes, as many Americans do, that teaching is a job that practically anybody can handle who has a desire to teach, a college degree, and a little on-the-job training, then these statistics are not particularly disturbing. If, on the other hand, one believes that a prospective teacher should have a good liberal education and a thorough knowledge of subject matter and how to teach it effectively to children with different interests, abilities, and backgrounds, then the statistics can only be viewed as appalling. Common sense suggests that well-educated, highly trained teachers will be more effective in promoting student learning than those without these qualifications, and there is now research evidence to support this conclusion.[16] The problem, of course, is not only to recruit well-qualified prospective teachers with the potential to develop into quality teachers but to keep them in schools, should they live up to their potential, and encourage them to make teaching a career.

RETENTION OF TEACHERS

At present, there are over three million teachers in the United States. Nearly half of these will need to be replaced this decade. Even if we could wave a magic wand and replace all of them with highly qualified teacher novices with the potential to develop into quality teachers, there remains, nevertheless, an ominous retention problem. Again, let us look at some statistics:

- Each year nearly twice as many teachers are prepared as actually enter teaching.[17]
- One-third of secondary teachers are obligated to teach one class a day for which they are not academically prepared.[18]
- Thirty-nine percent of the American Federation of Teachers membership work second jobs to make ends meet.[19]
- Less than one-fifth of first-year teachers receive mentoring.[20]
- In Miami Dade County, one of the largest school districts in the United States, 41 percent of the schools are packed with students 150 percent over capacity.[21]
- Nearly 19 percent of children in the United States—about 13.3 million—live in poverty, and there is evidence that concentrated poverty in schools is associated with lower achievement for both poor and nonpoor students who attend such schools.[22]
- The average teaching load for secondary teachers is 128 students and five classes per day.[23]
- Prior to the 1993-94 school year, about 286,200 teachers were newly hired by schools, but twelve months later, about 213,000 teachers—about 75 percent of those just hired—quit teaching altogether.[24]

These statistics alone would dampen the enthusiasm of many talented people from pursuing a career in teaching. There are other factors, however, that adversely affect the ability of school districts to recruit and retain quality teachers.

Salary

In their book, *Who Will Teach? Polices That Matter*, Richard Murnane and colleagues argued that teaching has become "particularly unattractive to the brightest and most talented" and that "the key to designing a successful strategy for improving the nation's teaching force is to recognize that the people we would most like to teach our children are college graduates with the best alternative career options. To attract them into teaching, we must adopt policies that increase the attractiveness of teaching relative to other occupations."[25] After documenting that salaries do indeed make a difference in how long teachers stay in the classroom, the authors concluded that "any strategy to increase the number of skilled teachers in the nation's schools must include competitive salaries."[26]

Salaries for American teachers clearly are not competitive. During the 1998–1999 school year, the average beginning public school teacher's salary was $26,639.[27] During this same year, teachers age twenty-two to twenty-eight made on average $7,894 less than other college-educated adults in the same age bracket.[28] The Organization for Economic Cooperation and Development (OECD) released a recent report comparing salary data submitted by fifteen countries, including Switzerland, Germany, the United Kingdom, and New Zealand, all countries that pay their secondary teachers more than the average college graduate. In analyzing the data, the authors noted that the gap between the average teacher's and the average college graduate's pay in the United States was the second largest of the fifteen countries participating in the study.[29]

The salary gap for older American teachers during the 1998–1999 academic year was even greater than for the younger ones. Teachers age forty-four to fifty earned $23,655 less than their counterparts in other occupations; those with a master's degree earned $32,313 less than nonteachers with the same degree. After adjusting for inflation, from 1994 to 1998, the average salary increase for master's degree teachers was less than $200 and for nonteachers with a master's, $17,505.[30] Since 1995, a period of unprecedented economic prosperity, teacher income increased only 11 percent.[31]

To compound the salary problem, we should note that 65 percent of teachers in America are women. In the past, the best of women became teachers; they had few other options. Now women can make much more money and can do so more and more frequently in occupations with considerably more status than public school teachers. Richard Riley, at the very end of his long tenure as secretary of the U.S. Department of Education during the Clinton administration, stated the seriousness of the salary issue in stark terms: "I have come to the conclusion that we will never really improve American education until we elevate the teaching profession and come to grips with the issue of teacher compensation."[32]

Teaching as a Career

Not only are salaries for teachers low, but teaching is essentially a dead-end profession—as long as one remains a classroom teacher. The salary of teachers is not significantly greater than it was when they first entered the classroom. When inflation is considered, teachers sometimes made more their first year of teaching than in the year of their retirement. In the United States, the only way for a teacher to make a decent salary and gain prestige in a school district is to abandon teaching and become a school administrator. Furthermore, in many schools, outstanding teachers receive little, if any, more salary than incompetent teachers.

School buildings. The physical working conditions for many teachers are poor at best and often abominable. In 1997, a conservative estimate of the cost of putting American school buildings into good condition was $112 billion.[33] More recently, the National Education Association put the figure at $332 billion, but this figure is skewed because the association included equipping the schools with new technology.[34]

Teacher education. With a little investigation, high school graduates contemplating teaching as a career will discover that departments, schools, and colleges of education are sorely underfinanced in comparison with other units of a college or university. In the 1984–1985 academic year, the cost of educating a teacher in undergraduate school was nearly half that of the cost of educating a K–12 student.[35] In this same year, a major state university spent from 50 to 60 percent more on educating engineers and business graduates than on educating teachers.[36]

Furthermore, school districts spend less than one-half of 1 percent of their budget on staff development;[37] and while nineteen states require districts to provide induction experiences for novice teachers, only ten pay for some or all of this costly but exceptionally important innovation.[38] Richard Wisniewski and Edward Ducharme sum up funding of teacher education in America: "Preparing teachers on the cheap has been and remains one of our profession's dirty little secrets."[39]

Intellectual ability. The brightest novice teachers, as measured by college entrance examinations, are the ones most likely to quit teaching.[40] During much of the twentieth century, teaching has managed to attract a significant number of people who are as intellectually bright as people in any other field, but teaching has also attracted a significant number of people who are below average academically. The good news is that the intellectual level of prospective teachers has risen in recent years. There are studies now that suggest that teacher education students compare favorably with arts and sciences students.[41]

Anti-intellectualism. As Richard Hofstadter documented, Americans have never highly valued intellectual work.[42] Politicians such as the late George Wallace well understand that every time they sneer and spit out the phrase "pointy headed intellectuals," the phrase will not be forgotten and will by itself sway not a few voters to support them. Albert Shanker concluded from a study of 200,000 students that neither students nor their parents take schooling very seriously.[43] In a Gallop Poll, only 15 percent of the respondents shunned the utilitarian value of education—getting a good job, for example—and supported knowledge for its own sake, that is, learning to think, to relate, and to understand. Americans apparently also act upon this belief, since few mothers said they worked closely with their children on academic tasks or encouraged them to work hard and be successful in school.[44] (In contrast, looking after the educational needs of children and young people is a national obsession in Japan and some other Asian countries and nearly a full-time job for many mothers.) In another survey, 40 percent of American parents said they never attend a school function and a quarter of them confessed that they had no idea how their children were doing academically in high school.[45]

The fact that two-thirds of American high school students during the regular school year have a job and half of them work more than fifteen hours a week is powerful evidence of the indifference of students and their parents to the kind of dedicated scholarly endeavor engaged in by students in many industrialized European and Asian nations.[46] Such students do not have time to work at McDonalds or their national equivalents. They must study.

Anti-intellectualism is not only rife among students, their parents, and American society in general, it far too often rears its ugly head in universities, of all places, as well as in public schools—especially among school administrators. For example, in the first year of the new millennium, a group of superintendents in Kentucky were pushing to *lower* the minimum scores of new teachers on a national test to measure their knowledge of the academic subject they plan on teaching.[47] In a survey of secondary school principals in 1992, the researchers found that the least important factor in the selection of teachers was their intellectual capacity. A 1996 study found that it made little difference to school district administrators whether teacher candidates had graduated from a college or university with a selective admissions policy and a reputation for academic excellence or from one with an indifferent academic reputation.[48] Diane Ravitch, a former assistant secretary in the U.S. Department of Education, asserted that there is a "strong strain of anti-intellectualism in American culture," but insisted that "it should be the role of the schools to combat anti-intellectualism, not to reflect it or foster it."[49]

State educational policies. During his long educational career, Albert Shanker made many thoughtful observations about the educational scene in America and abroad, but his most profound observation consists of one sentence: "No scheme ever works unless the people responsible for carrying it out want to make it work."[50] Historically, American legislators and state education department officials have paid little attention to H. L. Mencken's admonition that there is a simple solution for every complicated problem and it is typically wrong. In the 1980s alone, there were over 1,000 pieces of legislation regarding teachers; all this frantic activity in spite of the contention of respected researchers who claim, as the sociologist Edward Pauly did, that "there is no known school policy or program that consistently and predictably helps students learn more than any other school policy or program." Pauly argued that educational policies fail because "they prescribe how teachers and students are to go about the work of teaching and learning."[51] Micromanagement by the state of schools and teachers in them accomplishes little except to discourage good people from entering the profession and to encourage quality teachers to leave it as soon as possible.

Work environment. A quarter of a century ago, Daniel Lortie compared novice teachers to Robinson Crusoe. Contemporary teachers would have no argument with this comparison. Though beginning teachers are customarily assigned the most difficult classes nobody else wants, they must survive the first year of teaching on their own, without help from anybody else. The loneliness of neophyte teachers is equally applicable to more experienced ones. Once teachers close their classroom doors in the morning they are not only cut off from other adults but from their own colleagues. As Judith Renyi pungently put it, "The single greatest wasted resource in our country is the knowledge and experience of teachers who must individually reinvent their profession all of their lives as long as they remain isolated from each other in their classrooms."[52]

Teaching in America is exceedingly difficult not only because there is little time to work with colleagues to improve instruction and the curriculum; there is also little time to meet with students and parents, to plan and prepare lessons, to engage in nonclassroom activities such as supervising student teachers, to grade homework, and on and on. Teaching can indeed be exciting and rewarding, but the poor working environment makes it also, as Philip Jackson noted, a "daily grind."[53]

Empowerment. In most schools, teachers are not empowered; that is, they have little to say about decisions that effect their daily lives at school— their workload, assignment of classes, tests they give students, textbooks and other instructional materials, field trips (forbidden in many schools because of liability concerns), professional development activities, curriculum innovations, and so on. In Peters and Waterman's study of corporate excellence, they "observed, time and again, extraordinary energy exerted above and beyond the call of duty when the worker . . . is given even a modicum of apparent control over his or her destiny."[54] Teachers are no different than people in businesses or in any other occupation. They want to be treated with dignity and to have a strong say in things that affect their daily work lives.

Supply and demand. There is a chronic mismatch between teacher preparation in specific fields and the labor market needs for teachers. Among the reasons for this is that federal and state governments do not project demand by field and location, and colleges rarely try to recruit and prepare teachers to fill positions demanded by the labor market.[55]

Hiring practices. When it comes to hiring quality teachers, school districts are often their own worst enemies. Some districts do not even respond to a candidate's application. Others lose the application or a candidate's file or require a candidate to repeat a certain step, such as getting finger printed, not twice but three or four times. Many districts hire the cheapest teachers they can find, that is, the least qualified and experienced.

Most districts put a cap on the salaries they offer experienced candidates, which means that these candidates must take a cut in pay when moving to a new locality if they want to continue teaching. Many decide to change professions.[56] More than 350 of the 1,200 new teachers hired in Chicago in 1998 were not hired until after Labor Day. In the same year, Baltimore administrators began to fill 300 positions at a job fair held only twelve days before the start of the new school year. In New York City, new teachers are assigned at random to their schools. They are neither required to visit their schools nor to meet with the principal before the school year begins.[57]

There is little question that the inept, cumbersome hiring procedures of far too many school districts so frustrate teacher candidates that many decide never to put a foot inside a schoolhouse door.

In the remainder of this chapter, we suggest some steps that various organizations and institutions might take to improve the teacher recruitment and retention process.

IMPROVING TEACHER RECRUITMENT AND RETENTION

General Suggestions

- Equalize teacher salaries while simultaneously raising teacher standards.
- Standardize state teacher licenses so that teachers who cannot find a job in their own state can, with a portable license, move to a state where the jobs are.
- Grant a license to any out-of-state candidate who has earned National Board for Professional Teaching Standards certification, an advanced certificate awarded only to outstanding, experienced teachers.
- Develop national recruitment initiatives and online information technologies and modernize hiring procedures.
- Provide service scholarship programs, such as that provided by the North Carolina Teaching Fellows program, to attract and prepare highly capable candidates for fields with a shortage of teachers.
- Develop teacher-training programs in fields that need more teachers, such as mathematics, special education, physical science, and English as a second language.
- Create incentives for the development of more extended five-year teacher-training programs, since graduates of such programs are more likely than graduates of traditional four-year programs (and *much more likely* than graduates of short-term, alternative certification programs) to enter and remain in teaching.
- Develop intensive, quality induction programs for novice teachers because such districts as Cincinnati, Columbus, and Toledo, Ohio, and Rochester, New York, have found that those with such training are much less likely than those denied such programs to abandon teaching in the early years.
- Refuse to hire unqualified teachers because to do so only exacerbates the problem of finding and keeping quality teachers.[58]

Specific Suggestions

Linda Darling-Hammond argued in a 1999 report by the National Commission on Teaching and America's Future that "for any wide-scale reforms to succeed, there must be a congruence of effort. What goes on in classrooms between teachers and students may be the core of education, but it is profoundly shaped by what parents and principals do and by what superintendents, school boards, chief state school officers, state boards of education, governors, and legislatures decide. If the actions of federal and state governments do not support the work of local school districts, and if school districts do not support the work of schools, very little of worth can be accomplished."[59] What specifically can the different players in educational reform do to enhance recruitment and retention of quality teachers?

Federal government. Historically, the federal government has provided strong support to other professions such as medicine. In the 1960s, there was a shortage of doctors, and Congress tackled this problem by passing the 1963 Health Professions Education Assistance Act. This act sought to raise the quality of medical training by creating strong teaching hospitals, granting scholarships and loans to medical students, and establishing incentives for doctors to seek a specialization and settle in a location with too few doctors. This sustained effort lasted several decades and did much to increase the supply of doctors and to improve the quality of patient care throughout the country.[60] The government should do no less for schools and teachers in them. Senator Jeff Bingaman is proposing that the government "help districts fill unmet needs by supporting state efforts to increase the portability of teachers' pensions, certification, and years of experience so that qualified teachers can have greater mobility."[61] Most industrialized countries with top-notch school systems rely heavily on strong federal support in practically all educational areas. In what promises to be an increasingly competitive world in the twenty-first century, perhaps it is time for Americans to reassess their historic passion for local control of public schools, if for no other reason than to equalize funding of public school education, as most industrialized countries throughout the world have done long ago.

Governors and state legislators. The first thing the executive and legislative branches of state governments should do is to renounce micro-management of public school districts. The more rules and restrictions they place on teachers, the more difficult they make it to recruit and retain quality teachers. In making policy, the first question should always be, "How will this proposed policy put more quality teachers in schools and keep them there?" Specifically, governors and legislators should abandon quick fix panaceas and band-aid approaches to education reform and concentrate on the really difficult but essential things that in the long run will ensure better teachers and schools for all children in all public schools: equalize funding of school districts and beginning teacher salaries throughout the state; close all the loopholes that permit unqualified people to teach; make it easy for qualified people to teach in any state without losing salary or retirement benefits; make the salary and working conditions of teachers such that they will encourage a reasonable proportion of talented people to pursue teaching rather than engineering, medicine, law, business, high tech fields; drastically reduce the number of teacher-training programs and insist that those remaining adhere to high standards and focus on the training of teachers; adequately fund extended internships and mentoring programs for novice teachers; insist that public colleges and universities take teacher education seriously and provide prospective teachers, along with their work in education schools, with a well-thought-out, coherent liberal education and a solid knowledge of one or more academic disciplines customarily taught in public schools.

State boards of education. As governors and legislators, state boards of education must get out of the business of micro-managing school districts and teachers and stick to those things that will raise the quality of teaching and learning: eliminate substandard teaching certificates; base teacher licensure on high standards of subject matter to be taught, general (liberal) education subject matter, and pedagogical knowledge and skills; assist school districts in designing and implementing induction programs for beginning teachers; coordinate standards for teacher-training institutions, teacher licensure, and student learning in public schools; work with teacher unions to make it possible for recently retired teachers to return to teaching and receive a regular teaching salary and full retirement benefits.[62] Maryland initiated such a plan in 2000.

School districts. A few of the many things school districts should do is to streamline their hiring procedures, accept their responsibilities as teacher educators, encourage qualified teachers not currently teaching to resume teaching on a part-time basis, hire only qualified people, provide them with a mentor and a year-long induction program, and ensure that they and experienced teachers are assigned only courses they are qualified to teach. What school districts most need to do is to provide a school facility and working conditions appropriate for a professional person.

School districts might also utilize one of the cheapest, quickest, and easiest ways to get a good indication of whether finalists for a teaching position have the intellectual equipment to develop as a teacher. One way to approach this would be to require finalists to write a substantive essay on a significant teaching/learning problem. The number one priority of district personnel offices should be to hire candidates who know how to think because without this quality, regardless of what other qualifications they may have, it is impossible for them to develop into quality teachers.

Teacher unions. The responsibility of teacher unions for improving teaching and learning is discussed in chapter 12. Here, we will stress that much of their time should be devoted to helping school districts to develop professional development programs for experienced teachers and ongoing induction and mentoring programs for novice teachers. Preferably these programs should be delivered in schools specifically organized for professional development purposes, typically called professional development schools (PDS).

Subject matter associations. These associations can do much to assist school districts, states, and teacher-training institutions to establish high standards for prospective and experienced teachers not only in subject matter knowledge but in the pedagogical knowledge and skills essential to teach discipline content effectively. These associations can also do much to encourage a close collaboration between teachers and professors specializing in disciplines taught in public schools. A simple first step is to encourage their membership to join and participate actively in learned societies. In many European countries, secondary teachers, as a matter of course, join learned societies. Should American teachers do the same, the result could well be an appreciable rise in professorial respect for public school teachers and a greater willingness on the part of professors to support professional development activities in public schools and pre-service and graduate teacher training in their own institutions.

Businesses and philanthropists. Businesses and philanthropists and their foundations have a long tradition of donating large sums of money to institutions of higher learning, in particular to such elite institutions as Harvard, Yale, Duke, and Stanford. Lesser known colleges and universities also make a concerted, continuous effort to entice businesses and philanthropic giving to their institutions. What is needed is for governors, legislators, state departments of education, and teacher-training institutions to exert the same kind of effort as many higher education institutions to persuade philanthropists and businesses to devote a significant portion of their largesse to improving public schools and the teaching and learning in them. (Think of the incalculable benefits that would occur to schools and teaching training institutions if a huge international company such as Exxon/Mobil were to utilize its literally thousands of gas stations as an outlet for accurate, up-to-date, objective information—perhaps in collaboration with federal and state departments of education—about the needs, problems, and achievements of public schools and teacher-training institutions.) The message to potential donors is clear-cut and simple. Better teachers make better schools and better schools contribute to the economic and cultural well-being of the citizenry of any state.

Parents and community. A good school is supported by the community because the school makes members of the community part of the school by enlisting their time, energy, and resources to make the school the best it can be. When there is a sense of "we" between school and community, each will nudge the other to insist on quality standards for teachers and students.[63] In particular, schools and communities, along with teacher unions and the state boards of education, can work together to ensure top-quality induction programs for novice teachers.

Pre-collegiate student groups. People and organizations exerting some influence on teacher recruitment might well consider making a greater effort to stimulate capable middle and high school students to think seriously about teaching as a possible career. There are at present many such efforts to do this. A national survey of pre-collegiate teacher recruitment efforts in 1995 found 253 programs serving over 50,000 students. Considering the great imbalance between the race of teachers and that of their students, a particularly good feature of these programs is that 64 percent of the participants were youngsters of color. [64]

North Carolina has developed one of the more comprehensive pre-collegiate programs. The program, called the Teaching Fellows Program, receives $8 million a year from the state legislature and provides $20,000 scholarships to 400 academically talented high school seniors who enroll in one of the state's teacher education programs. Data indicates that three out of four fellows completed their four-year teaching obligations and continue teaching in the North Carolina public schools. Some teach in other states. Twenty-seven states now provide scholarships and loan-forgiveness programs for quality college students who make a commitment to teach in public schools. [65]

South Carolina provides a high school honors course, called the Teacher Cadet program, for academically talented students interested in exploring teaching as a career. This course is offered in approximately 75 percent of the state's secondary schools. The state also provides teaching clubs for middle school youngsters. These clubs make a special effort to encourage male students and members of minorities to consider teaching. There are at least fifty "teaching academy" projects nationwide that encourage high school students to pursue a career in teaching as part of their high school curriculum. [66] Finally, a few states have also tried to recruit community college students into teaching and to encourage school paraprofessionals to earn teaching licenses. [67]

Pre-collegiate teacher recruitment programs need not be state supported and as comprehensive as those in North Carolina and South Carolina. A program may be as simplistic as that started during the 2000 school year by two small school districts and a private academy adjacent to the Mobile, Alabama, area. The program, called Teen Tutors, provides volunteer high school students to tutor youngsters in grades three through six in the two districts and the academy free of charge in any school subject that may be desired. Fifty-five tutors have completed a training course and more will be trained throughout the year. Such simple, inexpensive programs as this should encourage more than a few talented teens to consider teaching as a career. [68]

The viability and importance of pre-collegiate teacher programs should not be underestimated. For example, Seymour Sarason argued that all youngsters, starting in the fifth or sixth grade, should experience the role of a teacher and that experience should continue throughout the school years. [69]

Teacher preparation institutions. The first thing teacher-training institutions should do to help resolve the teacher recruitment and retention problem is to set high standards of admittance to their programs for prospective teachers. What Ralph McDonald, the executive secretary of the

National Commission on Teaching and America's Future from 1946 to 1951, had to say on this subject is just as appropriate today as it was in the early 1960s:

So long as teacher preparing institutions admit just any student who applies for admission, or even the average student, we shall have a poor quality of teacher education. . . .

If we permit it to be weighted down by low standards, teaching will not have a chance to gain public esteem or adequate financial support.

Our experience shows that high standards of admission mean, over the years, a steadier and a larger supply of qualified teachers. It is sometimes assumed that the way to meet a teacher shortage is to lower standards of admission and thereby increase the potential supply by making a greater number of people eligible. This is just the reverse of the truth. Most of the states and school systems which have had the greatest turnover and the greatest number of emergency teachers have been among those which have the lowest standards. . . .

We can learn a profound truth from the history of professional progress in medicine, law, and dentistry. It is clear from the experiences of those professions that respect follows the enforcement of high standards. . . .

High standards are one key to good teaching. They are the one road to public esteem. They are also the sound approach to the securing of public support which will ensure adequate salaries and good working conditions. Any plan for educational advancement which does not rest on high standards of admission to teaching is like a house built upon the sand.[70]

Connecticut confirms McDonald's prophetic words of four decades ago. In 1986, Connecticut passed an Education Enhancement Act that linked dramatic increases in teacher salaries—they were doubled between 1985 and 1995—with significant equalization of funding across districts; higher standards for teacher education and licensing; and substantial investments in mentoring of novice teachers and lifelong professional development for all teachers that focused on improving their ability to increase student learning.

By increasing salaries in an equalizing fashion, teacher shortages were eliminated even in the cities, and a surplus of teachers existed within three years of the passage of the education act. By paying teachers well, insisting that they meet high academic standards, providing a state-supported mentoring program for novice teachers the first year on the job, the number of applications to the University of Connecticut's School of Education *tripled*. Furthermore, the grade point average of teacher trainees in this school are currently on average *higher* than those of ten of the eleven other schools on campus, which includes such schools as engineering, business, and nursing. To be admitted to a teacher education program in Connecticut, candidates must pass a basic skills test to gain admittance and then must major in an academic subject and maintain a grade point average of at least 3.0 in the courses taken for their major. Furthermore, they must pass a series of subject area tests before they can be licensed. Not surprisingly, since the reforms stipulated in the Education Enhancement Act were enacted, students in Connecticut public schools have made significant gains on the National Assessment of Educational Progress and have become one of the top-scoring states in the country in mathematics and reading.[71]

GOOD NEWS

We would be remiss if we did not punctuate our rather bleak description in this chapter of the teacher recruitment and retention scene with a brief recital of a few of the more positive educational developments relevant to this subject:

- During the 2000 campaign for the presidency of the United States, both Al Gore and George W. Bush said they wanted to be education presidents and made campaign promises that each believed would raise the quality of teaching and learning in public schools.[72]

- Many governors running for re-election stressed in their campaigns various measures to improve schools and the teachers in them.[73]

- The National Council for Accreditation of Teacher Education, the National Board for Professional Teaching Standards (NBPTS, the Board that awards advanced certification to outstanding, experienced teachers), and the Interstate New Teacher Assessment and Support Consortium (a consortium of some thirty states that joined together to develop more rigorous licensing and assessment standards for beginning teachers) are working to coordinate their efforts to change teaching from, in the words of John Goodlad, a "not-quite profession" into a legitimate profession.[74]

- In July of 2000, the governor of California signed into law a $20 million fellowship program designed to encourage teachers to teach four years in low-performing schools; a $15 million program to give bonuses to teachers who gain NBPTS certification; and a $43.6 million program to increase the number of interns with mentors.[75]

- Richard Riley, the secretary of the U.S. Department of Education, announced that the White House will request $1 billion from Congress to assist local communities to recruit and train teachers and to update the skills of current teachers. An additional $150 million is being sought to train teachers to use technology effectively.[76]

- In an effort to recruit and keep teachers, a number of school districts are increasing salaries, adding signing bonuses, and making the benefits packages more appealing.[77] A number of districts are also developing various programs to encourage their students to consider teaching as a career.

- Contrary to what some conservative pundits on television and in newspaper columns maintain, the American public overwhelmingly values and wishes to preserve the public school system.[78] Furthermore, a 1998 Louis Harris poll found that it is a very important goal to nine out of every ten respondents to have every classroom filled with a well-qualified teacher.[79]

- Leaders of the two major teacher unions in the United States, the National Education Association and the American Federation of Teachers, are now insisting that their members be as concerned with promoting quality teaching as with traditional bread and butter issues such as better salaries, retirement programs, and working conditions.[80] Teacher unions are also making, for the first time, a significant effort to communicate more effectively with the general public. The National Education Association, for example, has initiated a national advertising campaign aimed principally at informing the public why our democracy demands that the public schools be saved and improved.[81]

- There is a growing realization among teachers that they, like the unions, must also learn to communicate much more effectively with parents, community members, colleagues, and policy makers.[82]

- A number of departments, schools, and colleges of education have raised their admission standards for teacher candidates and made other innovations that should increase the quality of their graduates.[83]

- Since the 1980s, interest by students in pursuing a teaching career has steadily increased.[84]

- At the talking level, at least, it appears that many educational policy makers are beginning to recognize the paramount importance of quality teachers in raising student achievement.

- Some headway is being made in "empowering" teachers (that is, giving them a greater voice in decisions that effect them), and this is all to the good, since there is evidence that empowering teachers is positively associated with teacher retention.[85]

- Novice teachers appear to love teaching[86] and are determined to do a good job if substandard salaries and poor working conditions do not eventually wear them down and drive them out of the profession.

In spite of all this good news, there is thus far in our history a marked indifference of the American public to ensuring the right of *every* child and youth in America to well-qualified, trained teachers. We would like to think that a well-established democracy, such as in the United States, should demand that this right be enforced. Our country cannot afford, economically or morally, the incredible waste of human resources and funds involved in preparing a large percentage of teachers who do not teach or who soon leave the field.

In those countries that provide good working conditions for their teachers and pay them as much as or more than people with comparable education qualifications—Japan pays its teachers almost as much as doctors and lawyers, and Switzerland pays experienced teachers three times more than the average industrial wage—recruitment of quality people into teaching, and keeping them there, is not a significant problem. Americans have yet to take to heart Harry Judge's common-sense observation that "only when a significant number of prospective teachers can anticipate lifelong rewards comparable to those available to their contemporaries in other activities will a sufficient number of smart people wish to become teachers.[87]

NOTES

1. David Tyack, ed., *Turning Points in American Educational History* (Waltham, Mass.: Blaisdell, 1967), p. 155.

2. Tyack, *Turning Points,* p. 414.

3. Ann Bradley, "'The Not-Quite Profession,'" *Education Week,* 15 September 1999, p. 31.

4. Bob Chase, "A Teacher Speaks Out: Insights from the National Teacher of the Year," *Education Week,* 29 March 2000, p. 29.

5. Ibid.

6. Barbara Kantrowitz and Pat Wingert, "Who Will Teach Our Kids?" *Newsweek,* 2 October 2000, pp. 36–42; David J. Hoff, "Effort to Recruit Math, Science Teachers Urged," *Education Week,* 4 October 2000, pp. 1, 16.

7. Linda Darling-Hammond, *Solving the Dilemmas of Teacher Supply, Demand, and Standards: How We Can Ensure a Competent, Caring, and Qualified Teacher for Every Child* (Kutztown, Penn.: National Commission on Teaching and America's Future, 1999), pp. 6–7, <http://www.tc.columbia.edu/%7Eteachcomm/Conference-99/Solving/>.

8. Lynn Olson, "Finding and Keeping Competent Teachers," *Education Week,* 13 January 2000, p. 14.

9. "Quality Counts: A Report Card on the Condition of Public Education in the 50 States," *Education Week,* 22 January 1997, p. 40.

10. Richard M. Ingersoll, "Putting Qualified Teachers in Every Classroom," *Education Week,* 11 June 1997, pp. 46, 60.

11. Richard M. Ingersoll, "Why So Many Underqualified High School Teachers?" *Education Week,* 4 November 1998, p. 64.

12. Ann Bradley, "The Gatekeeping Challenge," *Education Week,* 13 January 2000, p. 24.

13. Ibid.

14. "Setting Policies for New Teachers," *Education Week,* 13 January 2000, p. 44.

15. Lynn Olson and Craig D. Jerald, "The Teaching Challenge," *Education Week,* 8 January 1998, p. 17; Dennis L. Evans, "Assistance for Underqualified Teachers: Differentiated Responsibilities," *Education Week,* 3 February 1999, p. 36.

16. See, for example, Ronald F. Ferguson, "Paying for Public Education: New Evidence on How and Why Money Matters," *Harvard Journal on Legislation* 28 (1991): 465–497.

17. Linda Darling-Hammond, *The Right to Learn: A Blueprint for Creating Schools that Work* (San Francisco: Jossey-Bass, 1997), p. 317.

18. Olson, "Finding and Keeping Competent Teachers," p. 14.

19. Ibid., p. 16.

20. Jeff Archer, "Teachers Suggest the Need for Better Training," *Education Week,* 3 February 1999, p. 12.

21. Tamara Henry, "School Rolls Hit Record," *USA Today,* 22 August 2000, sec. D, pp. 1, 7.

22. "High Poverty among Young Makes Schools' Job Harder," *Education Week,* 27 September 2000, pp. 40–41.

23. Richard Ingersoll, "The Problem of Underqualified Teachers in American Secondary Schools," *Educational Researcher* 28 (March 1999): 29.

24. Ibid., pp. 32–33.

25. Richard J. Murnane and others, *Who Will Teach? Policies that Matter* (Cambridge: Harvard University Press, 1991), pp. 4, 10.

26. Ibid., p. 37.

27. Reporter's Notebook, "AFT Backs Away from Charter School Support," *Education Week,* 12 July 2000, pp. 20–21.

28. Editors, "Who Should Teach? The States Decide," *Education Week,* 13 January 2000, p. 8.

29. David J. Hoff, "International Report Finds U.S. Teacher Salaries Lagging," *Education Week,* 17 May 2000, p. 5.

30. Editors, "Who Should Teach?" p. 8.

31. Kantrowitz and Wingert, "Who Will Teach," p. 40.

32. Quoted in Joetta L. Sack, "Riley Urges 'Review' of Standards," *Education Week,* 1 March 2000, p. 32.

33. "Quality Counts," p. 54

34. Alan Richard, "NEA Pegs School Building Needs at $332 Billion," *Education Week,* 10 May 2000, p. 3.

35. W. Robert Houston, "Lessons for Teacher Education from Corporate Practice," *Phi Delta Kappan* 68 (January 1987): 392.

36. Edward R. Ducharme and Russell M. Agne, "Professors of Education: Uneasy Residents of Academe," in *The Professors of Teaching: An Inquiry,* ed. Richard Wisniewski and Edward R. Ducharme (Albany: State University of New York Press, 1989), p. 80.

37. Linda Darling-Hammond, "The Quiet Revolution: Rethinking Teacher Development," *Educational Leadership* 53 (March 1996): 7.

38. Craig D. Jerald and Ulrich Boser, "Setting Policies for New Teachers," *Education Week,* 13 January 2000, p. 45.

39. Richard Wisniewski and Edward R. Ducharme, "Where We Stand," in *The Professors of Teaching: An Inquiry,* ed. Richard Wisniewski and Edward R. Ducharme (Albany: State University of New York Press, 1989), p. 156.

40. Editors, "Who Should Teach?" p. 9.

41. Willis D. Hawley, "United States," in *Issues and Problems in Teacher Education: An International Handbook,* ed. Howard B. Leavitt (Westport, Conn.: Greenwood Press, 1992), pp. 253–254.

42. Richard Hofstadter, *Anti-Intellectualism in American Life* (New York: Alfred A. Knopf, 1969).

43. Albert Shanker, "Where We Stand: Disengaged Students," *New York Times,* 2 June 1996, sec. E, p. 7.

44. David K. Cohen, "Rewarding Teachers for Student Performance," in *Rewards and Reform: Creating Educational Incentives that Work,* ed. Susan H. Fuhrman and Jennifer A. O'Day (San Francisco: Jossey-Bass, 1996), p. 94.

45. Debra Viadero, "Teen Culture Seen Impeding School Reform," *Education Week,* 5 June 1996, p. 10.

46. Ibid.

47. Tamara Henry, "A Principal Crisis in Education," *USA Today*, 22 August 2000, sec. D, p. 7.

48. Linda Darling-Hammond and others, "Teacher Recruitment, Selection, and Induction: Policy Influences on the Supply and Quality of Teachers," in *Teaching as the Learning Profession: Handbook of Policy and Practice*, ed. Linda Darling-Hammond and Gary Sykes (San Francisco: Jossey-Bass, 1999), p. 213.

49. Diane Ravitch, interview by Lynn Olson, *Education Week*, 13 September 2000, p. 6.

50. Albert Shanker, "Where We Stand: 'Break the Mold' Schools," *New York Times*, 6 October 1991, sec. E, p. 9.

51. Edward Pauly, *The Classroom Crucible: What Really Works, What Doesn't and Why* (New York: BasicBooks, 1991), pp. 109, 111.

52. Judith Renyi, "The Longest Reform," *Education Week*, 13 November 1996, pp. 34, 37.

53. Quoted in Pauly, *Classroom Crucible*, p. 38.

54. Thomas J. Peters and Robert H. Waterman, Jr., *In Search of Excellence: Lessons from America's Best-Run Companies* (New York: Harper and Row, 1982), p. xiii.

55. Darling-Hammond and others, "Teacher Recruitment," p. 223.

56. Ibid., p. 212.

57. Olson and Jerald, "The Teaching Challenge," p. 17.

58. The items listed under the subheading General Suggestions are paraphrased from Darling-Hammond, *Solving the Dilemmas*, pp. 16–20.

59. Ibid., p. 20.

60. Darling-Hammond, *The Right to Learn*, p. 319.

61. Jeff Bingaman, "The Role . . . the Federal Government Can Play in Improving Teacher Quality," *Educational Horizons* 78 (spring 2000), p. 115.

62. Martin Haberman, "Licensing Teachers: Lessons from Other Professions," *Phi Delta Kappan* 67 (June 1986): 724.

63. A cover story in the *U.S. News & World Report* powerfully illustrates the good things that can happen when schools and communities develop this "we" spirit. The article describes how five troubled high schools, scattered throughout the nation, worked cooperatively with parents and community members to resolve such serious problems as the indifference of many students, parents, and teachers to high academic standards. Ted Gest and others, "Fixing Your High School," *U.S. News & World Report*, 9 October 2000, pp. 64–73.

64. Darling-Hammond and others, *Teacher Recruitment*, p. 202.

65. Ibid., pp. 201–205.

66. Adrienne D. Coles, "High Schoolers Move to the Head of the Class," *Education Week*, 22 April 1998, p. 5.

67. Lynn Olson, "Sweetening the Pot," *Education Week*, 13 January 2000, p. 29.

68. Anne Clay Cernyar, "Program Offers Free Assistance to Students," *Baldwin Register*, 18 October 2000, pp. 1, 3.

69. Seymour B. Sarason, *How Schools Might Be Governed and Why* (New York: Teachers College Press, Columbia University, 1997), p. 146.

70. Ralph W. McDonald, "The Slow Climb Upward," in *Journey to Now: 1946–1961* (Washington, D.C.: National Education Association of the United States, 1961), pp. 10–12.

71. Jeff Archer, "Earning Their Stripes," *Education Week,* 13 January 2000, pp. 38–40, 43; Linda Darling-Hammond and Milbrey Wallin McLaughlin, "Investing in Teaching as a Learning Profession: Policy Problems and Prospects," in *Teaching as the Learning Profession: Handbook of Policy and Practice,* ed. Linda Darling-Hammond and Gary Sykes (San Francisco: Jossey-Bass, 1999) pp. 403-405.

72. Dale Mezzacappa, "Federal Involvement in Schools Likely to Become More Visible," *Birmingham News,* 8 October 2000, sec. A, p. 7; Joetta L. Sack, "Candidates' K–12 Policies Share Themes," *Education Week,* 6 September 2000, pp. 1, 50–51.

73. Bess Keller, "In Races for Governor, Education Out in Front," *Education Week,* 18 October 2000, pp. 14, 18.

74. Darling-Hammond, *Solving the Dilemmas,* pp. 3–4.

75. Jessica L. Sanham, "Calif. Sweetens Pot to Ease Teacher Shortage," *Education Week,* 12 July 2000, p. 32.

76. "Some States Can't Wait to Hire More Teachers," *USA Today,* 22 August 2000, sec. D, p. 7.

77. Julie Blair, "Districts Wooing Teachers Away with Bonuses, Other Incentives," *Education Week,* 2 August 2000, pp. 1, 17.

78. Darcia Harris Bowman, "Traditional Pubic Schools Win Vote of Confidence in Poll," *Education Week,* 6 September 2000, p. 12; William Raspberry, "Real Folks See School Issues Different," *Birmingham News,* 10 October 2000, sec. A, p. 7.

79. Jeff Archer, "Public Prefers Competent Teachers to Other Reforms, Survey Finds," *Education Week,* 25 November 1998, p. 6.

80. Bob Chase, "Double Duty: While Defending All Teachers' Rights, We Help Bad Teachers Depart," *Education Week,* 15 March 2000, p. 39; Sylvia Seidel and June VanderVeen, "Quality Teaching Is Achievable: A National Commitment Is Required," *Educational Horizons* 78 (Spring 2000): 139–140.

81. "Teaching and Learning: Ad Blitz," *Education Week,* 26 January 2000, p. 6.

82. Gary A. Griffin, "Changes in Teacher Education: Looking to the Future," in *The Education of Teachers,* pt. 1, Ninety-eighth Yearbook of the National Society for the Study of Education, ed. Gary A. Griffin (Chicago: University of Chicago Press, 1999), pp. 7–8.

83. David Imig, "Professionalization or Dispersal: A Case Study of American Teacher Education," *Peabody Journal of Education* 72(1) (1997): 25–34.

84. Darling-Hammond and others, "Teacher Recruitment," p. 188.

85. Jiamping Shen, "How to Reduce Teacher Attrition in Public Schools: Policy Implications from a National Study," *Educational Horizons* 76 (Fall 1997): 38–39.

86. *A Sense of Calling: Who Teaches and Why,* executive summary, 9 October 2000, p. 1, <www.publicagendaonline.com/specials/teachers/teachers.htm>.

87. Harry Judge, "Reforming Teaching Education: A View from Abroad," *Education Week,* 24 June 1987, p. 32.

11

Pre-Service Training of Teachers

The essence of teaching ... is taking something that you already understand and transforming it in a way that makes it meaningful to young people.

Lee Shulman

Pre-service training of teachers is that period of time, normally spent at a college or university, during which a prospective teacher is prepared to enter the teaching profession. It is often contrasted with in-service training, which is training for teachers who have already entered the profession. Over the next decade the United States will need to train more than two million new teachers.[1] Thus, the concept of pre-service teacher education is very much in the forefront of current discussions about teacher education. This chapter is divided into three sections—concepts, elements, and organization of pre-service training of teachers—and focuses on potential areas for reform. We conclude by noting some positive recent events and trends in pre-service teacher education.

CONCEPTS OF PRE-SERVICE TRAINING OF TEACHERS

The perspectives of the critics on pre-service training discussed in Part I vary considerably as do those of American citizens. At one end of the spectrum is Brameld's seven-year teacher education program, heavy on the professional component and comparable in quality and rigor to that provided to physicians. At the other end of the spectrum is a four-year undergraduate program proposed by Hutchins and Finn that provides no professional training for those interested in pursuing teaching as a career. The other critics, with the exception of Illich, fit somewhere between these two poles, as do most Americans.

Regarding pre-service teacher education, Dewey had three general suggestions. First, prospective teachers should take courses in academic subjects calculated to increase and strengthen their scholarship. Second, they should discuss and test principles of education based upon coursework in psychology. Third, they should study subject matter with reference to its use in secondary and elementary schools.

For Hutchins, the pre-service education of teachers would be identical to that of any liberally educated university graduate. Required courses in schools and departments of education and required degrees in education for teachers would be abolished. For Hutchins, the prospective teacher's general education would be identical with that of the lawyer, doctor, and clergyman.

Bestor maintained that the pre-service education of prospective teachers should be education in how to think; that is, it should be liberal education, training in those intellectual disciplines that have general applicability (that is, science, mathematics, history, English, foreign languages).

According to Conant, student teaching (with an accompanying methods course) is the one essential element in pre-service teacher education, although most prospective teachers should take six hours of coursework in two educational disciplines. Teacher training institutions should also provide teacher trainees with a two-year general education component consisting of a broad academic education.

Brameld was very specific regarding pre-service preparation. He proposed that prospective teachers complete a seven-year program of study consisting of two years of general education, two years of behavioral sciences, a year of education theory, a year of the subject specialty, and a year of internship.

Silberman urged colleges and universities to provide prospective teachers with "alternative pictures" of what teaching and learning can be, along with the methodologies needed to implement them. Silberman concluded that a central role in pre-service teacher education must be given to the history and philosophy of education, as well as to the psychology, sociology, and anthropology of education.

Illich, of course, would not support any pre-service teacher education requirements. Most skill models would need no educational training. Apprenticeship with a master teacher (a "pedagogue" in Illich's parlance) would be sufficient preparation for those who want to share their learning and aspire to be a professional educator.

Shanker had two recommendations regarding preparation programs for prospective teachers. First, we should eliminate generic instructional methods courses. Second, we should place more emphasis on teaching prospective teachers content.

Finn argued that pre-service teacher education should consist only of a solid general education and subject area knowledge. Prospective teachers need essentially the same education as any other college graduate. Finn would not require prospective teachers to have any professional knowledge.

The views of the critics regarding pre-service teacher education amply demonstrate the importance of this concept to the debate about education and teacher education. There are, no doubt, many more approaches to pre-service teacher education. However, an understanding of some of the alternative conceptions available, and the differences among those alternatives, should help frame the place of pre-service teacher education in the more general debate about education and teacher education.

ELEMENTS OF PRE-SERVICE TEACHER EDUCATION

According to Arthur Wise and Linda Darling-Hammond, two of the most knowledgeable American teacher educators, "The weight of research indicates that fully prepared and certified teachers are more effective in producing student learning than teachers without this training. Furthermore, this research shows that, beyond basic subject-matter knowledge, it is the extent of pedagogical training that makes the difference in teacher effectiveness."[2]

Despite these well-documented facts, secondary school teachers typically take only seven semester credit hours of work in teaching their discipline and four hours of work in educational foundations.[3] Even this small amount is further restricted by state legislation in some states.[4] While New York City has made improvements in recent years, in this city alone, of 4,600 uncertified teachers that were hired for the 1988–1989 school year, more than three-fourths had little or no training and only one out of five received mentoring or similar assistance on the job.[5]

This is the real world of teacher education, and this is the reason why reform is necessary. There are a number of elements that make up pre-service teacher education, but this section will focus on six of the most important: theory, practice, research, globalism, technology, and liberal education.

Theory

Work in educational foundations—the history, philosophy, psychology, sociology, and politics of education—is particularly suited to promoting the liberal education of trainees because education cannot be understood apart from its cultural setting. Education is a fundamental element of that setting—influencing culture and in turn being influenced by culture. Study of this continuous process of interaction between education and culture is basic to educational foundations.

Courses in foundations stress study of society, human behavior and thought, as they relate to the educational process. Emphasis is upon understanding, questioning, and evaluating fundamental ideas, concepts, scholarship, theory, and philosophies underlying educational practice. In contrast to courses stressing how to translate theory into practice, focus in educational foundations is on understanding the theory behind practice, systematizing different theories and viewpoints, discriminating among them, and placing them in historical and cultural perspective. A sociology of education course, for example, could address the concern of one teacher that "there should be sessions informing [pre-service] students about politics. You need to understand how things work and who's in charge."[6]

Seymour Sarason, a psychologist, concurs. He has made a strong case, indirectly, for greater exposure of teacher trainees to the foundations of education. In his extensive work with teacher trainees, he was struck by how "narrow their understanding of the school culture was" and by how much their interest and training were restricted to the "encapsulated classroom." In his words,

they were almost completely ignorant of how and why schools and school systems are organized and administered as they are; the nature and variety of decision-making processes and forums; the opportunities for and obstacles to change and innovation; the functions, status, and power of specialized nonteaching personnel; and issues of formal and informal power. Stated another way, they are, for all practical purposes, unequipped or not required to think about almost all the factors that will impinge on them, shape them as persons and professionals, determine their self-esteem or personal worth, and stimulate or inhibit their creativity and intellectual growth. . . . Our aim should be to prepare educators for the realities of schools and school systems, and how they transact with the dynamics of other parts of our social system."[7]

Practice

Gary Griffin sums up well what teacher educators should do with respect to the relationship between theory and practice:

If we expect teachers to be thoughtful about their practice, we should provide opportunities for guided practice to be informed by theory and theory to be tested against guided practice. If we expect teachers to be constantly inquiring into the nature and consequences of their work, we should provide individual and group opportunities to ask serious questions about practice and search for answers *in* practice as well as in theory. If we expect teacher education graduates to have an influence on the schools they enter as novices, we should work with them in ways that raise penetrating and thought-provoking questions rather than perpetuate acceptance of the norms of the schools and classrooms in which they find themselves.[8]

Teacher educators should also introduce teacher trainees to classroom and school-oriented research conducted by teachers who jointly examine a problem in their classes or school and come up with a solution. Teacher educators can arrange for teacher trainees to observe over time cooperative teams of teachers engaged in conducting research, sometimes called "action research." We discuss teacher research/study groups in the next chapter.

Whatever else teacher educators do, they must provide teacher trainees with the knowledge and skills essential to survive the first year or two of teaching. As a Yale graduate accepted into the Teach for America program put it after his first year of teaching, "The first hurdle, which took me months to clear, was simply writing daily lesson plans. This is one of the hardest points to make to non-teachers. Because the classroom is such a familiar and uncomplicated place for most people, it's hard to see that developing and executing a good curriculum is about as simple as composing and performing a good symphony."[9] A teacher must not only be educated, but *trained*.

The word "training" has an unjustified stigma in educational circles in America. It should not have. American doctors are well educated, but they are also well trained in the techniques of their craft. Teachers should also be well educated and well trained. Too often teachers enter the classroom not knowing how to make a lesson plan, to handle discipline problems, to talk with parents, to ask different questions on different levels of complexity, to work with small groups of children, to analyze learning difficulties, to grade papers, to give different kinds of tests, to conduct field trips, to involve students with widely different ability and achievement levels in overcrowded classrooms, to use computers and other instructional aids as teaching resources, to lead discussions, and on and on. As one American teacher put it, "I didn't have *any* 'nuts and bolts' knowledge to carry into battle."[10]

Teacher educators should also teach prospective secondary school teachers how to work with small groups. This is essential because secondary teachers tend to use the same methodology regardless of whether a class is large or small;[11] that is, they lecture. Over-reliance on lecturing by many secondary school teachers may explain in part why the older American students get, the lower their scores on the Third International Mathematics and Science Study (TIMSS). As Chester Finn noted, "Our fourth graders scored among the best in the world in math and science. But our eighth grade scores were mediocre, and our twelfth grade scores were downright miserable."[12] Can one of the reasons for this retrogression be that American secondary school teachers have much less work in pedagogy than elementary school teachers and, hence, rely excessively on the one teaching methodology, lecturing, most often modeled for them by their professors in the arts and sciences? It is a question worth pondering by people, such as Finn, who want to do away with pedagogical training for public school teachers.

Lack of technical knowledge often overwhelms beginning teachers and drives many of them from the profession. To be sure, teachers do need to be "students of teaching" and to develop a clear vision of what schools at their best should be—only with a predominance of such teachers can schools improve—but they also need at least three other things:

- basic skills that will enable them to survive the first year or two of teaching in schools as they are;
- a large stock of teaching techniques and methodologies that have proven effective in increasing student learning;
- a coherent curriculum that has continuity from month to month and year to year—it is indefensible to force teachers to reinvent continually, on their own cognizance, the curriculum wheel. The United States is the only industrialized country in the world that demands that teachers be, essentially, their own curriculum maker.

Research

Studies of decision making in teachers indicate that knowledge of research is not, at present, a significant source for guiding their practice.[13] For example, a National Education Association study concluded that the most important sources of teaching knowledge and skills were direct experience, consultation with other teachers, and observation of other teachers. To be relevant to teachers, researchers must focus their research on improving teaching effectiveness.

According to Kenneth Wilson, a Nobel Prize winner in physics, and Bennett Daviss, in their book on educational reform, "Teachers learn no repertoire of research-based classroom performance and management techniques that have proved to be consistently effective. Their profession has no structures through which to broadcast new understandings when knowledge of pedagogical methods or the psychology of learning advances."[14] To be sure, the knowledge base for teacher education has improved the past decade or so,[15] but still there is much that teacher educators—not only in the United States but throughout the world—do not know or know very imperfectly, for example:

- What specific knowledge and skills must a teacher master in order to enhance student learning?
- What should be the relationship between the professional and nonprofessional aspects of a prospective teacher's training?
- How many years of training is desirable for primary and secondary school teachers?
- Which parts of educational theory should trainees master before becoming a teacher and how should this theory be correlated with practice?
- What is the relationship between knowledge or skill mastery and subsequent success in practice?

- What kind of work should schools and teachers do with parents and how do different kinds of work affect student learning?
- What kind of cooperative arrangements between public schools and teacher training institutions are most effective in enhancing the knowledge and pedagogical skills of teacher trainees and classroom teachers?
- What kind of school structures and teacher workloads best promote student learning?
- How do different kinds of mentoring programs for beginning teachers affect student learning and retention of teachers?
- How may teachers best be prepared to do research and to be critical interpreters of educational research? What effect does possession or nonpossession of research skills have on teaching effectiveness? How may teachers and professors best work together on research projects to enhance teaching and learning in public schools?
- In addition to preparing classroom teachers, what other school related jobs—curriculum specialist, school research coordinator, community liaison—should teacher training institutions help teachers to assume?
- What are the fundamental ideas of academic disciplines taught in schools, and when and how should these ideas be presented to students of different ages, intellectual abilities, and socioeconomic backgrounds?
- What are the best ways for teacher interns and practicing teachers to demonstrate what they know and can do?

None of these questions has an easy, simplistic answer. For teacher education to rise in public respect, teacher educators must base their actions on a solid foundation of knowledge supported by quality research.[16] This means that teacher educators must be not only good teachers but active researchers as well. Production of a large number of quality educational researchers in teacher training institutions will not be easy.[17]

Most teacher educators have done little substantive research, and even if they had the desire and training to do so, most have little time to do it. Education professors typically have a heavier teaching load than their colleagues in the arts and sciences, and they must in addition supervise student teaching and consult with schools. Furthermore, it will be quite an adjustment for education professors to shift their research focus from individual, small-scale projects with questionable relevance to teaching to long-term, cooperative study of teacher-relevant issues such as the effect on student learning of class size, fully licensed teachers, nonlicensed teachers, advanced certification of teachers by the National Board for Professional Teaching Standards, teacher salaries, teacher work conditions, and so forth.

Educational research should be a high priority of government. It is not. The average federal agency in 1990 spent 4.7 percent of its budget on research and development, while the U.S. Department of Education spent only .8 percent. Furthermore, the federal government spends three times more money on research in agriculture and twenty-one times more in space research than it does on research devoted to improving schools.[18]

Long-term, large-scale, well-funded research efforts to improve education of teachers have no precedent in the United States. One is forced to agree with Del Schalock that "until such efforts are undertaken, and accompanied by research on the benefits and costs that accrue, teacher education will never progress in either its form or effectiveness far beyond what it is today."[19]

Globalism

There are a number of comparative education experts in America, but few colleges require undergraduate teacher trainees or administrators to take any courses in comparative education. As Philip Altbach, one of the best of these experts, noted: "Foreign experts are always studying American schools, American corporations, and American science. They feel that they have much to learn from us. They read our books and translate them for wider dissemination. But Americans seldom take seriously the experiences of other countries."[20]

Albert Shanker often bemoaned the provincialism of American educators and American society in general on educational matters around the world, especially in countries competing with us economically. He argued that the best way to improve schools is to learn from our competitors (nations such as Germany and Japan), to find out what they are doing that enables their students to achieve at higher levels than American students. In 1992, he noted some of the most important differences between the traditional schools in the competitor nations and those in America:

- Schools in these countries are run by professionals, with relatively little interference by lay persons.

- Schools are financed nationally or regionally. As a result, the disparity between wealthy and poor schools that is so destructive and shocking in the U.S. does not exist.

- For the most part, there is a national curriculum. Teacher training, textbooks, and assessments are geared to this curriculum. If students move from teacher to teacher or school to school, there is continuity.

- Assessments are curriculum-based and challenging. Teaching to the test is something positive when you have really good tests.

- These countries produce a higher percentage of students at top levels of achievement. Also, teaching is a relatively prestigious—in Japan, very prestigious—profession, so they can guarantee that all classrooms have teachers who have attained high levels of excellence.

- Like us, these countries track their students. However, we begin as early as first grade and they hold off until later. This means that all their kids get a more or less equal start. Ours don't.
- All these countries have clearly visible consequences for student performance. There are strict college-entry standards and clear employment standards. Students work hard, and their teachers and parents push them because success is rewarded in all tracks.
- Schools are relatively safe and free from disruption because the legal system supports school regulations needed to maintain a proper educational atmosphere.[21]

What we can learn most from such countries as Canada, Germany, and France is that Americans have low expectations for the education and training of our public school teachers. For example, in the province of Quebec in Canada, the guidelines for teacher training set by the ministry of education require a four-year education degree *after* the completion of a two-year pre-university program offered in publicly funded junior colleges. Thus, a prospective teacher would complete his or her training at age twenty-three, if there are no detours along the way. At the university level, teacher trainees must master specific professional competencies and spend 700 hours of different kinds of student teaching experiences spread out over their four-year program in increasing amounts each year and with increasing cooperation between the university and school. There are no shortcuts to becoming a certified public school teacher in Quebec province.[22]

In France, a certified teacher must have not only a university education but also two years of graduate study, including a year-long internship. In Germany, the certification requirements are equally high, so demanding in fact that a recent poll there ranked teachers second, only behind judges, on the "most respected" list of professionals.

The teaching profession in Germany adheres to a hierarchy similar to the apprentice, journeyman, and master levels of professional guilds and to the assistant, associate, and full professor ranks of professors in American universities. After completing university training, where the teacher candidate must earn a degree in two academic majors and successfully complete student teaching and pass the state's first certification examination, a novice teacher must then work for two years as an apprentice teacher under the close supervision of a "master" teacher. An apprentice teacher may advance to the journeyman level, which confers civil service status, only after completing advanced training at a teacher training institution, receiving a recommendation from the mentor teacher and outside master teachers, and passing the state's second certification examination. Many teachers remain at this level for the duration of their teaching career. Those, however, who desire to attain the highest professional rank, that of "master teacher," must continue teaching successfully for several years, gain the approval of two outside master teachers who observe them for three days, obtain the nomination for the rank from the school in which the applicant teaches, and pass a third state certification examination. Successful applicants for the master rank are qualified to serve on a part-time basis in leadership capacities devoted to professional development, teacher evaluation, campus administration, selection of instructional materials, and curriculum development. Obviously, German teachers must earn the public's high esteem.[23]

One of the most immediate needs in American education is to make comparative education an important component in the training of teacher educators so that they will in turn make comparative education an integral component in the training of schoolteachers and school administrators.

Technology

Teaching today requires a fundamental knowledge of technology and how to apply technology to enhance the instructional process. Teacher educators have a great responsibility to prepare teachers who not only know computers but also know specifically how to use them to increase their teaching effectiveness. For example, teacher educators might show teachers how computers can, in the words of former education editor of the *New York Times*, Edward Fiske:

[be] the most important new technology for writing instruction since the invention of the pencil—maybe even more so. Learning to write is essentially self-editing. The craft requires writing and rewriting. For little children, the biggest obstacle to learning to write is the physical act of moving the pencil across the paper, but computers make this unnecessary. For older students, word processing allows endless revisions. . . .

[be] powerful tools for working the curriculums of schools away from rote learning and toward the problem-solving skills that students will need in the workplace of the future. . . .

promote the value of respect for diversity. Whereas teacher talk appeals to the minority of students who learn best by hearing abstract ideas, computers offer a dazzling array of visual images. For a generation that has grown up on television and music videos, the significance of this is considerable. Moreover, since computers are inherently social devices—a document on a computer screen is public property—they enhance cooperative learning. Students work together naturally on computers.

make possible the creation of knowledge on the part of the student, not simply the dissemination of knowledge by teachers. . . . Technology helps the teacher to create an environment in which kids can build connections, not simply parrot their teachers, and to create knowledge that is new even to the teacher.

[promote] networks of learners . . . across town or around the world.

transform virtually all aspects of the factory-model school.[24]

The old factory-model of school that has hung on tenaciously in America throughout the twentieth century is clearly no longer appropriate for the twenty-first century. Just as the shift from the agricultural age to the industrial age demanded educational change, so shall the shift from the industrial age to the computer age. Rather than being tuba players at the back of bands in a festive parade—as teacher educators, for the most part, have always been—they can be drum majors and lead the bands by making sure that prospective teachers:

- understand the Internet, in particular the World Wide Web and e-mail;
- acquire three important skills essential for education in a computer age: skill in acquiring information, analyzing it, and communicating it—in short, teachers need to become information skill experts;
- become not only tolerant of computer technology and the changes it portends but embrace it enthusiastically as an essential tool in enriching their education and that of their pupils;
- understand children, of course, as leading educators have always admonished teachers, but in the computer age, teachers must also understand children as they relate to machines, and vice-versa;
- learn how to analyze software and use it for instructional purposes;
- are familiarized with different kinds of specialized computers as they come on the market, with their capabilities and potential instructional use.

Deans in schools of education must, of course, have professors who understand technology and its instructional use. This will require massive retraining of most professors, and it will require that new faculty members possess the necessary instructional technology knowledge and skills. Furthermore, deans who take the information technology revolution seriously should consider hiring as the number two administrator a person who is an expert not only in technology but an expert in the instructional process. Finally, schools must be adequately equipped with computers and Internet access if educators are to lead a technological revolution in school reform.

Liberal Education

Collectively, professors involved in a liberal education program should acquaint students with how knowledge is gained and verified by, for example, a mathematician, historian, biologist, or an anthropologist. The objective would be to give the general student some command, though limited, of the processes of thought employed by specialists in different disciplines. Such command is essential for young people and prospective teachers because they need to know that in a world of clashing opinions, in Bestor's words, "there are more orderly and cogent methods of gaining insight into the problems in hand than by subjecting oneself to the ceaseless battering of opposed controversialists."[25]

Regarding liberal education, we should stress three things. First, though the obstacles to getting a large number of arts and sciences professors to make a long-term commitment to improving liberal education are formidable, it is perhaps prudent to heed the words of E. B. White: "Somebody (I think it was I) once remarked that today's fantasy is tomorrow's news events."[26] Second, while liberal education demands superior teaching in each course comprising the program, great teaching in discrete courses does not necessarily make a liberal education *curriculum*. A sound curriculum must have not only good teaching but purpose, continuity, coherence. Each of its parts should fit together so rationally and effortlessly that students experience little difficulty in integrating their knowledge into a pattern that makes sense to them. Third, liberal education is a goal, not a prescribed set of courses. Some courses, of course, have more potential for liberal education than others, but any course can be illiberal. It all depends on how it is taught. Anton Chekhov once told a story about a man who tried to teach a kitten to catch mice. Whenever the kitten refused to give chase, the man beat it. After the animal grew up into an adult cat, it always cowered in terror in the presence of a mouse. "That," said Chekhov, "is the man who taught me Latin."

ORGANIZATION OF PRE-SERVICE TEACHER EDUCATION

Education professors provide on average no more than 21 percent of the degree program for secondary school teachers. Noneducation professors provide the rest of the program.[27] Teacher candidates model the teaching of their professors.[28] The professors they see most of the time are not education but arts and sciences professors. These professors, therefore, play an exceedingly important role in the education of future teachers. Thus, this section discusses several organizational constructs—collaboration, articulation, mentoring, elevation, customer orientation—which have the potential to improve the current conduct of pre-service teacher education.

Collaboration

To mitigate what Conant called the "feud" between teacher educators and their colleagues in other departments, we suggest that teacher educators take the initiative in developing a collaborative relationship that may in time—after many small steps, a little luck, and much hard work—blossom into one of mutual advantage. As Conant noted, such a relationship can greatly benefit future schoolteachers. Such an initiative is also in the interest of all professors because the production of *quality* schoolteachers can only be a plus for a college or university in a period of tight money and increasing demand by governors, legislatures, and the public at large for greater accountability on the part not only of schools but of institutions of higher learning.

Education professors could begin by making it clear to their academic colleagues that they are indeed committed to providing teacher trainees not only with pedagogical knowledge but with a solid liberal education and subject matter knowledge. They could, for example, play a prominent role in a university's efforts to clarify what a liberal education program should be and how professors individually and collectively can further its objectives. Professors will have somewhat different definitions of liberal education, of course, but most will probably agree that a well-thought-out liberal education program has the potential to give an added dimension to the lives of university students not only by providing them with sound knowledge of the principles of the fundamental intellectual disciplines, and their relationship to one another, but by assisting them to develop imaginative, critical thinking skills; aesthetic tastes; breadth of perspective; a zest for life; and a desire to continue learning throughout life.

Nobody needs this added dimension more than prospective teachers, for their ultimate professional objective should be to develop these same qualities in their students. What particular instructional and curricular practices might professors in education and the arts and sciences consider in developing a program to further the liberal education of teacher trainees and other undergraduate students?

Articulation

Some distinction should be made between courses taught for the purpose of enhancing the general student's liberal education and courses taught specifically for future specialists in a particular discipline. In the latter courses, professors must of necessity give attention not only to principles but to details and esoteric knowledge appropriate only for future specialists. In teaching liberal education courses for the general student, however, the objective might be to acquaint students only with those details and facts that support and clarify the major ideas and principles that undergird a particular discipline. They could point out to students the relationship of these ideas and principles to those in related disciplines. Perhaps of most importance, they could assist students in understanding how these ideas and principles are relevant to their everyday lives. The philosopher, Alfred North Whitehead made this point forcefully:

In my own work at universities I have been struck by the paralysis of thought induced in pupils by the aimless accumulation of precise knowledge, inert and unutilised. It should be the chief aim of a university professor to exhibit himself in his own true character—that is, as an ignorant man thinking, actively utilizing his small share of knowledge. In a sense, knowledge shrinks as wisdom grows: for details are swallowed up in principles. The details of knowledge which are important will be picked up *ad hoc* in each avocation of life, but the habit of the active utilisa-tion of well-understood principles is the final possession of wisdom.[29]

Mentoring

State reforms in teacher education almost never include resources that focus on enhancing the competencies or knowledge of the professorate, in schools of education or in schools of arts and sciences. For example, rarely does the training of a professor include substantive work on teaching effec-tiveness or research that has relevance and interest to: (1) people other than one's own colleagues in one's area of specialization; or (2) the improvement of education in general, for example, the assessment of what and how much students learn.

One area that might be fruitfully discussed by institutions of higher learning is the establishment of a mentoring program for neophyte profes-sors, headed by experienced professors highly regarded by their peers as fine teachers and researchers. New professors need on-the-job training as much as public school teachers. Mentors could provide their "trainees" with invaluable assistance in developing pedagogical skills, including as-sessment of student learning, and in understanding such things as the the-ory and practice of education at different levels, the relationship of their discipline to other disciplines and to the lives of students, the goals and ways to implement liberal education for all undergraduates, the relation-ship of the content and teaching of their discipline to promotion of liberal education, and the contributions they can make as teacher educators, as good models for prospective teachers.

Elevation

Nearly one-fifth of all states require a master's degree for initial teacher certification. Thus, the time when pre-service teacher training is elevated to primarily a graduate, professional enterprise supported by a pre-education undergraduate major may not be far off. This organizational model has a number of advantages.

First, it allows prospective teachers to concentrate on their liberal educa-tion as undergraduate students and requires them to master the skills of one or more disciplines. This should, in turn, improve the quality of teacher education applicants.

Second, it ameliorates, if not solves, the problem of curricular crowding and "turf wars" that are the cause of much animosity between arts and sci-ences professors and education professors. The removal of this systemic barrier should encourage a more collegial and collaborative atmosphere.

Third, it bases the education of teachers on the same model used by other professions such as law and medicine. This should help to raise the status of teacher education and hopefully decrease the funding disparities between teacher education and other professional programs.

Finally, elevation will make accountability and reform easier and more likely because the lines of responsibility are cleaner. This does not mean that collaboration is any less important, only that it is easier to separate and focus on problems in a professional model. In fact, collaboration between arts and sciences professors and education professors would be especially important in the undergraduate pre-education program.

We should also mention that a graduate professional school of education would also allow for cleaner lines of responsibility between academic preparation and clinical preparation. That is, if the clinical preparation of prospective teachers was primarily the province of the school system (as clinical preparation of physicians is now primarily the province of hospitals and medical clinics), then the lines of accountability would be much cleaner and therefore the chances of reform greater.

Customer Orientation

Just as teachers should listen carefully to their students, teacher educators should listen carefully to their clients—teacher trainees and practicing teachers. Public school teachers strongly believe that the teacher training institutions that trained them should be more committed to preparing them for the practice of teaching. What teachers are demanding are the details for putting a theory into action and the means—specific, systematic, structural methodologies, various kinds of equipment and high quality teaching materials—for doing so.

In a survey of American teachers by the Council for Basic Education, their responses suggest three major changes for teacher preparation: (1) require teachers to know well the content of subjects they plan to teach; (2) teach pedagogy always in the context of academic content; and (3) provide teacher trainees with numerous, varied school-based experiences. The responders also recommend that trainees be required to have at least a "B" average in an academic major; that they not be allowed to graduate without first passing an exit examination that assesses the breadth and depth of the subjects they plan to teach; and that the pedagogy courses offered by a teacher training institution be jointly developed by a team of classroom teachers, teacher educators, and professors in the arts and sciences. The teachers also suggested that the pedagogy courses be taught at the same time that trainees are having practical experiences in schools so that they can see how pedagogical ideas are applied in a classroom setting.[30] Each of these suggestions is reasonable and amenable to implementation, but of course not without some hard work and a firm commitment to get the job done. If medical, law, engineering, and business schools ignored suggestions by their graduates, they would soon be out of business. Survival is a powerful reason why teacher educators should listen carefully to what their graduates have to say about their training.

This same kind of customer orientation should also become a focus of the pre-service teacher training curriculum. Schools have become increasingly politicized in recent decades; yet, teachers have little knowledge about how to work effectively with parents and community members. As one teacher noted, "It would be good to develop how you communicate to the community. As teachers we're not prepared for this. We learn about our subject matter and how to teach it. But we really aren't trained at all on how to deal with developing an idea and taking it to the public."[31] Unfortunately, prospective teachers typically receive no training in working effectively with parents or the community (nor do their principals).[32] This could and should be changed.

CONCLUSION

Clearly, a typical present-day education school is a beleaguered institution. It strives to develop quality teachers but has limited success primarily due to inadequate human and financial resources and public backing. Still, education schools are the only stable entities with the necessary organization, experience, and potential of providing the nation with a huge number—over 200,000—of *qualified* teachers every year for an indefinite future. Furthermore, education schools have managed somehow over the twentieth century to provide the nation's schools with the kind of teachers Americans have been willing to pay for, while at the same time continually improving the qualifications of teachers. That is no small accomplishment.

Now, with the more sophisticated intellectual demands of the information age, teacher-training institutions must shift their focus from quantity of teachers to quality of teachers. There are a number of things going on in our nation that suggest there is reason for some optimism about the future of teacher education at the pre-service level.

Standards for admission to teacher preparation programs compare well with standards in such fields as engineering, journalism, business administration, library science, engineering, architecture, and pharmacy. Standards for prospective teachers also compare favorably with those for students majoring in the arts and sciences.[33]

There is some movement on the part of academic deans to work more closely with public schools. For example, a dean of arts and sciences created a new position in the science department for a faculty member to work closely with public schools. The dean plans on creating a similar position in the chemistry department.[34]

Some academic professors are reaching out to public school teachers. Assisted by a grant from the Edna McConnell Clark Foundation, teachers in Long Beach, California, are trying to improve their middle schools by working closely with the National Faculty. This faculty is an Atlanta, Georgia-based organization that brings together university professors and K–12 teachers. The primary objective is for professors to assist teachers to gain more depth and expertise in such areas as mathematics, social studies, writing, and science. The middle school teachers also work together with scholars in workshops and summer institutes devoted specifically to devising curriculum units geared to Long Beach's standards for students.[35] Obviously, the professors will also learn much from the teachers about schools and relating academic knowledge to children and young people of different ages, interests, social backgrounds, and academic abilities.

There is also an example of remarkable cooperation between an education and an arts and sciences dean at Northeastern University in Boston. These two deans are developing one of the nation's first education schools run primarily by professors outside the school of education. The objective is to make content knowledge in school-taught academic disciplines an integral part of teacher preparation. The key to achieving this objective, the two deans believe, is to involve professors in the arts and sciences in every aspect of the school of education, from conducting research to choosing curriculum and making hiring and tenure decisions. Joint appointments are given to all arts and sciences professors interested in the new teacher-training program. Thus far, 22 of 300 members of the arts and sciences faculty have signed up for the project. Under the new arrangement, these faculty members will continue to teach in their main disciplines but also will conduct research in education and take part in partnerships with Boston schools. Not everyone is sold on the new plan, but it is clearly a noble experiment that bears close study and possible replication, with appropriate modifications, in other universities.[36]

The 1998 Higher Education Act specifies that states must submit a report on the quality of their teacher education institutions, in particular to report the test results of students on teacher examinations for licensure. Since the reputation of a university at large is at stake, this act should be a powerful stimulus for professors to improve the quality of instruction for prospective teachers.[37]

Charles Reed, chancellor of twenty-three campuses comprising the California State University system, announced that one of his system's top priorities is to improve public schools; specifically, he wants universities to train better teachers, and more of them, to enter into partnerships with schools; to offer great support for teachers by doing such things as issuing warranties certifying their competency as neophyte teachers; and to provide experienced teachers with professional development opportunities.[38]

There are a number of innovative practices in education schools around the country. For example, in Millersville State University in Pennsylvania, the education school developed for teacher trainees one credit hour seminars to accompany various courses in arts and sciences. A liberal arts professor teaches a class such as Sociology of the Family, and an education professor sits in on it. Then, once a week, the sociology professor attends a pedagogical seminar conducted by the education professor. In the seminars, prospective teachers analyze how and why the course is taught as it is.[39]

The University of Virginia has developed computer-simulated classrooms for the training of teachers, and the Peabody College of Education at Vanderbilt University in Nashville now supplements field experiences for trainees with interactive videodiscs.[40] At the University of Louisville in Kentucky, full-time tenured, or on the tenure track, education professors spend on average one day a week in schools designated as professional development sites.[41]

In 1998, Texas was the first state to hold colleges and universities accountable for the scores of education students on the state's licensure tests. (Five other states, presumably, will soon follow suit.)[42]

Research has gone beyond the traditional research for generic teacher behaviors that a principal could check on a standardized form after visiting a teacher once or twice a year to a systematic search for the different kinds of knowledge that teachers must have to teach effectively.[43]

It is no longer unusual for the two major teacher unions, the American Federation of Teachers (AFT) and the National Education Association (NEA), to stress, along with the bread and butter issues of salary and working conditions, the quality of teaching of their members. AFT, for example, supports higher standards for admission to teacher education, demanding teacher licensing examinations and the elimination of emergency credentials.[44]

Scholars, other than education professors, are becoming increasingly involved in the study of schools and teachers. Some of the most interesting and well-designed educational research on teaching and learning during the 1990s has been done by economists. Though much of their work has been controversial and has received a cool reception by many educators, their entry into the field of educational research is welcome as is that of scholars in other academic disciplines. The more well-trained, objective scholars we have devoting serious attention to education, the more apt we are to improve the quality of teaching and the schools in which teachers work.[45]

There are not many, but there are some efforts by American educators to abandon their traditional international provincialism. For example, educators from the United States and the United Kingdom are meeting to exchange ideas on education in each other's countries. American educators are especially interested in finding out more about the national, nonpartisan British Inspectorate of Schools.[46]

For the first time to our knowledge there is a serious effort to adequately fund a few long-range, interdisciplinary studies on topics pregnant with significance for improving the teaching/learning process. For example, prominent educational researchers at the University of Michigan in Ann Arbor received a $4.1 million grant to identify the factors that account in part for the success of three comprehensive reform programs in schools with a significant concentration of poor students. Over a six year period, the researchers will study the progress of the three programs in 125 schools scattered around the country.[47]

The trustees of the State University of New York (SUNY) adopted a core curriculum required for all students entering the university in the fall of 2000.[48] Such a requirement is an essential first step in providing teachers and other students with a liberal education.

According to one survey of teacher trainees, the professors they valued most highly as models of good teaching were professors of education.[49]

In this chapter, we discussed a number of the most significant problems and challenges facing pre-service teacher education programs in colleges and universities and suggested some things teacher educators and arts and sciences professors might do to cope with them. Many of the pre-service teacher education trends of the past decade or so strike us as being in the right direction: closer links with K–12 schools; more emphasis on empowerment of teachers; more interest by the leadership of institutions of higher learning in teacher education; more work of education professors with schoolteachers; an increased amount of research on teaching; greater recognition by professors on the importance of modeling; greater recognition that teacher education should be an all-university function. Making sure that these fledgling trends become widespread and institutionalized, however, requires an ongoing commitment by all the vested interest groups associated with pre-service teacher education.

NOTES

1. Julie Blair, "Districts Wooing Teachers Away with Bonuses, Other Incentives," *Education Week*, 2 August 2000, p. 17.

2. Arthur E. Wise and Linda Darling-Hammond, "Alternative Certification Is an Oxymoron," *Education Week*, 4 September 1991, p. 46. For people who question this claim by Wise and Darling-Hammond, see Marci Kanstoroom and Chester E. Finn, Jr., eds. *Better Teachers, Better Schools* (Washington, D.C.: Thomas B. Fordham Foundation, 1999).

3. Donald R. Cruickshank, *Research that Informs Teachers and Teacher Educators* (Bloomington, Ind.: Phi Delta Kappa Educational Foundation, 1990), p. 113.

4. Robert A. Roth, "The Teacher Education Program: An Endangered Species," *Phi Delta Kappan* 71 (December 1989): 320.

5. Linda Darling-Hammond, "Achieving Our Goals: Superficial or Structural Reform," *Phi Delta Kappan* 72 (December 1990): 291.

6. Jeff Claus, "You Can't Avoid the Politics: Lessons for Teacher Education from a Case Study of Teacher-Initiated Tracking Reform," *Journal of Teacher Education* 50 (January–February 1999): 12.

7. Seymour B. Sarason, *How Schools Might Be Governed and Why* (New York: Teachers College Press, Columbia University, 1997), pp. 157, 160.

8. Gary A. Griffin, ed., *The Education of Teachers,* Ninety-Eighth Yearbook of the National Society for the Study of Education (Chicago: University of Chicago Press, 1999), p. 13.

9. Jonathan Schorr, "Class Action: What Clinton's National Service Program Could Learn from 'Teach for America,'" *Phi Delta Kappan* 75 (December 1993): 317.

10. Diana Wyllie Rigden, "How Teachers Would Change Teacher Education: A Survey's Results Lend Support—and a Voice—to the National Commission's Findings," *Education Week,* 11 December 1996, p. 48.

11. Richard F. Elmore, Penelope L. Peterson, Sarah J. McCarthey, *Restructuring in the Classroom: Teaching, Learning, and School Organization* (San Francisco: Jossey-Bass, 1996), p. 11.

12. Chester E. Finn, Jr., foreword to *A TIMSS Primer: Lessons and Implications for U.S. Education,* by Harold W. Stevenson (Washington, D.C.: Thomas B. Fordham Foundation, 1998), p. 2.

13. Robert B. Stevenson, "Educational Practitioners' Use of Research: Expanding Conventional Understandings," in *Transforming Schools and Schools of Education: A New Vision for Preparing Educators,* ed. Steven L. Jacobson and others (Thousand Oaks, Calif.: Corwin Press, 1998), p. 100.

14. Kenneth G. Wilson and Bennett Daviss, *Redesigning Education* (New York: Henry Holt, 1994), p. 80.

15. For knowledge-based research see W. Robert Houston, Martin Haberman, John Sikula, eds., *Handbook of Research on Teacher Education* (New York: Macmillan, 1990); M. C. Reynolds, ed., *Knowledge Base for the Beginning Teacher* (Elmsford, N.Y.: Pergamon Press, 1989); John Sikula, Thomas J. Buttery, and Edith Guyton, eds., *Handbook of Research on Teacher Education,* 2nd. ed. (New York: Simon & Schuster Macmillan, 1996); and Herbert J. Walberg, "Productive Teaching and Instruction: Assessing the Knowledge Base," *Phi Delta Kappan* 71 (February 1990): 470–478.

16. Chester Finn has long championed quality educational research. He supports the HR 4875 bill that is making, in his words, a "strong push for bona fide experiments, complete with control groups, which are normal in hard science and biomedical research but staunchly resisted by educational researchers." Chester E. Finn Jr., "Fixing Education Research and Statistics (Again)," *Education Week,* 20 September 2000, pp. 33, 48.

17. According to Page Smith, it is not easy to produce quality researchers in schools other than education. In his view, "the vast majority of what passes for research/publication in the major universities of America is mediocre, expensive, and unnecessary, does not push back the frontiers of knowledge in any appreciable degree, and serves only to get professors promotions." Quoted in Jianping Shen, *The School of Education: Its Mission, Faculty, and Reward Structure* (Baltimore, Md.: Peter Lang, 1999), p. 124.

18. Wilson and Daviss, *Redesigning Education,* p. 93.

19. Del Schalock, "Methodological Considerations in Future Research and Development in Teacher Education," in *The Education of Teachers: A Look Ahead,* ed. Kenneth R. Howey and William E. Gardner (New York: Longman, 1983), pp. 42–44.

20. Philip G. Altbach, "Needed: An International Perspective," *Phi Delta Kappan* 71 (November 1989): 244.

21. Albert Shanker, "Where We Stand: Improving Our Schools," *New York Times*, 17 May 1992, sec. E, p. 7.

22. Jon G. Bradley, "New Teacher Training Programs for Quebec," *Phi Delta Kappan* 77 (October 1995): 180–181.

23. In our comments on teacher education in Germany, we have drawn heavily on Ernest G. Noack, "Comparing U.S. and German Education: Like Apples and Sauerkraut," *Phi Delta Kappan* 80 (June 1999): 775–776.

24. Edward B. Fiske, *Smart Schools, Smart Kids: Why Do Some Schools Work?* (New York: Simon and Schuster, 1991), pp. 157–162.

25. Arthur Bestor, *The Restoration of Learning: A Process of Redeeming the Unfulfilled Promise of American Education* (New York: Alfred A. Knopf, 1956), p. 134.

26. E. B. White, *The Second Tree from the Corner* (New York: Harper & Row, 1984), p. xvii; For obstacles preventing a large number of arts and sciences professors from making a long-term commitment to improving liberal education, see Delbert H. Long, "Arthur Bestor on Education of Teachers," *The Educational Forum* 48 (summer 1984): 433–445.

27. Christopher J. Lucas, *Teacher Education in America: Reform Agendas for the 21st Century* (New York: St. Martin's Press, 1997), pp. 103–104.

28. Gary A. Griffin, "Changes in Teacher Education: Looking to the Future," in *The Education of Teachers*, ed. Gary A. Griffin, Ninety-Eighth Yearbook of the National Society for the Study of Education (Chicago: University of Chicago Press, 1999), p. 14.

29. Alfred North Whitehead, *The Aims of Education and Other Essays* (New York: Free Press, 1967), p. 37.

30. Rigden, "How Teachers," pp. 48, 64.

31. Claus, "You Can't Avoid the Politics," p. 12.

32. Dennis Kelly, "Training Teachers to Reach Out to Parents," *USA Today*, 17 June 1994, sec. D, p. 4.

33. Lucas, *Teacher Education in America*, p. 106.

34. "Teaching and Learning," *Education Week*, 26 January 2000, p. 6

35. Ann Bradley, "An Incomplete Education," *Education Week*, supplement to the 4 October 2000 issue, pp. 11–12.

36. Julie Blair, "Northeastern Rethinks Focus of Ed. School," *Education Week*, 3 November 1999, pp. 1, 14–15.

37. Anne C. Lewis, "High-Quality Teachers for All Americans," *Phi Delta Kappan* 81 (January 2000): 339.

38. Charles B. Reed, "Taking Action on K–12, University Cooperation," *Education Week*, 24 March 1999, pp. 53, 72.

39. Karen Diegmueller, "Teaching Our Teachers: Preparing Teachers for Elementary Schools Presents Special Challenges to Colleges of Education," *Education Week*, 13 February 1991, p. 18.

40. Ann Bradley, "Teaching Our Teachers: While All Agree on Value of Field Experience, Many Say Clinical Training Should be Redesigned," *Education Week*, 13 March 1991, pp. 29–30.

41. Betty Lou Whitford and Phyllis Metcalf-Turner, "Of Promises and Unresolved Puzzles: Reforming Teacher Education with Professional Development

Schools," in *The Education of Teachers,* ed. Gary A.Griffin, Ninety-Eighth Yearbook of the National Society for the Study of Education (Chicago: University of Chicago Press, 1999), p. 267.

42. Ann Bradley, "The Gatekeeping Challenge," *Education Week,* 13 January 2000, p. 26.

43. Richard J. Murnane and others, *Who Will Teach? Policies that Matter* (Cambridge: Harvard University Press, 1991), p. 98.

44. "Federal and State Teacher Quality Initiatives: American Federation of Teachers' Perspective," *Educational Horizons* 78 (Spring 2000): 127–128.

45. Bess Keller, "Economic Growth: More Practitioners of the 'Dismal Science' Casting an Eye Toward Education," *Education Week,* 25 October 2000, pp. 42–45.

46. Robert C. Johnston, "U.S., U.K. Swap Ideas at Gathering to Launch 'Education Diplomacy,'" *Education Week,* 25 October 2000, p. 8.

47. Debra Viadero, "Interdisciplinary Studies," *Education Week,* 11 October 2000, pp. 34–36.

48. Karen W. Arenson, "SUNY Trustees Are Poised to Adopt a Core Curriculum for All Students," *New York Times,* 12 December 1998, sec. A, p. 16.

49. Willis D. Hawley, "United States," in *Issues and Problems in Teacher Education: An International Handbook,* ed. Howard B. Leavitt (Westport, Conn.: Greenwood Press, 1992), p. 262.

12

In-Service Training of Teachers

Any teaching programme, any method of training, however good it may be, remains a dead letter having no real force, unless it becomes the conviction of the teachers.

K. D. Ushinskii, "father" of Russian teacher education

In-service teacher education is teacher training that occurs after a teacher is certified and employed. There are currently about 2.7 million teachers in schools in the United States.[1] Thus, the concept of in-service teacher education cannot be ignored in the more general discussion about teacher education.

In this chapter, we summarize the ideas of the critics on in-service teacher education and discuss how this component of teacher education might be enhanced by teaching training institutions, schools and school districts, and teacher unions. We conclude the chapter by noting some of the positive things that are happening around the country relevant to in-service teacher training.

CRITICS ON CONCEPTS OF IN-SERVICE TEACHER EDUCATION

Like pre-service teacher education, the thinking about in-service teacher education is exceedingly diverse. The diversity of viewpoints regarding the concept of in-service teacher education can be clearly seen in the writings of the critics discussed in Part I of this book.

Regarding in-service teacher education, Dewey said very little. Of course, it can be inferred that Dewey would encourage in-service programs that vary with the needs of individual teachers.

Hutchins saw no need for in-service teacher education. However, he did say that in-service teachers should be expected to belong to learned societies and that could be viewed as a form of in-service education.

Bestor said that the graduate training of teachers should be the same as their undergraduate training—more training in the fundamental intellectual disciplines. The graduate courses should be structured to the peculiar needs of a teacher, although the courses should be offered by the regular departments of liberal arts and sciences.

Concerning in-service education, Conant proposed that such work not be tied to course credits and that it be directed as a "group attack" on a matter of mutual concern to a group of teachers in a particular school or school district. Both academic and education professors, at the taxpayer's expense, should assist teachers in coping with the mutual concerns they identify.

Brameld was silent regarding in-service teacher education. However, since he embraced the medical model for pre-service teacher education, it might be inferred that he would have favored the type of in-service education that physicians typically receive (that is, voluntary professional seminars, occasional meetings with commercial vendors regarding new products, and so on).

Silberman said very little about in-service education of teachers. However, he did insist that learning to teach is a lifelong endeavor and that teacher education (and presumably in-service teacher education) should be a cooperative effort of public schools and education and arts and sciences professors.

Illich, of course, would not have supported any in-service teacher education requirements. Both pre-service and in-service training in a deschooled society would take the form of apprenticeships.

Shanker thought it important to devote a sufficient amount of time and money for teacher in-service. He pointed out that the automobile industry devotes ninety-two hours of training and thousands of dollars a year per employee, and suggested that it will take at least that much time and money for professional development to keep teachers up to date.

Finn believed that entry to teaching should be opened up to mid-career people and to young college graduates with degrees in academic fields who want to try teaching. To give them a reasonable chance of succeeding as teachers, he urged schools to provide neophyte teachers with on-the-job supervision, mentoring, and pointers on classroom management.

The perspectives of the critics on in-service education, as on pre-service education, is as varied as that of the American general public. What accounts for the highly divergent views in American society on in-service and pre-service teacher education? A partial explanation starts with the close interrelationship of two questions: (1) What should be the purpose or purposes of public schools? and (2) What kind of preparation does a teacher need? Let us explain.

The critics recognize that education is more than learning to read, write, and calculate and that it takes place not only in a class but in the home and community. If by education we mean what shapes, directly or indirectly, a person's social, aesthetic, ethical, emotional, and intellectual development, certainly schools and teachers play a vital role in this process, but so do parents, the community, the government, the judicial system, the church, and the mass media. Considering, then, that the school is only one of several educational institutions, and the school teacher only one of several "teachers" that exert educational influence on a child, the big question is what emphasis should schools and the teachers in them give to developing the skills, understandings, and attitudes that make a person what he or she is. People in general, and the nine critics highlighted here in particular, differ on how they answer this question, which put simply is: Should the schools expand or contract their role in the total development of children and young people. The trend during the twentieth century has clearly been for the school to expand its responsibility for the development of the so-called whole child. Some of the critics welcome this trend; others oppose it.

At the turn of the past century, Dewey gave impetus to the trend toward expansion of the role of the school beyond the teaching of the 3 Rs and the moral standards of the McGuffey readers, with his insistence that the aim of education and the school is identical. This aim is to develop in students the capacity for continuous growth in all areas that enable people to lead lives suffused with meaning and purpose. In contrast, Hutchins and Bestor, in particular among our critics, called for a sharp contracting of the functions of the American public school. They do not deny that an educated person should be able to think, feel, and act. They do deny that the school should put emphasis on all three functions. They believe the school should concentrate on doing what it was set up to do. It was established, they argued, to teach students to think. If the schools do not teach students this fundamental skill, they are convinced no other institution will.

The starkly contrasting views of our critics help us better understand why Americans have such strong, divergent views on what kind of training our teachers need. The critics agree that teachers need, of course, the kind of training essential to achieve the objectives of public school education. But since they disagree about those objectives, they also disagree about both pre-service and in-service teacher training.

PROFESSIONAL DEVELOPMENT OF TEACHERS

One by-product of this lack of agreement regarding the proper objectives of American education is the lack of a serious commitment by teacher training institutions, schools and school districts, and teacher unions to the lifelong professional development of teachers. Since the research is clear that student growth is dependent on teacher growth, this lack of commitment is especially troubling.

Teacher Training Institutions

Teacher training institutions, which play the predominant role in pre-service teacher education, continue to have important in-service responsibilities as well, such as:

- continuing the effort, started in undergraduate school, of encouraging teachers to devote much of their time and energy to advancing their own professional development and that of their colleagues as well;
- updating teacher qualifications and skills through courses, seminars, workshops, and conferences;
- utilizing outstanding public school teachers as instructors at their institutions;
- preparing, in cooperation with public schools, outstanding teachers to specialize in such roles as coordinator of school research and coordinator of community resources;
- orienting a significant amount of their research to problems relevant to public school teachers;
- assisting school districts in acquainting teachers with the results of research relevant to the classroom;
- providing teachers with the knowledge and skill necessary to plan, conduct, and evaluate classroom-oriented research;
- conducting joint research with teachers;
- providing interested teachers advanced training in master's and doctoral degree programs with academic standards comparable to those in other university programs;
- designing, conducting, and analyzing sociological studies of teachers and the teaching profession.

One other responsibility that teacher training institutions share with school districts requires some elaboration. There is common agreement that school principals can be a powerful force for or against development of schools where both students and teachers are constantly expanding their knowledge and skills. While detailed discussion of the training of school principals is beyond the scope of this book, we should nevertheless like to make one suggestion that is directly related to in-service training of teachers: Principals should be outstanding teacher educators. This means first of all that administrators should be as broadly educated as we expect teachers to be. If teachers are to be broadly educated, it simply will not do to have school principals who rate the intellectual capacity of teachers as the *least important factor in the selection of teachers for employment in a school district*.[2]

Nor will it do to have guidelines for the evaluation of administrators that ignore their responsibility for the vitality and quality of the workplace culture as the incubator for student and teacher learning.[3]

In the training of school administrators, the trend now is for more mentoring and for field and clinically oriented training.[4] Such training obviously is important, but administrators also need a solid, *continuous* liberal education focused on providing them with the knowledge and skills necessary to think, as expected of teachers, critically, objectively, humanely, and logically.

One of the authors of this book is a trained school administrator and worked as such for several years. The other author has been an administrator at the university level. Both the authors have worked closely over the years with many principals and school superintendents. The school administrators we have known are hardworking and devoted to promoting the welfare of public school education. But many know little about what it takes to really know and be able to teach an academic discipline effectively because they often do not have such training. Many know little about leadership in other fields, such as the military, business, and public and hospital administration because their training has not provided them with such knowledge.[5] Many know little about how to evaluate teachers fairly and objectively because they are often unclear about what it takes to be a quality teacher. Not without reason do teachers often cite poor principals as a chief reason for their dissatisfaction with teaching.

The first step in peeling away some of the provincialism of principals is for teacher-training institutions and public school systems to give them a vision of what principals as teacher educators might look like and then develop a program that makes this vision a reality. Here, we restrict ourselves only to selection of a compelling vision, not to its implementation, which of course is the exceptionally difficult part. One cannot find a better model of a principal/teacher educator than the great Soviet educator, Vasilii Sukhomlinskii, who worked for thirty-five years as a teacher/principal of a grade one through ten rural school in the Ukrainian Republic. We suggest Sukhomlinskii as a model first because of his wisdom and second because he wrote extensively about his work, and the best of his publications are available in English. Some of his books should be required reading for future school administrators.[6]

As principal, Sukhomlinskii called in his administrative bursar each day before classes began and spent ten to fifteen minutes taking care of administrative matters and spent the rest of the day working with teachers, pupils, and parents. In short he devoted practically all his time to being an educational leader and a teacher educator.

As a teacher educator, Sukhomlinskii believed that his most important task was to ensure that teachers become thoughtful researchers with a real thirst for knowledge. Creative teaching demands teachers with such attributes. Research, he observed, promotes ideas about teaching, and these ideas in turn stimulate the faculty to engage in joint research work. Sukhomlinskii considered this work to be the "most interesting and vital activity in school life." Without a thirst for knowledge, Sukhomlinskii insisted, a teacher could not understand a child. His rationale for this belief was simple. A "true master of his profession, an artist, a poet of the classroom" has a wide range of knowledge, infinitely wider than the school curriculum, and thus during a lesson his or her attention is focused not on presentation of content but on the pupils, "their mental activity, their thought processes and the difficulties they encounter in their mental activity."

What must teachers do to gain knowledge and insight into the mental operations of children? The solution to Sukhomlinskii was reading. In his words, the real intellectual wealth of a teaching staff is "first and foremost their individual reading. The true teacher is a book-lover." Sukhomlinskii developed in his school an intellectual climate in which each teacher felt a strong need for wide reading.

Sukhomlinskii obviously succeeded in encouraging his teachers to be book lovers. The personal libraries of his teachers totaled over forty-nine thousand books. Individual teachers had a library of 1,000 to 1,800 books. Sukhomlinskii recognized, however, that teachers need time to read. Hence, he stressed the necessity of relieving teachers as much as possible of everything not directly related to the teaching process. Sukhomlinskii well understood that the more teachers were tied down with things extraneous to good teaching, the more likely they would burn out and have nothing more to give to their pupils. Time, he repeated again and again, "is an all-important source of intellectual enrichment for the teacher."

American teachers typically do not conduct research with their colleagues, nor do they mention in surveys that reading is an important source of their teaching knowledge. Should a principal be able to encourage and make it easier for teachers to conduct joint research and to read widely on professional matters, this by itself would indeed be a notable accomplishment. It must be acknowledged, however, that the current overemphasis in American education on rules and regulations create pressures on public school principals that require them to spend an inordinate amount of time on administrivia. Thus, it is difficult for them to mimic the schedule and behavior of Sukhomlinskii even if they had the desire and training to do so. Until the system is redesigned to encourage this kind of principal schedule and behavior, in-service teacher education will remain an unloved stepchild.

Schools and School Districts

A 1998 survey by the National Center for Education Statistics on Teacher Quality indicated that participation of teachers in professional development activities during the previous twelve months typically lasted from only one to eight hours, the equivalent of one day of training or less.[7] With this minuscule amount of time devoted to a professional development activity, it is not surprising that only two out of five teachers consider themselves sufficiently well prepared to implement new teaching methods, and only a little over one-third believe they are well prepared to implement higher standards for students.[8] If schools are to improve significantly, school districts must give teachers the support and incentive essential for them to advance their professional development and that of their colleagues. Thus far, the overwhelming majority of school districts have not done this.

School districts provide little financial support for professional development. A typical school spends only 0.5 percent of its budget on professional development. A typical private-sector company spends four times as much.[9]

School districts provide little financial incentive for teachers to engage in professional development that *specifically enhances their teaching effectiveness*. With few exceptions, teacher salaries throughout the nation are based not on teaching effectiveness but on experience and education credentials.

In a U.S. Department of Education study, fewer than one-fifth of the teachers in the study had received mentoring.[10]

There are many factors critical to enhancing the in-service training of teachers. Among the most important are time, teacher study groups, technical culture, professional development schools, and "pedagogical gymnasiums."

Time. Lack of time to improve instruction is the curse of public school teachers. Secondary school teachers teach at least five periods a day, and primary school teachers barely have a free minute during the day when they are not teaching or supervising children. In contrast, it is rare for a teacher in China to teach classes more than three hours a day. In Japan, it is the law that teachers may teach children no more than four hours a day.

Albert Shanker flatly asserted that "teachers in the United States are teaching longer and harder than teachers anywhere else in the world,"[11] and then backed it up with some statistics. In an international survey of hours taught by American teachers and those in schools in fifteen European countries, in spite of all other countries having a longer school year, American teachers, at all levels, teach hundreds of more hours per year than teachers in other countries. The Americans, for example, have 1,019 hours of classroom instruction per year in the upper grades of secondary school while the mean for teachers in other countries is only 745 hours. What accounts for this apparent paradox: American teachers work far fewer days per year than other teachers in the survey but teach far more hours during the school year?

The answer obviously is that they teach more class periods every day of the school year. In other countries, the fifteen to twenty hours a week when a teacher is not instructing a class is devoted to professional development—to discussing with other teachers how better to plan their lessons, to measure student progress, confer with parents, improve teaching techniques and methodologies, conduct a group or class discussion, and so on. The workday of American teachers is about the same as that of teachers in Europe and in such Asiatic countries as Japan. The big difference is that American teachers do their planning alone at home and other teachers do it together at school, as part of their regular workload. For example, one of the hardest teaching skills to learn is how to ask good questions at different levels of complexity and for different purposes.

According to Harold Stevenson and James Stigler, who made a fascinating study of Japanese and Chinese education, "in the United States, the purpose of a question is to get an answer. . . . In Japan, teachers ask questions to stimulate thought." To formulate such questions is very difficult, and American teachers must gain this skill by themselves. Unlike American teachers, Japanese teachers have the time during the regular school day to work together to decide specifically what kinds of questions for specific academic material will best get students involved in thinking and discussing the material. Teaching students to think takes time, and Japanese teachers—unlike their American colleagues who too often are in a great hurry to speed through the lesson in order "to cover" the material mandated by the state—give their students time to think, to reflect, to discuss. In short, they want students to understand the material.[12]

Both the National Assessment of Education Progress (NAEP) and the Third International Mathematics and Science Study's (TIMSS) Videotape Classroom Study provide evidence that teaching American students to really understand the subject matter at hand is not a high priority in American classrooms. The NAEP, for example, found that "only 5 to 10 percent of students can move beyond initial readings of a text; most seem genuinely puzzled at requests to explain or defend their points of view."[13]

The authors of the Videotape Classroom Study comparing the teaching of eighth-grade mathematics in Germany, Japan, and the United States found that American teachers require less high-level thinking than teachers in Japan and Germany and that the goal of American teachers is to teach students how to do something while the goal of Japanese teachers is to help students to understand mathematical concepts.[14]

Teacher study groups. When Japanese teachers devote considerable time to resolving how best to ask thought-provoking questions relevant to this or that academic content, this is an example of teacher study groups at its best because it should result in teaching that enhances student learning. It should be noted that Japan is at the top or near the top in all international assessments of student learning. Teacher study groups are clearly the most prominent feature of in-service training in Japan.

Professional development is taken very seriously indeed in Japan. It has been estimated that Japan spends 8 percent of the public school budget on professional development.[15] A very large percentage of this is reserved for collaborative development activities in individual schools.[16] In schools in Japan where there is more than one novice teacher, the superintendent of schools appoints a full-time mentor from among the experienced teachers to work with the beginning teachers.[17] The novice teacher is on probation for the first year of teaching, and during this time receives ninety days of in-service training, mostly at the school but also at training centers set up by prefectures. After five, ten, or twenty years of teaching, and sometimes more often, teachers are required to undergo intensive in-service training programs at prefectural centers. The traditional Japanese cultural values of collegiality and the importance of obtaining consensus on decision making strongly support the belief that professional development should be primarily school based and that the responsibility for this development should be assumed by all the teachers in the school.

Since Japanese teachers are restricted by law to teach no more than four hours of classes a day, they have adequate time to work together to improve the instructional process. The objective of most teacher study groups in Japan is to improve the lesson. To understand the paramount importance of a lesson in Japanese pedagogy, it is useful to compare a teacher's lesson plan in Japan and in America. An American lesson plan is very brief, perhaps a paragraph, designed for one day and then to be discarded. The plan mentions a few grand concepts, but these concepts are to be developed spontaneously by the teacher on the spur of the moment when and how he or she thinks best. In contrast, a Japanese lesson plan is a dense text of several paragraphs specifying a detailed set of concepts replete with illustrations and methods of teaching the concepts.[18] The lesson plan will be used time and again with whatever adjustments the teacher and his or her colleagues deem necessary as a result of their study group sessions.

All this detail may suggest that a lesson in Japan is mechanistic. Such an impression is incorrect. According to the two principal researchers of the TIMSS Videotape Study, James Stigler and James Hiebert,

The typical eighth-grade mathematics lesson in Japan . . . focuses on one or sometimes two key problems. After reviewing the major point of the previous lesson and introducing the topic for today's lesson, the teacher presents the first problem. The problem is usually one that students do not know how to solve immediately but for which they have learned some crucial concepts or procedures in their previous lessons. Students are asked to work on the problem for a specified number of minutes and then to share their solutions. The teacher reviews and highlights one or two aspects of the students' solution methods or presents another solution method. Sometimes this cycle is repeated with another problem; other times, students practice the highlighted method or the teacher elaborates it further. Before the lesson ends, the teacher summarizes the major point for the day. Homework is rarely assigned.[19]

Stigler and Hiebert concluded that "Japanese lessons include high-level mathematics, a clear focus on thinking and problem solving, and an emphasis on students' deriving alternative solution methods and explaining their thinking."[20]

Japanese teachers, beginners and experienced, are required to perfect their teaching skills by interacting with their teacher colleagues. The vice-principal and head teachers at their school organize the meetings, and the more experienced teachers advise and guide their younger colleagues. The head teachers are also responsible for organizing meetings devoted to discussion of teaching techniques and development and improvement of lesson plans and handouts. The discussions are pragmatic and concentrate on developing better teaching techniques and lesson plans.[21] In "lesson study groups" small groups of teachers meet once a week on a regular basis to collaboratively evaluate, implement, and revise lessons. A number of these groups spend a whole school year perfecting only a few lessons.[22]

Japanese education has its problems, and it would be ill-advised to totally adopt this or that feature of education in Japan or Germany or any other country because education and teacher education appropriate for any one country must be an outgrowth of that country's history and cultural traditions. It would be equally ill-advised, however, not to study carefully what is going on educationally in Japan, Germany, and other countries because such study has the potential of broadening our perspective. A broadened perspective may well give us a clearer grasp of what it is we could and should be doing to improve our schools and the quality of teachers in them.

Teacher study groups are far from common in schools in the United States, but there are some and should be more in the near future, thus inching teaching more toward a legitimate profession. A number of "theme," or alternative schools, have been created in New York City, for example, that are doing some interesting things made possible by emphasis on professional development. The goals of one of these schools, the Central Park East Secondary School (CPESS) in Harlem, reflect five "habits of mind" that permeate the entire curriculum: weighing evidence, understanding different viewpoints, perceiving relationships, speculating on possibilities, and assessing personal and social values. Through imaginative block scheduling and student programming, the school has freed up several hours of time each week for the faculty to engage in collaborative teacher planning, staff development, and faculty governance. CPESS and other theme schools also have yearly retreats, summer institutes, and additional days devoted to professional development.[23] Obviously, much of this professional development time is devoted to study of how better to achieve the goals of the schools, as, for example, reflected in the five "habits of mind" that unite and guide the actions of faculty and students at CPESS.

At the other end of the country, the Selma (Oregon) Elementary School was disappointed with their third-grade scores on a state assessment and worked all year to do something about it. The principal, the school's nine teachers, and other staff members analyzed their reading program, identified the barriers blocking their goal, and brainstormed about how best to remove them. Then the study group initiated a plan of action and started working to solve their problem.[24]

Technical culture. An important by-product of teachers having the time and administrative support to engage in teacher study groups is that in countries such as Japan, teachers are building up an admirable technical culture. Most Japanese schools, for example, are equipped with a twenty-volume reference work titled *Arithmetic and Mathematics Educational Practice Lectures.*[25] This collection has over three thousand articles written—not by university professors of mathematics—but by some six hundred school teachers who have been nominated for this honor by university professors and boards of education throughout the country. Multiple volumes are devoted to discussions of how best to teach various mathematics skills, and there are articles on making lesson plans, setting goals for a lesson, evaluating student performance, using equipment in class, understanding trends in mathematics education, and so on. Every Japanese school has comprehensive reference materials such as this. There is no legitimate reason why every school in America should not have the same kinds of material; and there is no legitimate reason why American teachers should not have the time, support, and incentive to engage in an American version of teacher study groups, which at best would raise their morale, stimulate their intellectual faculties, make them part of a team with common goals, hone the skills essential for an "empowered" teacher, and most important of all, enhance their teaching effectiveness.

Arthur Powell put his finger on perhaps the greatest barrier to teaching in America becoming a legitimate profession. Unlike some other fields, Powell said that education has not learned how "to codify, preserve, and transmit the lore of successful experience."[26] Stigler and Hiebert agreed: "Our biggest long-term problem is not how we teach now but that we have no way of getting better. We have no mechanism built into the teaching profession that allows us to improve gradually over time. . . . We have no way of harvesting the best ideas of the thousands of teachers who work, by themselves, to improve their own teaching."[27]

Professional development schools and "pedagogical gymnasiums." One way that some school districts and teacher training institutions have collaborated is in the creation of professional development schools (PDS). PDS are similar in concept to teaching hospitals in medicine. They are designed to provide extended internships for prospective teachers (normally in a five-year program), year-long induction experiences for novice teachers, and professional development activities for veteran teachers. Professors and teachers working in these schools also conduct research and experimentation that is relevant to improving the teaching/learning process. These schools have the potential to be a viable means of enhancing both pre-service and in-service teacher training, but only if both institutions have given careful study to the matter beforehand and are strongly committed to providing the human and financial resources essential to its successful implementation and continuation.

Considering the significant growth of specialized public schools in recent years, some of the larger urban school districts may want to consider establishing a school that has some of the characteristics of "pedagogical gymnasiums" located in such Russian cities as St. Petersburg and Moscow. Such gymnasiums have encouraged many talented students to enter teaching and have served as an excellent vehicle for involving professors and schoolteachers in collaborative teacher education activities.

In one of the first pedagogical courses that pupils take in the eighth grade in the Moscow gymnasium, they are asked by the teacher to imagine themselves as teachers and pupils in a school in ancient Greece. One plays the role of the teacher and the rest, the role of pupils, and they try to imagine, built on their knowledge of ancient Greece, how the teacher teaches and how the pupils learn. In short, they are playing school. While this is a game, it is an integral part of the pedagogical curriculum. They not only play school in ancient Greece, but also in other countries at different historical periods. They make costumes appropriate for a particular country at a certain historical period, bring appropriate food, and so on. Focus is always on helping pupils understand the peculiarities of communication between a teacher and children. Teachers stress to the pupils that teachers and children are all different, and prospective teachers must recognize this and prepare themselves accordingly.

In the ninth grade, pupils are acquainted with the great pedagogues of the past and with their writings. Each year, different people are studied, depending on the interest of the children. During the 1995–1996 school year, Plato, Rousseau, Sukhomlinskii, Makarenko, Ushinskii, and Kamenskii were studied.

In the tenth grade, pupils participate in various workshops where they can get acquainted with such twentieth-century educators as Rudolf Steiner and Maria Montessori. They also study contemporary Russian schools following the ideas developed by various teacher-innovators. These schools are called "author schools." It is not obligatory for pupils to attend all these workshops, but they may attend any that interest them. According to A. G. Kasprzhak, the principal of the gymnasium, the goals of the courses in the ninth and tenth years are quite different from the tra-ditional pedagogical courses. We don't try to make them learn pedagogical theory systematically. We want them to get acquainted with different theories or to get fas-cinated with them. Normally, when they start their work with one or another the-ory, this short course starts with an introductory lecture. Then they work with the original writings of one of the great pedagogues, not with a textbook. The next as-signment is for them to find a place where an educational theory is actually being put into practice. For example, when they attended a workshop on Rousseau, one of the school principals here in Moscow came to the workshop, the last session of course, and told the children what ideas of Rousseau are actually implemented in his school.[28]

After attending numerous workshops over a two-year period, pupils se-lect during their senior year a research topic relevant to their pedagogical training at the gymnasium and write a substantive paper on it. While writ-ing the paper, pupils attend a course on research methodology, and they are assigned a tutor/consultant who will assist them in their research and in writing the paper.

Students in the gymnasium do a great deal of pedagogical work with younger children (the gymnasium has children in grades 1 through 11). As much as possible, the teachers and the principal try to put teacher trainees and younger children in natural situations where they interact freely with each other as friends. In the same way, teachers and their pupils try to meet together, to work together, to compete together as friends, as members of a family might do. John Dewey would have nodded in approval. He never tired of saying that a good school should resemble a good family.

Pedagogical Gymnasium No. 24 in St. Petersburg has an agenda some-what comparable to that of the one in Moscow. The St. Petersburg gymna-sium, however, puts a greater emphasis on joint research, conducted by the gymnasium faculty and professors, for the most part, at the Herzen Peda-gogical University. For example, one research team is developing a packet of programs consistent with the academic plan of the gymnasium that fo-cuses on the formation of the personality of pupils so that they are oriented not only to the pedagogical profession, but also to the "demands of the modern society." Another team is developing diagnostic methods and tools for determining at what level certain pedagogical skills and abilities should be fostered. Yet another team is trying to clarify on a continuum the interrelated responsibilities of curators (typically one of the most experi-enced, respected, and popular teachers in the school who is directly respon-sible for working with pupils in the pedagogical classes), class leaders, and leaders of pedagogical practice. There are many more research projects than those we have mentioned. Thus, in Russian pedagogical gymnasiums pre-service and in-service teacher education is collaborative, and the lines between these two activities is blurred. The result is that the transitions from student to student teacher to teacher to teacher trainer are smoother, and the value of research and training is infused throughout the entire teacher education system.

Let us conclude this section by briefly mentioning a few other things that school districts might do to be more actively involved in teacher education. First of all, they should work carefully with people in their communities to help them to better understand why student learning is dependent on professional development of teachers and why this development should be a top priority of their districts. This means allocation of substantial funds to professional development and restructuring how schools are organized and run so that teachers have the opportunity to grow continuously. In-service education must receive careful attention by teachers, administrators, and school board members in order to make it a highly planned, systematic process that always focuses on the real, practical needs of classroom teachers.

Second, school districts should develop a mentoring program for first and second year teachers. We do not expect new doctors to have all the polished skills of experienced doctors. They are inducted into full membership in their profession slowly through an internship and a residency program. Nor should we expect neophyte teachers to assume immediately full responsibilities of experienced teachers. Just as doctors, young teachers need time and mentoring help if they are to cope successfully with the many demands of successful teaching.

Third, school districts should be as actively involved in pre-service teacher education as in in-service teacher education. This means that both pre-service and in-service training of teachers should be a dual responsibility of school districts and schools of education. School districts should make being a supervising teacher of teacher trainees involved in field experiences and student teaching an honor to be sought after by the best teachers in the school district. To be a good supervising teacher takes time, energy, considerable human relations skills, and commitment. Such requirements cannot be met if teachers do not have sufficient time during the school day to even prepare adequately for their own lessons. School districts can honor supervising teachers by paying them substantially more than regular teachers, by reducing their teaching load, and by providing them, in collaboration with teacher training institutions, specialized training appropriate for a supervising teacher.

Fourth, school districts should make it possible for meritorious teachers to acquire specialized skills that will permit them not only to remain in the classroom with a reduced teaching load but to serve as their schools' specialist in such areas as curriculum development, research design, student evaluation, community liaison, community educational resources, school of education liaison, and so on.

Fifth, school districts should pay teachers more for their teaching effectiveness than for their academic credentials and years of experience.

Finally, school districts should start treating teachers as professionals by actively involving them in *all* school reform efforts and by providing them with principals who devote practically all their workday to being teacher educators. School districts can also do a number of smaller—but very important—things such as providing teachers with the following:

- private offices, if no more than a cubby hole, and telephones;
- a well-stocked professional library;
- a room specifically designed for teachers to engage in teacher study sessions;
- a clean, attractive, well-maintained school building on property that is well landscaped and pleasing to the eye;
- a routine system of getting into the hands of teachers the results of research relevant to teaching effectiveness;
- the funds and released time necessary to attend workshops and seminars that focus on enhancing teaching effectiveness;
- the technological means necessary for communication with other teachers in the district, state, nation, and world;
- a teachers' lounge with some comfortable chairs where teachers can catch their breath and, yes, perhaps close their eyes and rest for a few minutes—good teaching is extraordinarily hard work. It is unlikely that any conscientious teacher, at any educational level, from kindergarten to graduate school, would disagree with Jacques Barzun's claim that "steady teaching is a task that would fray the nerves of an ox."[29]

To sum up, professional development of teachers should be embedded in all the daily activities of a school. Schools for the twenty-first century should become learning schools for both students and teachers.

Teacher unions. To some people, such as Governor John Engler of Michigan or Governor Tom Ridge of Pennsylvania, teacher unions are the enemy who fight every effort to improve schools, teachers, and student learning, and these two governors did indeed mount a successful campaign during the 1990s to demonize the unions and—due to the unions' intransigent opposition to all their reform proposals, even the very sensible ones—succeeded in large measure in breaking their once considerable power.[30]

The general public has mixed feelings about teacher unions. In a Recruiting New Teachers/Louis Harris poll, a 55 to 34 percent majority agreed that "teacher unions support setting high standards for teachers," but a similar 53 to 32 percent majority believed that "teacher unions often stand in the way of real reform."[31] When asked in a Gallup poll whether unions helped, hurt, or made no difference concerning the quality of public school education, 26 percent believed they hurt, 27 percent said they helped, 37 percent thought they made no difference, and 10 percent said they did not know.[32] Two 1997 books provide sharply different answers to this question. In the *United Mind Workers*, the authors believe that the unions can make a significant contribution to improvement of schools and the teaching learning process. The subtitle of the second book expresses clearly the view of the author on teacher unions—*How the NEA and the AFT Sabotage Reform and Hold Students, Parents, Teachers, and Taxpayers Hostage to Bureaucracy.*[33]

Whatever the accuracy of these polls may be, leaders of the National Education Association (NEA) and the American Federation of Teachers (AFT)—but not necessarily the membership—are convinced that they are in deep trouble and must change dramatically if they are to play a significant role in educational debates at the state and national levels. The president of the NEA, Bob Chase, expressed this need for change bluntly: "Every child deserves a quality teacher. No exception, no excuses. . . . We cannot hide behind the old union axiom—'We didn't hire 'em—we can't fire 'em."[34] The NEA is in trouble, according to Chase, because "for the last 25 years or so, we have allowed our union role to dominate *at the expense* of our professional, educational role." Virtually no one, he adds, in the education, political, or social environment views the NEA "as a creative, positive, and influential leader in making America's public schools better."[35] In a 1997 speech to the National Press Club, he called for a reinvention of the union by ending industrial-style adversarial tactics and by building partnerships with administrators to improve school and teacher quality.[36] Albert Shanker, the long-time president of AFT until his death in 1997, started sounding this alarm in 1985 and repeatedly called on the membership to stress quality as much as the bread and butter issues of pay, retirement benefits, working conditions, and so on. His successor, Sandra Feldman, continues to make the same point.

Teacher unions can make a significant, positive contribution to raising the quality of teachers and student learning, but it will not be easy, as the following items attest:

Unions are rather schizophrenic on testing of teachers. They have supported rigorous testing of new teachers but have opposed testing of current teachers.[37]

In an NEA convention in July 2000, the delegates voted against a resolution calling for pay for performance even though the leaders of the union backed the measure.[38]

Industrial-style adversarial relations between union and administration continue to exist in many school districts. For example, in 1999, the Birmingham (Alabama) Education Association, an affiliate of NEA, called a strike *at the very beginning of the school year* because the teachers received a minuscule raise while the superintendent and other top administrators received a large raise. The strike infuriated many otherwise staunch supporters of public school education. The union for administrators in Rochester, New York, sued the school district and the teachers union over the peer assistance and review program. The administrators claimed that permitting teachers to evaluate one another violated their rights. The case was eventually dropped by the state's supreme court.[39]

Labor laws in the United States are still based on an industrial model in which collective bargaining assumes that the employee should be concerned only with such bread-and-butter issues as pay, job security, benefits, and general conditions of employment while the employer is responsible for everything else, including the mission of the institution and how the work is conducted.[40] Teacher unions, for example, have traditionally allocated the evaluation of teachers to management and protection of teachers to the union. Such a stance makes it difficult for organized teachers to fight for professional standards of practice when they have had little say in the definition and implementation of those standards.[41] New labor laws are needed that take into consideration the great changes that are taking place in the nature of work, but thus far "no legislature has yet tackled the question of whether labor statutes should encourage unions to organize around educational quality."[42]

In spite of the opposition of a number of governors and legislatures, teachers by and large remain devoted to the single salary schedule based not on performance but on academic credentials and years of experience.

School administrators and union staff, while opponents at bargaining sessions, are often united in support of industrial unionism.

According to union staff and officers, it is very difficult to persuade teachers to support and work to implement reform ideas.

To gain greater support from school boards, administrators, governors, and legislators for quality professional development of teachers, national and state teacher organizations must start showing as much interest in the welfare of children as in the welfare of teachers. Among other things, they should stop blocking and start leading the way in getting rid of incompetent teachers because the few bad apples stigmatize all the good teachers. They should cease their opposition to evaluating teaching effectiveness just because it is hard to do and make a determined effort to seek ways of doing it as fairly as possible. It can be done because it is done all the time in American universities. Is it done fairly? Not always. Are mistakes made? Of course. But it is better to make a few mistakes than to have no serious system of teacher evaluation. Taxpayers quite rightly resent paying all teachers the same, the brilliant, the average, and the totally incompetent.

Unions should stop opposing the testing of teachers because they claim the tests are culturally biased against minority groups. Rather, they should help develop tests that are not culturally biased. We need the most intelligent, competent people we can get into teaching. A good testing program upon entrance to college and graduation from college is one way to increase the odds that intelligent, competent people will enter the teaching field.

Teacher unions—in collaboration with legislatures, school administrators and school board members, state and federal departments of education, and institutions of higher learning—should wage a continuous public relations effort to explain clearly and carefully what good teaching is and how American citizens from all walks of life, with or without children, can help provide the conditions in schools and the communities they serve that are essential if good teaching is to flourish and if students are to learn all they are capable of learning.

Teacher unions—in collaboration with school administrators and school boards—sorely need to prove to the general public that they are adamantly against wasting money provided by tax payers. Patrick Welsh, a teacher of English in Massachusetts, notes in his book, *Tales Out of School*,[43] that in the early 1960s in the schools in his district, he and other teachers were able to educate students without so-called curriculum specialists to help them plan their courses. At the time he wrote this book, his school district had nine curriculum specialists who did no teaching at all, and three who taught only two periods a day. They cost taxpayers more than $350,000 a year.

Union leaders are now talking a good game; that is, they have worthwhile intentions for promoting quality teaching. What they and their membership should consider doing now is to adhere more closely to that old truism—actions speak more clearly than words. For example, to demonstrate their interest in students, they could enact two suggestions by Arthur Powell: (1) each teacher stays after school two days a week to hold office hours for students and parents; and (2) each teacher and administrator accepts responsibility for eight or ten student advisees and becomes committed to knowing each one well.[44] A more difficult, long-range thing to do is to study carefully the successes, stand-offs, and failures of the most progressive element of both the NEA and the AFT, the so-called local TURN (Teacher Union Reform Network) organizations and implement on a wider scale their successful endeavors. These local teacher unions are at the forefront of trying to implement innovative, collaborative arrangements with school administrators and school boards. For example, the Denver Public Schools and the Denver Teachers Association have agreed to a two-year pilot program that bases pay for teachers in participating schools on performance.[45]

GOOD NEWS

If polls are accurately reflecting public sentiment, the good news is that the general public is beginning to recognize more clearly the centrality of well-trained, quality teachers to student learning. In one poll, roughly nine out of ten Americans believe that the best way to improve achievement of students is to guarantee that every classroom has a qualified teacher. In another poll, it was found that the public concurs with the proposition that teaching demands special training and skills, not simply a good general education. In this same poll, the public expressed strong support for the value of teacher education.[46]

In spite of the apparent moral support of Americans for well-qualified, quality teachers, progress in improving in-service training of teachers remains slow, erratic, tenuous, and limited to a relatively small percentage of schools and school districts. Still, the following items suggest reasons for guarded optimism about the future of in-service professional development:

- Action research and teacher study groups are beginning to appear in a number of schools around the country.
- States are stiffening the requirements for the recertification of teachers.[47] For the first time, teachers in the state of New York, for example, will have to meet professional development requirements in order to keep their licenses.[48]
- California passed legislation that requires novice teachers to be involved in a two-year induction program in order to earn a permanent license.[49]
- North Carolina has developed a three-stage system of initial, continuing, and advanced licenses, all of which are predicated on a teacher's performance rather than on academic credentials and years of experience.[50]
- The leaders of both the NEA and AFT have strongly supported the lifelong education of teachers and have encouraged their membership to play an active role in improving this process.
- The Professional Development Reform Act, S.1442, will fund such activities as opportunities for teachers to visit each others' classrooms to model effective teaching practices, mentoring, curriculum-based content training, and time for collaborative lesson planning.[51]
- Of the three questions that governors, business people, and educational leaders focused on at the 1998 National Education Summit, the first was, "What will it take to recruit, prepare, support, and retain a quality teaching force capable of teaching to much higher student-learning standards?" Participants at the summit stressed that professional development of teachers was a top priority.[52]
- School districts in Texas that implemented high quality induction year programs had significant gains in retention of novice teachers over a five year period.[53]
- More and more teachers are accepting responsibilities for leading and managing their schools.[54]
- Of various ways to improve teacher quality, the public most prefers mentoring programs, raising the requirements for teacher licensing, and raising teacher salaries.[55]
- In Alabama, a state at or near the bottom in several indices of educational quality, the governor announced in December 2000 that the state would raise the pay of any teacher who achieves advanced certification by the National Board for Professional Teaching Standards (NBPTS) by $5,000 a year for ten years. Each certi-

fied teacher will also receive a one-time $5,000 grant for classroom instruction. The state also pays the assessment fee for taking the examination.[56]

- In 1999, 14 percent of teachers in the state of New York did not have certification and most of them worked in poorly performing schools. A state policy enacted in New York in 1998 bans uncertified teachers from public schools by 2003.[57]

In summary, all is not doom and gloom. In fact, in-service teacher education is receiving more support and attention than previously. The bad news is that there is a huge distance to go before it reaches a level appropriate to its importance.

NOTES

1. *The Condition of Education* (Washington, D.C.: U.S. Department of Education, National Center for Education Statistics, U.S. Government Printing Office, 1999).

2. Linda Darling-Hammond and others, "Teacher Recruitment, Selection, and Induction: Policy Influences on the Supply and Quality of Teachers," in *Teaching as the Learning Profession: Handbook of Policy and Practice,* ed. Linda Darling-Hammond and Gary Sykes (San Francisco: Jossey-Bass, 1999), p. 213.

3. Milbrey McLaughlin, "What Matters Most in Teachers' Workplace Context?" in *Teachers' Work,* ed. Judith Little and Milbrey McLaughlin (New York: Teachers College Press, 1993), pp. 79–103.

4. Tamara Henry, "A Principal Crisis in Education," *USA Today,* 22 August 2000, sec. D, p. 7.

5. Lynn Olson, "New Thinking Emerges on What Makes a Leader," *Education Week,* 19 January 2000, p. 16.

6. See, especially, Vasily Sukhomlinsky, *To Children I Give My Heart* (Moscow: Progress, 1981); *V. Sukhomlinsky on Education* (Moscow: Progress, 1977). In describing Sukhomlinskii's ideas on education and teacher education, we rely primarily on *V. Sukhomlinsky on Education.* All Sukhomlinskii quotes in the text are from this book.

7. Laurie Lewis and others, *Teacher Quality: A Report on the Preparation and Qualifications of Public School Teachers, NCES 1999-080* (Washington, D.C.: U.S. Department of Education, National Center for Education Statistics, U.S. Government Printing Office, 1999), p. 6.

8. Dennis Sparks and Stephanie Hirsh, *A National Plan for Improving Professional Development,* 2000, p. 4, <http://www.nsdc.org/library/NSDCPlan.html>.

9. Ibid.

10. Jeff Archer, "Teachers Suggest the Need for Better Training," *Education Week,* 3 February 1998, p. 12.

11. Albert Shanker, "Where We Stand: 'Less Is More,'" *New York Times,* 28 May 1995, sec. E, p. 7.

12. Harold W. Stevenson and James W. Stigler, *The Learning Gap: Why Our Schools Are Failing and What We Can Learn from Japanese and Chinese Education* (New York: Summit Books, 1992), pp. 157–160.

13. Quoted in Linda Darling-Hammond, "The Implications of Testing Policy for Quality and Equality," *Phi Delta Kappan* 73 (November 1991): 221.

14. James W. Stigler and others, *The TIMSS Videotape Classroom Study: Methods and Findings from an Exploratory Research Project on Eighth-Grade Mathematics Instruction in Germany, Japan, and the United States* (Washington, D.C.: U.S. Department of Education, National Center for Education Statistics, U.S. Government Printing Office, 1999), p. 7, <http://nces.ed.gov/pubs99/timssvid/index.html>.

15. *Education Policy Analysis* (Paris: Organisation for Economic Co-operation and Development, 1998), footnote 6, p. 7.

16. Ibid.

17. Nobuo K. Shimahara and Akira Sakai, *Learning to Teach in Two Cultures: Japan and the United States* (New York: Garland, 1995), p. 235.

18. Thomas P. Rohlen and Gerald K. LeTendre, *Teaching and Learning in Japan* (Cambridge: Cambridge University Press, 1996), pp. 13–14.

19. James W. Stigler and James Hiebert, "Understanding and Improving Classroom Mathematics Instruction: An Overview of the TIMSS Video Study," *Phi Delta Kappan* 79 (September 1997): 18.

20. Ibid.

21. Stevenson and Stigler, *The Learning Gap*, p. 160.

22. Stigler and Hiebert, "Understanding and Improving," p. 20.

23. Linda Darling-Hammond, "Restructuring Schools for High Performance," in *Rewards and Reform: Creating Educational Incentives that Work*, ed. Susan H. Fuhrman and Jennifer A. O'Day (San Francisco: Jossey-Bass, 1996), pp. 147–179.

24. "Inquiring Minds: Creating a Nation of Teachers as Learners," *Education Week*, 17 April 1996, p. 49.

25. Kenneth G. Wilson and Bennett Daviss, *Redesigning Education* (New York: Henry Holt, 1994), pp. 87–88.

26. Quoted in Geraldine Joncich Clifford and James W. Guthrie, *Ed School: A Brief for Professional Education* (Chicago: University of Chicago Press, 1988), p. 352.

27. Stigler and Hiebert, "Understanding and Improving," p. 20.

28. Quoted in Delbert H. Long and Roberta A. Long, *Education of Teachers in Russia* (Westport, Conn.: Greenwood Press, 1999), pp. 116–117. The discussion on pedagogical gymnasiums draws on this book.

29. Jacques Barzun, *Teacher in America* (Garden City, N.Y.: Doubleday, 1955), p. 29.

30. William Lowe Boyd, David N. Plank, and Gary Sykes, "Teachers Unions in Hard Times," in *Conflicting Missions? Teacher Unions and Educational Reform*, ed. Tom Loveless (Washington, D.C.: Brookings Institution Press, 2000), p. 177.

31. Recruiting New Teachers, "The Essential Profession," 30 November 2000, p. 3, <http://www.rnt.org/publications/essential.html>.

32. Lowell C. Rose and Alec M. Gallup, "The Thirtieth Annual Phi Delta Kappa/Gallup Poll of the Public's Attitudes Toward the Public Schools," *Phi Delta Kappan* 80 (September 1998): 41–56.

33. Charles Kerchner, Julia E. Koppich, and Joseph G. Weeres, *United Mind Workers: Unions and Teaching in the Knowledge Society* (San Francisco: Jossey-Bass, 1997); Myron Lieberman, *The Teacher Unions: How the NEA and AFT Sabotage Reform and Hold Students, Parents, Teachers, and Taxpayers Hostage to Bureaucracy* (New York: Free Press, 1997).

34. Bob Chase, "Double Duty: While Defending All Teachers' Rights, We Help Bad Teachers Depart," *Education Week*, 15 March 2000, p. 39.

35. Bob Chase, "Letters," *Rethinking Schools* 11 (Summer 1997): 5.

36. Robert Chase, "A New Approach to Unionism—It's Not Your Mother's NEA," Speech to the National Press Club, Washington, D.C., 1997.

37. Dale Ballou and Michael Podgursky, "Gaining Control of Professional Licensing and Advancement," in *Conflicting Missions? Teacher Unions and Educational Reform*, ed. Tom Loveless (Washington, D.C.: Brookings Institution Press, 2000), p. 80.

38. Jeff Archer, "NEA Delegates Take Hard Line Against Pay for Performance," *Education Week*, 12 July 2000, pp. 21–22.

39. Charles Taylor Kerchner and Julia E. Koppich, "Organizing around Quality: The Frontiers of Teacher Unionism," in *Conflicting Missions? Teacher Unions and Educational Reform*, ed. Tom Loveless (Washington, D.C.: Brookings Institution Press, 2000), p. 291.

40. Julia E. Koppich and Charles Taylor Kerchner, "Organizing the Other Half of Teaching," in *Teaching as the Learning Profession: Handbook of Policy and Practice*, ed. Linda Darling-Hammond and Gary Sykes (San Francisco: Jossey-Bass, 1999), p. 318.

41. Boyd, Plank, and Sykes, "Teachers Union," p. 202.

42. References for this and the rest of the items may be found in Kerchner and Koppich, "Organizing around Quality," pp. 282, 291, 293, 299, 302.

43. Patrick Welsh, *Tales Out of School: A Teacher's Candid Account from the Front Lines of the American High School Today* (New York: Penguin Books, 1987), p. 180.

44. Arthur G. Powell, *Lessons from Privilege: The American Prep School Tradition* (Cambridge: Harvard University Press, 1996), pp. 246–247.

45. Kerchner and Koppich, "Organizing around Quality," pp. 294, 298.

46. Recruiting New Teachers, "The Essential Profession," pp. 1–2.

47. Ulrich Boser, "States Stiffening Recertification for Teachers," *Education Week*, 3 May 2000, pp. 1, 16.

48. Ann Bradley, "Zeroing in on Teachers," *Education Week*, 11 January 1999, p. 50.

49. Ibid.

50. Ann Bradley, "Panel Reports Ample Action on Teaching," *Education Week*, 26 November 1997, p. 9.

51. Senator Jack Reed, "The Importance of Professional Development for Teachers," *Educational Horizons* 78 (Spring 2000): 117.

52. Robert Schwartz and Matthew Gandal, "Higher Standards, Stronger Tests: Don't Shoot the Messenger," *Education Week*, 19 January 2000, p. 40.

53. Linda N. Lucksinger, "Teachers: Can We Get Them and Keep Them?" *Delta Kappa Gamma Bulletin* 67 (Fall 2000): 13.

54. James H. Lytle, "Teacher Education at the Millennium: A View from the Cafeteria," *Journal of Teacher Education* 51 (May–June 2000): 176–177.

55. Jeff Archer, "Public Prefers Competent Teachers to Other Reforms, Survey Finds," *Education Week*, 25 November 1998, p. 6.

56. David White, "Master Teachers in State Rise to 144," *Birmingham News,* 9 December 2000, sec. A, p. 2.

57. Abby Goodnough, "In New York, Back to School with a Worsening Teacher Shortage," *New York Times,* 5 September 2000, sec. A, p. 26.

III

Future (2000–2100)

13

Quality and Teacher Education

Quality is never an accident; it is always the result of high intention, sincere effort, intelligent direction and skillful execution; it represents the wise choice of many alternatives.

William A. Foster

The quality of the teachers in our educational system has been an issue of national concern since at least the early 1900s.[1] However, interest in educational quality seemed to have intensified during the second half of the twentieth century. In the 1980s alone more than three hundred task forces on education were appointed at the state level.[2]

According to Lewis Mayhew, the author of *Quest for Quality*, recent interest in education quality can be traced to concerns about the quality of American goods in general. It started with cameras and stereos in the 1960s, continued with televisions and automobiles in the 1970s, and moved on to electronics and other consumer goods in the 1980s. The decline in the industrial status of the United States was linked to the poor performance of our educational system, and the result was an increased interest in education quality.[3]

This spotlight was focused squarely on teacher quality in 1997 when President Bill Clinton devoted an unprecedented one-quarter of his State of the Union address to education and issued a "Call to Action for American Education." He set a number of national goals, including "There will be a talented, dedicated, and well-prepared teacher in every classroom."[4] In his 2000 State of the Union address, President Clinton kept the spotlight shining by proposing a one billion dollar initiative to improve teacher quality.[5]

CONCEPTS OF TEACHER QUALITY

The concept of quality lies at the heart of most debates about education and teacher education. Without a clear understanding of this concept, that debate will not be advanced. Both the centrality and the diversity of the concept of quality can be clearly seen in the views of the critics discussed in the first part of this book.

Dewey argued that quality teachers can best be developed in a laboratory setting because it develops habits that are theoretical rather than empirical. A quality teacher has the ability to think scientifically, an unusual love and aptitude in some one subject, genuine insight into all subjects, and the ability to communicate love of learning to others. Moreover, just as Dewey's definition of quality education varies depending on the needs of the individual child, his definition of quality teacher education is dependent on the needs of individual teachers.

For Hutchins, a quality teacher is one who has mastered the three R's, the liberal arts, and "the greatest works that the human race has produced." Quality teachers are masters of their intellectual subject matter as well as the arts of pedagogy, which are the abilities to organize, express, and communicate knowledge.

Quality teachers in Bestor's perspective are experts in how to think; that is, they are well educated in those intellectual disciplines that have general applicability. They have the ability to consider evidence according to the reasoning processes and critical methods accepted by the discipline involved. Quality teachers are so dedicated to gaining knowledge and intellectual power that their learning inspires learning in their students.

Conant concluded that a quality teacher is one who has been judged competent during student teaching by a quality clinical professor. Quality teacher education requires a team approach involving institutions of higher learning, state departments of education, and local school systems, with each having clearly defined responsibilities.

Brameld said that quality teachers have the same characteristics as quality physicians: (1) a well-rounded, challenging general education; (2) a solid knowledge in the subject area, which is most necessary to all practitioners; (3) a thoughtful theory or philosophy of their profession that helps them understand the contributions of their profession to the growth of civilization; (4) an abundance of rich experiences in effective practice—that is, in the techniques of their profession.

Silberman believed that quality teaching consists in finding the right balance between individual growth and fulfillment and the transmission of definite skills, intellectual discipline, and bodies of knowledge. Quality teachers have a sense of purpose or a philosophy of education; they know about the ramifications of the subject or subjects they teach, about how those subjects relate to other subjects and to knowledge—and life—in general.

According to Illich, a quality teacher is simply one who demonstrates a skill well and can attract a sufficient number of students. Furthermore, quality skill centers are those that are judged highly by customers (on their results, not on the personnel they employ or the process they use). Quality network builders and administrators keep themselves, and others, out of people's way and facilitate encounters among students, skill models, educational leaders, and educational objects.

Before being licensed, Shanker would have had graduates of teacher education programs pass a bar exam like doctors and lawyers currently do. Quality would also be determined by a system of peer review developed by teacher unions in collaboration with their school districts. In this system, master (i.e., experienced and excellent) teachers define quality. At the conclusion of the probationary period, these master teachers would make recommendations about who should be offered tenure and who should be let go.

Finn insisted that quality teachers are well grounded in facts; teach to the test; adapt their pedagogy to the backgrounds, abilities, and interests of their students; adjust instructional strategies to the values of parents; and organize the instructional process so that students learn what they are supposed to learn. Quality schools are those that survive in the marketplace (i.e., those that are chosen by parents). Parental choice, Finn believed, forces schools to be more competitive, and hence, exhibit higher quality.

The views of the critics regarding quality amply demonstrate the importance of the concept to the debate about education and teacher education. There are, no doubt, as many definitions of education quality as there are educators. But without an understanding of at least some of the alternative conceptions available, and the differences among those alternatives, any progress toward consensus will be chimerical.

DIMENSIONS OF TEACHER QUALITY

Teacher quality is a complex phenomenon, and there is little consensus on what it is or how to measure it.[6] However, the two most common definitions focus on teacher qualifications and teacher practices. Moreover, it is typically assumed that high quality teacher preparation results in high quality teaching.[7]

Perhaps the most traditional approach to characterizing teacher quality is the one that focuses on "expert" teachers, teachers who have been identified as successful by their administrators or peers. Using this approach, the Interstate New Teacher Assessment and Support Consortium (INTASC) established ten key principles it believes to be central tenets of effective teaching. These principles include statements that teachers should be able to understand their subject matter and relate it to students; adopt teaching strategies that are responsive to different learners; employ diverse instructional strategies; create active, meaningful learning environments; measure student development; and engage in continual curriculum evaluation and professional development.[8]

Just as definitions about teacher quality differ, so do the ways in which it has been measured. Approaches to measuring teacher quality have usually taken four forms: (1) classroom observations of teachers; (2) written examinations of teachers measuring their basic literacy, subject-matter knowledge, and pedagogical skills; (3) student performance and achievement; and (4) large-scale surveys of teacher qualifications, attitudes, behaviors, and practices.[9] In summary, the dimensions of teacher quality are diverse and polymorphous.

Perhaps the most relevant characterization of quality is the oft-quoted passage from Robert Pirsig's *Zen and the Art of Motorcycle Maintenance*, "even though Quality cannot be defined, you know what Quality is!"[10] Having worked for many years with literally hundreds of student teachers and their supervising teachers in every possible kind of elementary, middle, and high school, we conclude that quality teachers are those who genuinely like young people and have a natural empathy for their problems, self-doubts, and their fumbling efforts to understand themselves and to find a niche in life where they can fit in. They learn all they can about their students—their psychological development and family and social backgrounds—so as to better motivate them to learn.

Quality teachers know that students learn more if they are convinced that a teacher likes, enjoys, and respects them and treats them always in a fair, consistent way. They try to develop a family atmosphere in their classrooms because they have learned from long experience that such an atmosphere encourages and inspires young people to become the best they can become as people and as young scholars.

Quality teachers are understanding, yes, but also very demanding. They understand that difficult but reasonable learning objectives can inspire students to work hard and to do quality work. They insist, along with their colleagues, that students learn the best that has been written and thought or produced in literature, mathematics, the natural and physical sciences, history, and the arts.

Quality teachers make every effort to show the relevance of academic material to the lives of their students and to show the connectedness of knowledge in one field to that of knowledge in other fields. To do this effectively requires: that they be broadly educated, a proud possessor of a sound liberal arts education; have in-depth knowledge of one, two, or more academic fields of study; and have a thorough grounding in pedagogical knowledge and teaching skills.

Quality teachers take seriously their role as teacher educators by providing expert assistance to student teachers and interns, and they work closely with other teachers to advance their academic and pedagogical knowledge and teaching skills.

Quality teachers are lifelong learners. What the novelist and playwright Somerset Maugham said about the writer is equally true for teachers: "The writer can only be fertile if he renews himself and he can only renew himself if his soul is constantly enriched by fresh experience."[11] All master teachers, without exception, have a burning desire to impart knowledge to their children. To these teachers, knowledge not shared with others, is inert, meaningless.

Quality teachers offer a great gift to children—passion for their subject matter and a love for learning in general. They do this in many ways but especially by being, if a music teacher, a musician; if an English teacher, a poet or author; if a chemist or physicist, a scientific researcher; if a history teacher, a historian; if a drama teacher, an actor; if a lover of antiquity, an anthropologist; if a lover of nature, an ornithologist or geologist.

Quality teachers model for their children what it means to lead a humane life with numerous intellectual interests. They realize that their love and enthusiasm for their subject(s) and outside interests and for learning in general will rub off on their students.

Quality teachers know how to think carefully, logically, philosophically—and they instill these qualities into their students. They think, all the time, not only about the needs of their students but also about their own needs as professionals. They continually ask themselves such questions as, What is it my colleagues and I should be doing and why with this particular group of students?

Finally, quality teachers never give up on any of their students. They use every bit of knowledge and skills they have to ensure that their students have every opportunity and encouragement to live up to high moral and scholarly standards. This brief description of quality teachers is, of course, incomplete and idealistic, but not unrealistic if—and it is a big *if*—the training and work environment of teachers are dramatically improved.

CURRENT STATUS OF TEACHER QUALITY

There have been a number of recent reports on teacher quality that present statistics on teacher preparation, qualifications, working conditions, salaries, workload, diversity, and attrition rates. In general, they focus on the need to improve teacher quality.

In its 1996 report, *What Matters Most: Teaching for America's Future,* the National Commission on Teaching and America's Future found that:

- Twelve percent of all newly hired teachers enter the workforce without any training at all, and another 15 percent enter without having fully met state standards. Annually, 50,000 enter teaching on emergency or substandard licenses.

- Only 500 of the nation's 1,300 education schools meet common professional standards.

- Twenty-three percent of all secondary teachers do not have even a college minor in their main teaching field. This is true for more than 30 percent of mathematics teachers.

- Fifty-six percent of high school students taking physical science courses and 27 percent of those taking mathematics courses are taught by teachers who do not have backgrounds in these fields. The proportions are much higher in high-poverty schools and in lower track classes.

- Teachers make up 43 percent of total school employment in the United States. Teaching staff in other countries comprise 60 to 80 percent of school employment. The United States has the lowest ratio of core teaching staff to nonteaching staff (less than 1:1), well behind the leaders, Belgium (4:1), Italy (3.5:1), and Japan (3.4:1).

- Most elementary school teachers have only 8.3 minutes of preparatory time for every hour they teach, while high school teachers have just 13 minutes of prep time per class hour.

- Teaching loads for high school teachers generally exceed 100 students per day and reach nearly 200 per day in some cities.

- The average class size is twenty-four students, with some areas having as many as thirty students per classroom.

- School districts spend 1 to 3 percent of their resources on teacher development. The percentage is much higher in most corporations and in other countries' schools.

- Teachers earn substantially less than other professionals.[12]

In a 1998 report entitled *Promising Practices: New Ways to Improve Teacher Quality,* the U.S. Department of Education found that:

- While a third of America's students are minorities, only 13 percent of their teachers are and that gap is growing.

- Students in the schools with the highest minority enrollments—usually schools in high-poverty areas—have less than a 50 percent chance of having a science or math teacher with a license or degree in the field he or she teaches.

- Attrition rates for new teachers in urban districts can sometimes reach 50 percent in the first five years of teaching because of inadequate preparation (particularly for those entering teaching on emergency permits or waivers), challenging assignments, and the paucity of high-quality mentoring and induction programs available for novice teachers.[13]

Finally, an *Education Week* report entitled "Quality Counts 2000: Who Should Teach?" reported the following:

- Thirty-nine states require prospective educators to pass a basic skills test, but thirty-six of those states have loopholes that allow at least some people to teach who have failed such exams.

- Twenty-nine states require high school teachers to pass tests in the subjects they plan to teach, and thirty-nine require them to have a major, a minor, or an equivalent number of course credits in their subjects. Yet all of those states, except New Jersey, can waive those requirements, either by granting licenses to individuals who have not met them or by permitting districts to hire such people.

- Fewer than half the states expect middle school teachers to earn secondary school licenses in the subjects they plan to teach. The rest allow them to use "generic" elementary school certificates. Only nine states require all middle school teachers to pass tests in their subjects.

- Eleven states do not require special permission for teachers to spend part of the day teaching outside their areas of expertise. Only twenty-two states have the authority to penalize schools or districts for having out-of-field teachers, such as by revoking accreditation or cutting state aid. Only one state requires notification of parents when out-of-field teachers teach their children. No state has published information about out-of-field teaching on school report cards for the public.

- Only Massachusetts and Maryland offer "signing bonuses" to lure talented people into teaching.

- Twenty-seven states have scholarship or loan-forgiveness programs for prospective educators, but only eighteen target such programs to specific shortage fields such as math and science. Only ten aim those programs at candidates who are willing to work in urban or rural schools, schools in impoverished neighborhoods, or low-performing schools.

- Forty states have programs that provide an accelerated pathway into teaching, particularly for career-switchers and liberal arts graduates. But with the exception of California, New Jersey, and Texas, such alternative routes serve few comers.

- Teachers aged twenty-two to twenty-eight earned an average $7,894 less per year than other college-educated adults of the same age in 1998. Teachers aged forty-four to fifty earned $23,655 less than their counterparts in other occupations. Teachers with master's degrees aged forty-four to fifty earned $32,511 less than nonteachers with the same degree.

- From 1994 to 1998, the average salary for master's degree holders outside teaching increased 32 percent, or $17,505, after adjusting for inflation; the average salary for teachers with master's degrees increased less than $200.

- Forty-nine percent of the 1992–1993 college graduates who prepared to teach while in school had never worked in a K–12 public school four years later.

- Both those who prepared to teach as undergraduates and those who went on to do so were less likely to have scored in the top 25 percent on college entrance exams than their peers who chose other professions.

- Of the college graduates who began teaching by 1993–1994, nearly one in five had left within three years. The brightest novice teachers, as measured by their college-entrance exams, were the most likely to leave.

- Teachers who did not participate in an induction program, who were dissatisfied with student discipline, or who were unhappy with the school environment were much more likely to leave than their peers.[14]

In summary, every report concludes that the quality of teachers in our schools needs to be improved. Unfortunately, their recommendations on how to solve this problem are diverse and often contradictory. For example, some reformers want to increase the length, rigor, and regulation of teacher preparation and certification[15] while others want to de-regulate the teacher education system and open up the teaching profession to unlicensed but well-educated individuals.[16]

QUALITY AND TEACHER EDUCATION

By 2008, America's public and private schools will educate nearly three million more children than they do today—a total of more than fifty-four million youngsters. These enrollment increases are occurring just as teacher retirements are beginning to accelerate. This means that over the next decade more than two million teachers will need to be trained and hired. Thus, there is a need to prepare more teachers in a shorter period than during any other time in our history.[17]

Currently, the more than 1,300 teacher education programs graduate about 100,000 potential teacher candidates each year. That means that these programs may supply only one-half of the teachers who will be needed.[18] The teacher supply and demand problem is closely linked to teacher quality. During the twentieth century there have been several cycles of teacher surplus followed by teacher shortage. In times of teacher surplus, schools and teacher education institutions have typically raised standards. In times of teacher shortage, standards have usually been lowered or ignored.[19]

Two contradictory solutions have been proposed to the current teacher shortage problem: (1) more flexible certification standards and shorter teacher education programs, and (2) more rigorous certification standards and extended teacher education programs. Proponents of the first solution argue that flexible standards and shorter preparation programs will both solve the shortage problem and increase teacher quality because they will attract more people and more academically able people to the teaching profession.[20] Proponents of the second solution argue that more rigorous standards and extended preparation programs will increase teacher quality by improving classroom instruction and will also be more effective in the long run regarding the shortage problem.[21] The evidence seems to favor the second solution.

Studies have found that teachers prepared in extended teacher education programs enter and remain in teaching at higher rates than teachers in traditional four-year programs and remain at much higher rates than those prepared in short-term, alternative certification programs. It actually costs substantially less to prepare a candidate in an extended program than it does to prepare candidates in shorter programs who leave much sooner.[22]

Moreover, there is evidence that an increase in teacher quality results in an increase in student achievement. In fact, investments in teacher knowledge are the most productive means for increasing student learning; more productive than reducing class size, increasing salary, or increasing experience. Furthermore, knowledge of subject matter and, especially, the knowledge of teaching and learning acquired in teacher education are strongly correlated with teacher performance in the classroom.[23] Over one hundred studies indicate that high quality teacher preparation makes a difference. Fully prepared teachers are more able to recognize students' individual needs and customize instruction for them and are more able to establish a positive climate.[24]

In addition, there is evidence that student achievement is related to quality teacher education. Research demonstrates that the states that invested most in improving the quality of teacher education (as measured by NCATE accreditation standards) over the past decade experienced the greatest gains in student performance in that period of time.[25] A 1999 study by the Educational Testing Service (ETS) found that graduates of NCATE-accredited colleges of education pass ETS content examinations for teacher licensing at a higher rate than do graduates of unaccredited colleges. Teacher candidates who attend NCATE colleges boost their chances of passing the examination by nearly 10 percent. Thus, NCATE-accredited institutions produce proportionally more qualified teachers than unaccredited institutions.[26]

TEACHER QUALITY IN THE INFORMATION AGE

In the early 1900s, just 10 percent of the nation's jobs required a college-level education. In contrast, more than half of the jobs created today require some college, and over 70 percent of all jobs require technological literacy.[27] This is just one indication of a socioeconomic transition from the Industrial Age to the Information Age. This transition has direct implications for economic productivity and quality and indirect implications for educational productivity and quality.

Because of the high cost of industrial production, mass consumption was the goal of Industrial Age producers. Products needed to be sold, and therefore produced, many times over in order to generate a profit. In order to make a profit, producers needed to identify a market need and flood the market. Production quality standards utilized criteria such as the following:

- consistency (how close the finished products came to the ideal as defined by market research);
- scalability (how easily the product could be mass-produced); and
- customer satisfaction (usually limited to a local marketplace).

The Industrial Age economy required an educational system that produced workers who could, in turn, produce the same product to the same specifications time after time after time. Thus, production standards were translated into academic standards in the following ways:

- consistency: Carnegie units, grades, standardized tests, minimum competency exams, class rankings, diplomas;
- scalability: lectures, multiple choice tests, standardized textbooks, standardized curricula, bell schedules; and
- customer satisfaction: parent-teacher nights, school newsletters, state accreditation agencies, student evaluation instruments, school report cards.

Thus, in the Industrial Age, quality meant that the product was mass produced to certain standards and possessed a set of characteristics a customer would normally expect. Likewise, graduates of an Industrial Age educational organization also were expected to possess certain basic skills as well as an understanding of a generally agreed upon canon of knowledge.

Because of the low cost of information production and the concomitant proliferation of producers as well as the emergence of a global market, the goal of production in the Information Age is serving a niche (as opposed to mass) market. In order to make a profit, producers need to create (as opposed to identify) a market need and produce a product more quickly than their competitors. Information Age production quality standards utilize such criteria as the following:

- visionary (the ability of the product to create a new market);
- cycle time (how quickly the product can be designed, produced, and delivered); and
- consumer delight (in a global marketplace).

An Information Age economy requires an educational system that produces workers who thrive on challenge, change, and speed. Thus, Information Age production standards will be translated into academic standards in ways such as the following:

- visionary: individualized programs of study, student-designed portfolios, unique student products designed for commercial use;
- cycle time: time/date-stamped student projects, student projects designed by commercial entities; and
- consumer delight: tracking of the frequency of consumer utilization of student products, consumer testimonials about student products.

Thus, in the Information Age, quality means that the product is unique and possesses characteristics that consumers would not anticipate. Likewise, graduates of Information Age educational organizations will be expected to possess specialized skills and have a track record of creating products that amaze and delight consumers.

Because an Industrial Age economy can only support a small percentage of highly educated workers, teachers had to function as quality control engineers and focus on rejecting all but the highest quality students. An Information Age economy requires a high percentage of highly educated workers. Thus, Information Age teachers must function as learning advocates or ombudspersons who try to ensure that every student learns to his or her maximum potential. Quality teaching will be measured by how many students succeed rather than by how many students fail.

In the Industrial Age, instructional quality was defined by, among other things, a small student-teacher ratio, intensive face-to-face contact between students and teachers, and standardized content, delivery, and schedule. In the Information Age, instructional quality will be defined by, among other things:

- Intensive student-information interaction. Online interactive learning environments diminish the need for intensive student-teacher interaction.

- Fast delivery of on-demand student-teacher virtual contact. Online interactive learning environments diminish the need for constant in-person supervision.

- Customized content, delivery, and schedule. Online interactive learning environments diminish the need for standardization.

There is a growing recognition of this transition within teacher education as witnessed by NCATE's 1999 announcement of its intention to establish a paperless accreditation process.[28] However, though the NCATE 2000 Standards[29] do pay lip service to advances in educational technology, they do not recognize the fundamental change in quality that has occurred in the Information Age.

For example, NCATE 2000 Standards still focus primarily on disciplinary knowledge. In the Industrial Age, when the knowledge base was relatively stable, it made sense for teachers to master a body of knowledge. However, in the Information Age, when knowledge doubles every five years, knowledge of a discipline is not sufficient. Quality teacher education in the Information Age will require standards—in addition to teaching dispositions, discipline knowledge, and pedagogical knowledge and skills—that emphasize information skills, customization skills, and asynchronous (i.e., independent of space and time) teaching skills.

In summary, the Information Age will change the meaning of quality. This new definition of quality will change the meaning of educational quality, which in turn will redefine educational research, policy, and practice. Thus, the debate about teacher quality will continue, but the nature of the debate, and the statistics that buttress it, will change. Furthermore, this new definition of quality will have dramatic ramifications for the conduct of teacher education and teacher education accreditation.

NOTES

1. Roben J. Maaske, "Analysis of Trends in Teacher Supply and Demand," *Journal of Teacher Education* 2 (1951): 263–68.

2. Lewis Mayhew and others, *The Quest for Quality: The Challenge for Undergraduate Education in the 1990s* (San Francisco: Jossey-Bass, 1990), p. 3.

3. Ibid, pp. 3–4.

4. *President Clinton's Call to Action for American Education in the 21st Century* (Washington, D.C.: U.S. Department of Education, 1997), <http://oeri2.ed.gov/updates/PresEDPlan/>.

5. *Address Before the Congress on the State of the Union* (Washington, D.C.: The White House, 2000), <http://www.pub.whitehouse.gov/uri-res/I2R?pdi://oma.eop.gov.us/2000/01/27/15.text.1>.

6. Susan S. Stodolsky, "Should SASS Measure Instructional Processes and Teacher Effectiveness?" in *The Schools and Staffing Survey: Recommendations for the Future*, ed. John E. Mullins and Daniel Kasprzyk (Washington, D.C.: U.S. Department of Education, 1996), <http://nces.ed.gov/pubs/97596.html>.

7. *Teacher Quality: A Report on the Preparation and Qualifications of Public School Teachers* (Washington D.C.: U.S. Department of Education, National Center for Education Statistics, 1999), <http://nces.ed.gov/pubs99/1999080.htm>.

8. Interstate New Teacher Assessment and Support Consortium, *INTASC Core Standards* (Washington, D.C.: Council of Chief State School Officers, 1995), <http://www.ccsso.org/intascst.html>.

9. *Teacher Quality*, <http://nces.ed.gov/pubs99/1999080.htm>.

10. Robert M. Pirsig, *Zen and the Art of Motorcycle Maintenance* (Toronto: Bantam, 1975), chapter 17, <http://www.virtualschool.edu/mon/Quality/PirsigZen/part3.html>.

11. W. Somerset Maugham, *The Summing Up* (Garden City, N.Y.: Doubleday, 1938), p. 94.

12. *What Matters Most: Teaching for America's Future* (New York: National Commission on Teaching & America's Future, 1996), <http://www.tc.columbia.edu/~teachcomm/>.

13. *Promising Practices: New Ways to Improve Teacher Quality* (Washington, D.C.: U.S. Department of Education, 1998), <http://www.ed.gov/pubs/PromPractice/index.html>.

14. "Who Should Teach? The States Decide," *Education Week*, 13 January 2000, p. 8.

15. *What Matters Most*, <http://www.tc.columbia.edu/~teachcomm/>.

16. Marci Kanstoroom and Chester E. Finn, Jr., eds., *Better Teachers, Better Schools* (Washington, D.C.: Thomas B. Fordham Foundation, 1999), <http://www.edexcellence.net/better/tchrs/teachers.html>.

17. *Promising Practices*, chapter 1.

18. Ibid., chapter 3.

19. W. Timothy Weaver, *America's Teacher Quality Problem: Alternatives for Reform* (New York: Praeger, 1983), chapter 1.

20. *The Teachers We Need and How to Get More of Them* (Washington, D.C.: Thomas B. Fordham Foundation, 1999), <http://www.edexcellence.net/library/teacher.html>.

21. Linda Darling-Hammond, *Solving the Dilemmas of Teacher Supply, Demand, and Standards: How We Can Ensure a Competent, Caring, and Qualified Teacher for Every Child* (New York: National Commission on Teaching & America's Future, 1999), <http://www.tc.columbia.edu/~teachcomm/CONFERENCE-99/SOLVING/solving.htm>.

22. Ibid.

23. Ibid.

24. Linda Darling-Hammond, "Teaching and Knowledge: Policy Issues Posed by Alternative Certification of Teachers," *Peabody Journal of Education*, 67 (1992): 123–154.

25. *Doing What Matters Most: Investing in Quality Teaching* (New York: National Commission on Teaching & America's Future, 1997), <http://www.tc.columbia.edu/~teachcomm/dwhat.htm>.

26. *The Academic Quality of Prospective Teachers: The Impact of Admissions and Licensure Testing* (Princeton, N.J.: Educational Testing Service, 1999), p. 25.

27. J. D. Haselkorn, "Shaping the Profession that Shapes America's Future," Paper prepared for the U. S. Department of Education's National Forum on Attracting and Preparing Teachers for the 21st Century, Washington, D.C., April 1997.

28. *Accreditation for the 21st Century: An NCATE Technology Update* (Washington, D.C.: National Council for the Accreditation of Teacher Education, 1999), <http://ncate.org/specfoc/techplans.htm>.

29. *NCATE 2000 Standards* (Washington, D.C.: National Council for the Accreditation of Teacher Education, 2000), <http://ncate.org/>.

14

Educational Reform and Teacher Education

Education reform is an especially difficult area; it is strewn with pitfalls because, before you can reform education, you have to reeducate the educators.

Sir Karl Popper

American attitudes toward the public schools have changed radically in the last fifty years. In 1946, public opinion polls showed that 87 percent of Americans were satisfied with the public school system.[1] By the 1990s, however, many Americans believed that the school system was in need of reform. In the November 1998 congressional elections, voters in nearly every state ranked education reform as the number one or number two issue on their minds.[2]

This change in attitude began in the 1960s and 1970s, but a 1983 U.S. Department of Education report entitled *A Nation at Risk* was a seminal event.[3] By linking U.S. economic troubles in the late 1970s and early 1980s to problems with U.S. education, *A Nation at Risk* brought education reform to the forefront of national consciousness. It has remained there ever since.

CONCEPTS OF TEACHER EDUCATION REFORM

The concept of reform, like the concept of quality, lies at the heart of most debates about education and teacher education. Without a clear understanding of this concept, that debate will not be advanced. Both the centrality and the diversity of the concept of reform can be clearly seen in the views of the critics discussed in the first part of this book.

Dewey proposed reforming teacher education by creating two different kinds of teacher training institutions: (1) schools that train rank and file

teachers using already well-established principles, and (2) schools that educate the leaders of educational systems (teachers in normal and training
schools, professors of pedagogy, superintendents, and principals of
schools in large cities) and devote themselves to pedagogical discovery and
experimentation.

Hutchins' suggested reforms included the elimination of accreditation,
certification, and requisite degrees for teachers because they made the system less flexible, perpetuated vested interests, and created occupational
monopolies. Hutchins insisted that the prospective teacher's general education should be identical with that of the lawyer, doctor, and clergyman
and that a good education in the liberal arts (grammar, rhetoric, logic, and
mathematics) would provide teachers with the basic rules of pedagogy.

Bestor attributed the need for educational reform primarily to the faulty
thinking of educationists: teacher educators, school administrators, and
educational bureaucrats. Teacher education in Bestor's perspective should
be education in how to think; that is, it should be liberal education, training
in those intellectual disciplines that have general applicability.

Conant viewed the feud between education professors and academic
professors as the major obstacle to teacher education reform. He recommended limiting the role of the National Council for Accreditation of
Teacher Education (NCATE) and regional accrediting associations to advisory bodies for local school boards and teacher education institutions. For
certification purposes, Conant required only that a teacher candidate hold
a bachelor's degree and complete a state-approved student teaching program.

Brameld warned that only audacious reform that places preparation for
any kind of educational service on a level at least equal in standards to that
of the medical profession would suffice. Teacher educators should concede
that current programs in teacher education are appallingly weak. However, instead of "cringing" before the pressures of liberal arts and sciences
critics, they should construct a much better professional program than any
that the critics could propose.

Silberman asserted that no matter how outstanding a teacher preparation program at a university might become as a result of reforms, its influence will be short lived if schools are characterized by docility, passivity,
conformity, and lack of trust. The most needed reform at the university
level in Silberman's view is that teacher education needs to be a
universitywide function involving not only education professors but professors in the arts and sciences.

Illich did not want to reform the existing educational system but rather
to abolish it. He wanted, for example, to abolish compulsory attendance
laws and all academic credentialing. Furthermore, he believed that most of
the traditional functions of the school should either be eliminated or assigned to other agencies in society. Illich's plan for teacher education in a

deschooled society combined the most ancient model of teacher education, apprenticeship, with the technology of a computer society.

Shanker espoused several reforms including raising standards for both students and teachers and giving teachers the ability (through collective bargaining) to control their own profession. He also insisted that unless the country is willing to significantly improve the working conditions of teaching (e.g., salaries, pension, benefits, and site-based decision-making authority), we will never be able to attract a sufficient number of high quality teachers into the profession.

Finn believed that revolutionary educational reform must, on the whole, be initiated and sustained not by educators but by political leaders, business leaders, and the general public. Since the education profession is rife with such dubious notions as facts are unimportant, it cannot be trusted to reform the school system.

The views of the critics regarding reform amply demonstrate the importance of the concept to the debate about education and teacher education. Just as with the concept of education quality, there are as many variants of education reform as there are reformers. But without an understanding of at least some of the reforms being proposed, and the reasoning behind those proposals, any progress toward consensus will be illusory.

HISTORY OF EDUCATION REFORM

A Nation at Risk was not the first report to critique the U.S. public school system. Various groups have found fault with the system ever since it was established. Many of these critics issued reports to back up their claims, such as the *Report of the Committee of Ten on Secondary School Studies*[4] in 1893, *The Cardinal Principles of Secondary Education*[5] in 1918, and *The American High School Today*[6] in 1959.

The agenda for reform fluctuated dramatically during the twentieth century. The *Report of the Committee of Ten on Secondary School Studies* favored instituting a standardized, rigorous course of study. The *Cardinal Principles of Secondary Education* concentrated on students who were not college bound. The 1930s and 1940s emphasized a progressive or child-centered curriculum. Reforms enacted during the 1950s focused on math and science in an effort to educate the next generation of leaders in science. Reformers stressed equity for minority children in the 1960s and 1970s. In 1983, *A Nation at Risk* recommended a return to basics such as reading and math in order to boost U.S. competitiveness in the international economy. In the 1990s, vouchers, or school choice programs, were championed by many reformers.[7]

In 1991, spurred by the founding of the New American Schools Development Corporation (now called New American Schools) by American business leaders, a new emphasis on systemic reform flourished. The purpose of NAS was to identify and provide financial support for the developers of promising "break the mold" school designs. Today, there is a $150 million federal program to subsidize the adoption of these designs, and currently over 1,500 schools in forty-five states are using NAS designs.[8]

A number of current education reformers and organizations have developed wildly disparate models of curriculum and instruction that are meant to transform entire schools. For example:

- Robert Slavin's Success for All
- E. D. Hirsch's Core Knowledge
- Henry Levin's Accelerated Schools
- Theodore Sizer's Coalition of Essential Schools
- Chris Whittle's Edison Project
- James Comer's School Development Program
- Howard Gardner's Multiple Intelligences
- Siegfried Engelmann's Direct Instruction
- Kurt Hahn's Expeditionary Learning Outward Bound
- National Alliance for Restructuring Education's America's Choice

Today there are literally dozens of reform models and radical designs, most of them being vigorously marketed and some of them fairly widely implemented.[9]

Perhaps the only statement accepted by all sides in the debate over school reform is that the problem lies not with any single practice or set of practices, but with the educational system. The educational system, as it was originally designed, is not able to meet all of the demands that we place on it. The time is past for piecemeal reform; it is time to reform the entire system.

In her 1997 book, *The Right to Learn,* Linda Darling-Hammond observed that during the last two decades of the twentieth century we moved through four waves of reform. The first wave sought to raise achievement through course and testing mandates. The second wave argued for improvements in teaching and teacher education. The third wave focused on defining more challenging standards for learning while restructuring schools so they can produce dramatically better outcomes. Now we are in the fourth wave, which is concerned with transforming the education system rather than merely getting schools to do better than what they have already done.[10]

The problem is that different reformers have entirely different conceptions of what a redesigned education system should look like. Thus, there is consensus on the need for improvements in education and teacher education, but there is fundamental disagreement about the nature and details of those improvements. In short, reformers agree on very little, except that change must be systemic.

CURRENT STATUS OF EDUCATION REFORM

In general, education reform movements rarely meet their goals. An examination of reforms during the twentieth century reveals that while national commissions can succeed in calling attention to potential problems, the remedies suggested are often ambiguous and their implementation ill defined. Open space, individualization, community-based education, whole language, heterogeneous grouping, authentic assessment, team teaching, flexible scheduling, inclusion, and many other reforms have simply failed to meet expectations.[11]

Test scores are often cited in the debate over education reform, and analysis of test score trends is a perennial topic among reformers. Some use tests like The National Assessment of Educational Progress (NAEP),[12] a federally sponsored testing program, to argue that scores have remained flat for many years. Others use international test data from the Organization for Economic Cooperation and Development (OECD) to argue that U.S. students do not measure up.[13] Test critics respond that the tests are not accurate and only measure lower level rote thinking skills.

By the 1980s, a number of states had put in place a series of steps to improve education. Frequently, state education reforms included increasing high school graduation requirements, particularly in math and science; instituting statewide testing programs; offering more Advanced Placement courses; promoting the use of technology in the classroom; and instituting new teacher evaluation programs.[14]

There is no single reform effort that crosses all state boundaries, but some states have initiated programs to evaluate and rate public schools. According to an *Education Week* report, nineteen states issued public ratings of individual schools, and fourteen states rewarded successful schools with increased funding. The report also found that nineteen states identified low-performing schools in an effort to help them improve, while sixteen states took over failing schools. So far, these state takeovers have usually solved fiscal shortcomings, but have not always increased student achievement.[15]

Some researchers, however, contend that poor student performance is not the fault of the educational system, but the result of socioeconomic conditions such as poverty or inadequate parenting. They note, for example, that nearly 20 percent of U.S. children live in poverty. The 1995 book *The Manufactured Crisis* offered a great deal of evidence that most education problems are concentrated in poverty-stricken areas, such as the inner cities, and are not inherent in the public school system.[16]

The need for federal reform of education culminated in the 1989 National Education Goals. America's governors and the president developed the original six goals, and the U.S. Congress added two new goals. The goals stated that by the year 2000:

- All children in America will start school ready to learn.
- The high school graduation rate will increase to at least 90 percent.
- All students will leave grades 4, 8, and 12 having demonstrated competency over challenging subject matter in the core academic subjects.
- U.S. students will be first in the world in mathematics and science achievement.
- Every adult American will be literate and will possess the knowledge and skills necessary to compete in a global economy and exercise the rights and responsibilities of citizenship.
- Every school in the U.S. will be free of drugs, violence, and the unauthorized presence of firearms and alcohol and will offer a disciplined environment conducive to learning.
- The Nation's teaching force will have access to programs for the continued improvement of their professional skills and the opportunity to acquire the knowledge and skills needed to instruct and prepare all American students for the next century.
- Every school will promote partnerships that will increase parental involvement and participation in promoting the social, emotional, and academic growth of children.[17]

These national goals were a direct outgrowth of the state-led education reform movement of the 1980s. Despite past education reform efforts, there was bipartisan agreement that students and schools were not measuring up to the high standards required to maintain a competitive economy and a strong democracy. It is too early to judge the success of Goals 2000, but there is no reason to believe that this program will have any more impact than previous reform attempts.

EDUCATION REFORM AND TEACHER EDUCATION

The release of *A Nation at Risk* brought public attention to the need to reform American schools. Nevertheless, colleges of education typically were neither leaders of reform, nor considered key elements in implementing change. Two major reports released in the late 1980s began to change this trend. The reports of the Carnegie Forum on Education and the Economy and the Holmes Group identified improvements in the preparation of new teachers as a critical link to educational reform. Then during the 1990s, the American Association of Colleges for Teacher Education,[18] the Association of Teacher Educators, [19] the Council for Chief State School Officials,[20] and the National Council for the Accreditation of Teacher Education[21] made efforts to codify knowledge needed by new teachers. In addition, several other influential reform-oriented documents on teacher education were published during this time period.[22]

In its 1986 report, *A Nation Prepared: Teachers for the 21st Century*, the Carnegie Forum's Task Force on Teaching as a Profession—made up of business and government leaders and union and school officials—called for sweeping changes in education policy. Among the eight recommendations, two were specific to the preparation of new teachers: (1) require a bachelor's degree in the arts and sciences as a prerequisite for the professional study of teaching; and (2) develop a new professional curriculum in graduate schools of education leading to a Master in Teaching degree, based on systematic knowledge of teaching, internships, and residencies in the school.[23]

Another influence for reform has been the Holmes Group, a coalition of deans from the graduate schools of education at research universities. Their 1986 report, *Tomorrow's Teachers*, developed a common agenda that included eliminating the undergraduate education major, strengthening and revising both the undergraduate curriculum and graduate professional training of teachers, creating new professional examinations for entry into the profession, and connecting higher education institutions to schools, through the development of professional development schools.[24]

The Holmes Group issued another report in 1995 entitled *Tomorrow's Schools of Education.* That report called for education schools to revamp their curricula, establish clinical professorships in professional development schools (analogous to teaching hospitals), create student cohorts encompassing all educational roles (e.g., teachers, counselors, administrators), conduct case study research, and create partnerships with local schools and other units in the university.[25]

The Holmes Group's agenda has not met with universal acceptance. Many educators have decried the exclusivity of the organization. There is also concern about the creation of one specific model of teacher preparation, especially one that required a four-year liberal arts major followed by a fifth year of graduate study in education. As a result, in 1989 the Renaissance Group was formed. The Renaissance Group is composed of twenty reform-minded state colleges and universities, the largest producers of teachers. Their 1994 report, entitled *Teachers for the New World: A Statement of Principles,* listed twelve principles for the preparation of teachers including that teacher education is an all-campus responsibility and that it should be integrated throughout a student's university experience and not reserved for the student's final year.[26]

Nearly every observer of teacher education during the last century has noted its resistance to change. Calls for reform have been tempered by acknowledgments of the many reform barriers such as mission uncertainty, instability of academic leadership, faculty powerlessness, insufficient resources, regulatory burdens imposed by the state, program fragmentation, faculty isolation, scholarly expectations, reward and promotion systems that fail to recognize service to schools, lack of time, lack of effective communication, lack of agreement on how and what to reform, lack of money, faculty turnover, faculty apathy, lack of central-university support.[27]

In summary, after a slow start there has been a fair amount of activity in the teacher education reform arena. However, like education reform in general, the results have not been impressive.

REFORM OF EDUCATION AND TEACHER EDUCATION IN THE INFORMATION AGE

Two major barriers limit attempts to reform education and teacher education in America—size and priority. The U.S. public school system is huge. In the year 2000, the U.S spent roughly $314 billion on education. The school system included 5.4 million employees (2.7 million of which were teachers) and 46 million students.[28] The sheer size of the system makes overcoming inertia exceedingly difficult.

Furthermore, schooling in America is not a high priority. For example, 65 percent of U.S. students work during the school year compared to only 2 percent of Japanese students.[29] Andrew Shapiro reports in *We're Number One* that among the seventeen major industrialized nations, the United States ranks: first in fewest homework hours, fifteenth in days spent in school, last in rewarding teachers, and last in public spending on education.[30]

Perhaps the most telling juxtaposition of educational size and priority is included in the following statistic: In 1999, the United States spent about $313 billion on public K–12 education, but invested less than 0.1 percent of that amount to determine what educational techniques actually work and to find ways to improve them.[31]

Demographics clearly demonstrate why schooling is not a priority in the United States and why it is not likely to become a priority in the near future:

- Only 20 percent of U.S. adults have children in school.[32]
- There are more people over age sixty-five than teenagers.[33]
- The fastest growing population group in the U.S. is people over eighty-five.[34]
- The American Association of Retired Persons is now the largest individual member organization in the United States.[35]

These statistics have grave implications for education. As people get older, they become less interested in youth issues. Their own health and financial security take top priority. As many communities have learned, it is hard to pass school bond issues when large numbers of voters are over sixty-five.

If these barriers are as intractable as they seem, then how is it possible to reform schools and teacher education in the twenty-first century? The answer to this question lies in the socioeconomic revolution that society is currently undergoing. After the agricultural and industrial revolutions, the Information Age is the third great socioeconomic revolution.[36] Like the others, it will reshape where and how we live and work and that will reshape how we educate. Consider the following statistics:

- In 1998, corporations spent $100 million on Internet-based training; by 2002 they will be spending $7 billion per year.[37]
- In 1999, there were 20 million teleworkers (defined as employees or independent contractors who work at home during normal business hours at least one day a month) in the U.S. workforce. That equals about 10 percent of the U.S. adult population.[38] It is predicted that more than 137 million workers (68 percent of the U.S. workforce) will be involved in some sort of remote work by 2003.[39]
- In 1999, consumers spent $7 billion shopping online[40] and that amount is expected to grow to more than $2 trillion by 2005.[41]
- In 2000, 60 percent of U.S. homes were connected to the Internet and that number is expected to increase to 80 percent by 2005.[42]
- In 2000, the United States had over 130 million Internet users, and it is predicted that the United States will have over 200 million Internet users by 2005.[43] The average person in 2000 spent two hours a day online.[44]
- In 2000, the Internet contained more than one billion unique documents,[45] and 72 percent of Americans said that the Internet improved their lives.[46]

In the twentieth century, reform of our educational system moved at a glacial pace. However, the current socioeconomic revolution may speed up the pace of reform in the twenty-first century. For example, the Internet is infiltrating society faster than any other technology in the history of civilization. Radio was in existence thirty-eight years before fifty million people tuned in; TV took thirteen years to reach that benchmark; the personal computer took sixteen years. Once it was opened to the general public, the Internet crossed that line in four years.[47]

The explosive growth, both current and future, of the Internet can be explained by two technological "laws" that have held true for more than three decades. Moore's Law states that computing power doubles every eighteen months, or conversely, the price of computing power halves every eighteen months. Metcalfe's Law states that the value of a network grows exponentially with the number of users (in other words, the larger a network grows, the larger it is likely to grow in the future). The Internet rests at the intersection of these two laws. Thus, the ratio of the cost of Internet access to the value it provides plummets over time. This dynamic fuels rapidly increasing usage that, in turn, generates capital for expansion and upgrading. The bottom line is that the Internet is not a fad, but rather the most obvious manifestation of a socioeconomic revolution.[48]

What are the implications of this socioeconomic revolution for reform of education and teacher education? The most effective reform strategy may be to support the development of information technologies that are consistent with life and work in the twenty-first century. For example, education reformers should lobby for a free, ubiquitous, high-speed information infrastructure such as Next Generation Internet (NGI)[49] that would give all Americans instant access to infinite resources including the world's great libraries, museums, and universities. Education reformers should also lobby for free, multimedia, interactive, Internet-based information databases, repositories, communication devices, and training programs available at any time and any place to every citizen. These lobbying activities, if successful, may do more to advance reform of education and teacher education than any direct attempt to reform the educational system .

The socioeconomic revolution known as the Information Age now makes such an approach to education reform both possible and affordable. However, it does not make it inevitable. For example, although information technology accounted for one-third of U.S. economic growth from 1995–1997, the U.S. government spent less than 2 percent of the federal research and development (R&D) budget (about $1.5 billion) on information technology research in 1998. The 1999 report of the President's Information Technology Advisory Committee recommended doubling the budget for information technology R&D. More to the point, the report outlined the roles of six government agencies—Department of Energy, Department of Defense, National Aeronautics and Space Administration, National Institutes of Health, National Oceanic and Atmospheric Administration, and National Science Foundation—in this new effort but neglected to even mention the Department of Education.[50]

Thus, if education reformers want to harness the power of the Internet, they cannot depend on government to do it for them. Instead, they should support efforts such as the National Learning Infrastructure Initiative (NLII). The NLII is a coalition of colleges, universities, nonprofit organizations, publishers, software companies, and information technology businesses that work to enhance and improve teaching and learning environments through innovative applications of information technology.[51]

Some critics argue that today's technologies are simply the latest in a long line of innovations that have failed to transform schools. For example, it is argued that although computers have found their way into schools in large numbers, they have failed to transform schools. Most teachers can and do ignore them and schools remain much as they were fifty years ago. As a school reform tool, technology has had about as much effect as other reform tools—very little.[52]

Clearly, however, industrialization changed schooling and teacher education (think of bell schedules, Carnegie units, and so on), as did the agricultural revolution before it (e.g., the nine-month school calendar). The information revolution is beginning to leave its mark on our educational system already. For example, nearly all U.S. schools have websites, and nearly all U.S. colleges and universities offer courses online.

Moreover, the history of human civilization clearly demonstrates that new technologies change society and that social change begets educational reform.[53] In 1999, 72 percent of U.S. colleges offered entire programs online, and education was the third most common online subject area (behind only business and social sciences).[54] By 2002, it is predicted that the number of students taking online courses will represent 15 percent of all higher education students.[55]

REFORM OF THE EDUCATION AND TEACHER EDUCATION PROFESSIONS

There has been much talk about the relationship between education reform and the education profession. Typically, reformers have called for increasing the power and prestige of educators as a way of improving education.[56]

Professions have a long history, having evolved from medieval guilds. These guilds regulated the occupations and preserved a monopoly on each craft. Craft guilds of the period were called "mysteries," a term derived from the Latin word for occupation, "ministerium." Secrecy was a prerequisite for joining a guild, since the guild members knew their livelihood would be threatened if the techniques of the trade became common knowledge. For this reason, the progress of an apprentice to journeyman to master craftsman was long and arduous.[57]

Today, some professional associations (e.g., in medicine and law) fulfill some of the functions of the old guilds but are rarely given that name. Lawyers, professors, doctors, and ministers have traditionally been considered professionals. In recent years, however, other occupations have vied for professional status (e.g., accountants).

In the nineteenth century, medicine was not a high status occupation. Indeed, the local barber often doubled as the town doctor. However, at the dawn of the twenty-first century physicians reign supreme in terms of power and status. This change can in part be attributed to advances in medical technology. It has often been observed that a physician who was magically transported from 1900 to 2000 could not function in a modern medical facility while a teacher transported from 1900 would be quite at home in a modern school.

Modern medical technology has made medicine a mysterious, powerful profession. The average citizen is in awe of CAT scans, pacemakers, and other medical technologies. Recent advances in educational technology, particularly the Internet, now make it possible for educators to follow the precedent set by physicians. Computers and computer programming have the ability to convey mystery and power to the education and teacher education professions. Embracing educational technology and the associated information skills (e.g., information acquisition, analysis, and display) may be the most effective way of both improving the status of educators and reforming the education professions.

Fundamental reform of schools and teacher education will happen in the twenty-first century. The Information Age is here. The real questions are what shape will the reform take and who will control the reform? Education reformers should concentrate on aligning our education system and professions with our new socioeconomic system. In addition to the twentieth-century requirements of possessing a great knowledge of at least one discipline and a sufficiently expansive liberal education so that they know how these disciplines relate to other disciplines and to the lives of their students, teachers must embrace the requirements of a new century. To do this, teacher educators should become masters of information skills and educational technology while educators should become journeymen and education students should become apprentices.

If it were indeed possible to transport people from 1900 to the present, teachers and teacher educators should be as dysfunctional as physicians. However, educational reformers in search of a quick, revolutionary fix should heed the cautionary words of the dean of American diplomats, George F. Kennan:"I think it's dangerous to try to create great changes in human nature in any short space and time. If you're going to change a civilization, it can be done only as the gardener does it, not as the engineer does it. That is, it's got to be done in harmony with the rules of nature and can't all be done overnight. That's why I'm against practically all revolutions—because they usually end badly by trying to do too much at once."[58]

NOTES

1. George H. Gallup, *The Gallup Poll: Public Opinion, 1935–1971* (New York: Random House, 1972), vol.1, p. 597.

2. Michael W. Kirst, "Special Report: The Debate over Education Reform," *Microsoft Encarta Encyclopedia 99,* <http://encarta.msn.com/events/education/backtoschool/feature.asp>.

3. *A Nation at Risk* (Washington, D.C.: U.S. Department of Education, National Commission on Excellence in Education, 1983), <http://www.ed.gov/pubs/NatAtRisk/risk.html>.

4. NEA, *Report of the Committee of Ten on Secondary School Studies* (New York: American Book Co., 1894).

5. Commission on the Reorganization of Secondary Education, "The Cardinal Principles of Secondary Education," in *The Development of Secondary Education*, ed. Frederick M. Raubinger and others (New York: Macmillan, 1969).

6. James Bryant Conant, *The American High School Today* (New York: McGraw-Hill, 1959).

7. David Tyack and Larry Cuban, *Tinkering Toward Utopia: A Century of Public School Reform* (Cambridge: Harvard University Press, 1995), pp. 49–54.

8. New American Schools, <http://www.naschools.org/>.

9. James Traub, *Better by Design: A Consumer's Guide to Schoolwide Reform* (Washington, D.C.: Thomas B. Fordham Foundation, 1999), <http://www.edexcellence.net/library/bbd/better_by_design.html>.

10. Linda Darling-Hammond, *The Right to Learn: A Blueprint for School Reform* (San Francisco: Jossey-Bass, 1997), p.5.

11. Tyack and Cuban, *Tinkering Toward Utopia*, chapter 1.

12. *National Assessment of Educational Progress* (Washington, D.C.: U.S. Department of Education, National Center for Education Statistics, 1969–2000), <http://nces.ed.gov/nationsreportcard/site/home.asp>.

13. *Education at a Glance* (Paris: Organization for Economic Cooperation and Development, 1999), <http://www.oecd.org/publications/figures/>.

14. Tyack and Cuban, *Tinkering Toward Utopia*, chapter 5.

15. "Who Should Teach? The States Decide," *Education Week*, 13 January 2000, pp. 8–9.

16. David Berliner and Bruce Biddle, *The Manufactured Crisis: Myths, Fraud, and the Attack on America's Public Schools* (Reading, Mass.: Addison-Wesley, 1995).

17. *The National Education Goals* (Washington, D.C.: U.S. Department of Education, 1994), <http://www.ed.gov/pubs/goals/summary/goals.html>.

18. Maynard C. Reynolds, ed., *Knowledge Base for the Beginning Teacher* (Elmsford, N.Y.: Pergamon Press, 1989).

19. W. Robert Houston, Martin Haberman, and John Sikula, eds., *Handbook of Research on Teacher Education* (New York: Macmillan, 1990).

20. Interstate New Teacher Assessment and Support Consortium, *INTASC Core Standards* (Washington, D.C.: Council of Chief State School Officers, 1995), <http://www.ccsso.org/intascst.html>.

21. *NCATE 2000 Standards* (Washington, D.C.: National Council for the Accreditation of Teacher Education, 2000), <http://ncate.org/>.

22. *Teacher Quality: A Report on the Preparation and Qualifications of Public School Teachers* (Washington D.C.: U.S. Department of Education, National Center for Education Statistics, 1999), <http://nces.ed.gov/pubs99/1999080.htm>; *What Matters Most: Teaching for America's Future* (New York: National Commission on Teaching & America's Future, 1996), <http://www.tc.columbia.edu/~teachcomm/>; Marci Kanstoroom and Chester E. Finn, Jr., eds., *Better Teachers, Better Schools* (Washington, D.C.: Thomas B. Fordham Foundation, 1999), <http://www.edexcellence.net/better/tchrs/teachers.html>; John Goodlad, *Teachers for Our Nation's Schools* (San Francisco: Jossey Bass, 1990).

23. *A Nation Prepared: Teachers for the 21st Century* (New York: Carnegie Forum on Education and the Economy, 1986, p. 90.

24. *Tomorrow's Teachers: A Report of the Holmes Group* (East Lansing, Mich.: Holmes Group, 1986).

25. *Tomorrow's Schools of Education* (East Lansing, Mich.: Holmes Group, 1995).

26. Renaissance Group, *Teachers for the New World: A Statement of Principles* (Cedar Falls, Iowa: University of Northern Iowa, 1994), <http://www.uni.edu/coe/rengroup/otherpubs/newworld.html>.

27. David G. Imig and Thomas J. Switzer, "Changing Teacher Education Programs: Restructuring Collegiate-Based Teacher Education Programs," in *Handbook of Research on Teacher Education,* ed. John Sikula, Thomas J. Buttery, and Edith Guyton, 2nd ed. (New York: Simon & Schuster Macmillan, 1996), pp. 213–14.

28. *The Condition of Education, 1999* (Washington, D.C.: U.S. Department of Education, National Center for Education Statistics, 1999), <http://nces.ed.gov/pubs99/condition99/>.

29. Dean C. Corrigan and Ken Udas, "Creating Collaborative, Child- and Family-Centered Education, Health, and Human Service Systems," in *Handbook of Research on Teacher Education,* ed. John Sikula, Thomas J. Buttery, and Edith Guyton, 2nd ed. (New York: Simon & Schuster Macmillan, 1996), chapter 41.

30. Andrew L. Shapiro, *We're Number One* (New York: Vintage Books, Random House, 1992), chapter 1.

31. David Shaw, "K–12 Education: Acting on Ignorance," testimony to the Web-based Education Commission, 14 September 2000, cited in Bob Kerrey and others, *The Power of the Internet for Learning: Moving from Promise to Practice,* Report of the Web-based Education Commission to the President and Congress of the United States (Washington, D.C., December 2000), <http://interact.hpcnet.org/webcommission/Research_and_Development.htm>.

32. *Statistical Abstract of the United States* (Washington, D.C.: U.S. Department of Commerce, 1999), <http://www.census.gov/statab/www/>.

33. Ibid.

34. Ibid.

35. American Association for Retired People, <http://www.aarp.org/>.

36. *The Emerging Digital Economy* (Washington, D.C.: U.S. Department of Commerce, 1998), <http://www.ecommerce.gov/emerging.htm>.

37. *Employing Critical IT Talent in the 21st Century* (Framingham, Mass.: International Data Corporation, 1999), <http://www.idc.com/Press/default.htm>.

38. Joanne H. Pratt, *1999 Telework America National Telework Survey* (Washington, D.C.: The International Telework Association & Council, 1999), <http://www.telecommute.org/>.

39. GartnerGroup, <http://gartner12.gartnerweb.com/public/static/home/home.html>.

40. Jupiter Communications, <http://www.jup.com/company/pressrelease.jsp?doc=pr000113>.

41. ActivMedia Research, <http://www.activmediaresearch.com>.

42. Harris Interactive, <http://www.harrisinteractive.com/>.

43. Computer Industry Almanac Inc., <http://www.c-i-a.com/199911iu.htm>.

44. eMarketer, <http://www.emarketer.com/>.

45. Inktomi WebMap, 18 January 2000, <http://www.inktomi.com/webmap/>.

46. The Gallup Organization, "Americans Say Internet Makes Their Lives Better," 23 February 2000, <http://www.gallup.com/poll/releases/pr000223.asp>.

47. *The Emerging Digital Economy,* p.4.

48. Kevin Werbach, *Digital Tornado: The Internet and Telecommunications Policy* (Washington, D.C.: Federal Communications Commission, 1997), <http://www.fcc.gov/Bureaus/OPP/working_papers/oppwp29pdf.html >.

49. Next Generation Internet (NGI), <http://www.ngi.gov/>.

50. *Information Technology for the Twenty-First Century (IT2): A Bold Investment in America's Future* (Washington, D.C.: National Coordination Office for Computing, Information, and Communications, 1999), <http://www.ccic.gov/it2/>.

51. NLII: National Learning Infrastructure Initiative, <http://www.educause.edu/nlii/>.

52. Larry Cuban, *Teachers and Machines: The Classroom Use of Technology since 1920* (New York: Teachers College Press, 1986).

53. Thomas Kuhn, *The Structure of Scientific Revolutions* (Chicago: University of Chicago Press, 1962).

54. Market Data Retrieval, "The College Technology Review, 1999–2000," 28 March 2000, <http://www.schooldata.com/datapoint43.html>.

55. *Online Distance Learning in Higher Education, 1998–2002* (Framingham, Mass.: International Data Corporation, 1999), <http://www.idc.com/Press/default.htm>.

56. Linda Darling-Hammond, "Teachers and Teaching: Signs of a Changing Profession," in *Handbook of Research on Teacher Education*, ed. W. Robert Houston, Martin Haberman, and John Sikula (New York: Macmillan, 1990), pp. 268–270.

57. George Clune, *The Medieval Gild System* (Dublin: Brown and Nolan, Ltd., 1943).

58. Quoted in Nicholas Lemann, "The Provocateur," *The New Yorker*, 13 November 2000, p. 98.

15

Trends in Teacher Education

Some problems are just too complicated for rational, logical solutions. They admit of insights, not answers.

Jerome Wiesner

By studying the future, people can better anticipate what lies ahead. More importantly, they can decide what would be desirable in the future and then work to achieve it. People have speculated about the future since the dawn of civilization. Futurism as an academic field of study, however, did not emerge until the 1950s when military and economic uses were the driving forces in the development of systematic futures research and techniques. Futurism has not been commonly applied to the field of teacher education. This is especially unfortunate given the fact that educational systems are frequently criticized for lagging behind society.[1]

It is noteworthy that, except for Illich, and to a lesser degree Brameld, the future does not play a large part in the ideas of the education critics discussed in the first part of this book. They are all (except Illich and Brameld) firmly grounded in their present, rather than the future. This traditional lack of future focus regarding thinking about teacher education may partially explain why educational systems lag behind society.

In previous chapters, we have discussed at some length the necessity of preserving and improving such traditional features of teacher education as liberal education, subject matter knowledge, pedagogical knowledge and skills, and educational practice and theory. In this chapter, we argue that our society is being transformed from an industrial paradigm to an information age paradigm and that this latter paradigm has profound implications for the future of American teacher education. In short, while teacher education should continue to give careful attention to the traditional features just named, the Information Age demands additional kinds of knowledge and skills for school children and teachers. The demands of the

Information Age for teacher education have been virtually ignored by educational reformers, policy makers, and critics. Thus, in this chapter, we concentrate heavily on what these demands might be and suggest a few ways teacher training institutions might react to them.

The first part of this chapter uses current and historical trends in education and teacher education to predict the short-term future of teacher education over the next decade. This section is organized by concepts that currently define teacher education—recruitment, selection, preparation, clinical experiences, certification, induction/retention, in-service education, governance, and status.

The second part of this chapter focuses on a topic that is tightly linked to the future of education and teacher education—technology. The evolution, current status, and the future of education technology is discussed. The research on the effects of education technology is also examined.

This chapter concludes with some thoughts about the long-term future of teacher education through the year 2100. The reader should be cautioned that short-term predictions of the future are often too optimistic, while long-term predictions are often too conservative. There is nothing to suggest that this chapter will be different in that regard.

SHORT-TERM TRENDS IN TEACHER EDUCATION

Recruitment

Demographic trends suggest that the demand for teachers will increase in the short-term future. The National Center for Education Statistics forecasts that the number of classroom teachers is expected to increase from 3.03 million in 1996 to 3.46 million by the year 2008, an increase of 14 percent. This increase is due mostly to increases in school enrollment, but also reflects an expected decline in the pupil-teacher ratio from 18.6 in 1996 to 17.0 in 2008.[2]

Historical trends suggest that the number of teachers per capita will also increase. In 1900, in the United States, there were roughly 400,000 public school teachers for a population of 76 million (a ratio of 1:190).[3] By the year 2000, there were roughly 3 million public school teachers for a population of 280 million (a ratio of 1:93).[4] More than anything, this trend reflects the increasing importance of education in our society. There is nothing on the current horizon to indicate that this trend will not continue.

Thus, in both the long-term and short-term future, it is likely that there will be more teachers, more teachers per pupils, and more teachers per capita. Recruitment of teachers, therefore, will continue to be an important aspect of teacher education.

Selection

Demographic trends suggest that in the short term the teaching force in the United States will not reflect the characteristics of the general population. Our society is inevitably becoming more multicultural. In 1990, 35 percent of school age children came from minority racial or language groups.[5] By 2035, that percentage will increase to 50 percent.[6] However, only 13 percent of the teachers in public schools are minorities[7] and only 8 percent of education school graduates are minorities.[8] Thus, the under representation of minorities in the teaching force will continue to get worse in the short-term future.

U.S. population trends also suggest that selecting teachers who can function in urban communities will continue to be important because 80 percent of the population live in urban areas.[9] Again, these demographic trends do not by themselves guarantee a change in the teaching force. In 1989, less than 10 percent of education school graduates sought positions in urban areas.[10]

Gender balance is also a problem. Although 50 percent of elementary students are male, more than 90 percent of elementary school teacher education students are female. Furthermore, more than 50 percent of teacher education professors and more than 50 percent of elementary school principals are male.[11]

These trends suggest that the selection of teachers who reflect the general population will continue to be an important issue in teacher education in both the short-term and long-term future.

Preparation

Formal preparation of teachers is the joint responsibility of a number of vested interest groups—public and private colleges and universities, professors in teacher education, professors in liberal arts and sciences, and teacher educators in local schools. Moreover, there are a large number of institutions involved in teacher preparation. In 1900, there were roughly 300 institutions preparing teachers.[12] In 1988, there were roughly 1,300 (that number has been relatively stable for thirty years). Teacher education institutions are currently much more numerous than other professions. For example, in 1988, there were 202 business schools, 243 engineering programs, 172 law schools, 127 medical schools, and 74 journalism schools.[13]

Because of the large number of vested interest groups and institutions involved in the preparation of teachers, fragmentation and diversity in teacher preparation programs and practices are likely to continue in the short term. However, it should be noted that from 1900 to 2000 the type of institution preparing teachers has changed from normal schools to teacher colleges to colleges and universities.[14] If this trend continues, then perhaps in the future most teachers will be prepared in graduate schools of education. This would then reduce the number of vested interest groups and insitutions involved in teacher preparation, which would, in turn, reduce the fragmentation and diversity.

Clinical Experiences

The earliest method of preparing teachers was the apprenticeship model used during the Middle Ages. In the United States, however, formal teacher education gradually evolved into an academic enterprise conducted away from the actual school. Student teaching requirements appeared in the 1920s as a reaction to this separation of theory and practice. Pre-student teaching clinical experiences became common during the last quarter of the twentieth century. By 1985, all fifty states required prospective teachers to engage in student teaching, and thirty-five states had standards pertaining to pre-student teaching clinical experiences.[15]

Policies in England and France appear to be moving toward more field-based preparation of teachers.[16] In the United States, the period devoted to student teaching has gotten increasingly longer during the twentieth century.[17] Recently, several universities have adopted fifth-year programs and internships.[18] In general, in the short-term future, it appears likely that clinical experiences will continue to increase in length and importance.

Certification

Historically teacher certification (the legal right to teach) began as an oral test given by local authorities. This was gradually replaced in the first half of the twentieth century by the awarding of teaching certificates by approved college programs. In the 1980s, college programs were augmented by teacher competency tests such as the National Teacher Examinations. In the 1990s, the National Board for Professional Teaching Standards was established and administered a voluntary national teacher certification process for experienced teachers seeking advanced certification.[19]

Clearly the trend is toward centralization and more governmental involvement in teacher certification. However, the movement toward national teacher certification is hindered by the fact that education is constitutionally a function of the states, not the federal government. Thus, it is unlikely that national certification will become widespread in the short term.

In 1900, no states required a bachelor's degree for teachers. By the year 2000, all states did.[20] Currently, nearly half of all U.S. teachers have a master's degree,[21] and over a fifth of the states require a master's degree for certification. The historical trend is clearly for certification to be linked to higher levels of education, and it seems likely that this trend will continue in the short-term future.

Forty states currently provide alternative certification, but the number of teachers certified in this manner is small.[22] History suggests that alternative certification is a function of supply vs. demand.[23] Since it is likely that the supply and demand for teachers will continue to fluctuate from year to year, it is also likely that alternative certification will continue to exist and that the frequency of use will correlate with teacher supply and demand.

Induction/Retention

Induction is the transition from student of teaching to teacher or the period between pre-service and in-service. Prior to 1980, there were very few teacher induction programs, but they steadily increased in number during the last two decades of the twentieth century to the point where there are now several hundred.[24] A 1996 study of teacher induction programs found that twenty-one states had programs and an additional five states were piloting or planning programs. Still, nearly 50 percent of beginning teachers do not participate in anything more than school orientations.[25]

Currently, one-third of teachers participated in an induction program when they first began teaching. However, newer teachers were more likely to have participated in some kind of induction program at the beginning of their teaching careers than were more experienced teachers. Sixty-five percent of teachers with three or fewer years of experience participated in an induction program versus 14 percent of teachers with twenty or more years of experience.[26]

Induction programs exist in part to counter trends in teacher retention. Each year nearly twice as many teachers are prepared as actually enter teaching.[27] Approximately 30 percent of beginning teachers leave the profession during their first two years (the overall teacher turnover rate is 6 percent per year).[28] Induction has a short history and a relatively small body of research associated with it. Thus, it is difficult to predict the future for induction as a component of teacher education. However, in the short term it is unlikely that all these relatively new induction programs will disappear. Thus, it is possible that teacher retention rates may improve as a result. However, since retention is also related to other factors (such as salaries and working conditions) that show little progress, any increase in retention rates is not likely to be significant.

In-service Education

There is a worldwide trend in general society toward lifelong learning and nearly half of all U.S. adults participate in some form of education or training annually.[29] There is also evidence that in the field of education this concept, in the form of in-service education of teachers, received increased emphasis during the last quarter of the twentieth century.[30]

However, the overwhelming majority (90 percent) of all corporate and government training occurs on paid time.[31] In public schools, teachers report that just over a third (39 percent) of their professional development occurs on paid time.[32] Japanese teachers spend about 40 percent of their paid time on professional development and collaboration compared with about 14 percent for their American counterparts.[33] While virtually all U.S. teachers currently participate in some kind of professional development activity,[34] less than one percent of the typical school budget is devoted to staff development.[35]

Thus, it is likely that in the short-term future in-service education will remain common, but low funding and lack of time will continue to hamper its effectiveness.

Governance

In the United States, teacher education is governed by the 50 states, more than 1,300 higher education institutions, and over 5,000 local school districts. In addition, there are a number of organizations that exert influence. Below is a partial list:

- U.S. Department of Education
- National Education Association
- American Federation of Teachers
- American Association of Colleges for Teacher Education
- Association of Teacher Educators
- Teacher Education Colleges in State Colleges and Universities
- Association of Independent Liberal Arts Colleges for Teacher Education
- Association of Colleges and Schools of Education in State Universities and Land Grant Colleges
- Affiliated Private Universities
- Holmes Group
- Interstate New Teacher Support and Assessment Consortium
- National Board for Professional Teaching Standards
- National Council for the Accreditation of Teacher Education (NCATE)

One governance trend that is likely to continue in the short term is increasing federal involvement in teacher education. For example, in 1998 the U.S. Congress required all states and institutions of higher education that prepare teachers and receive Title IV funds to develop and publish report cards describing the performance of teacher preparation graduates on state teacher assessments. Thus, by federal law, nearly all teacher preparation programs will become publicly accountable by 2003.[36]

A second trend that is likely to continue in the short term is the debate over national accreditation in teacher education. Currently, only 40 percent of the over 1,300 organizations preparing teachers are accredited by NCATE.[37] Thus, it is likely that accreditation will continue to be a contentious issue in the short-term future.

Status

Historically, teachers and teacher educators have been accorded relatively low status. Two manifestations of this phenomenon are that teacher education has been underfunded,[38] and teacher education faculty have relatively low salaries compared with other fields.[39]

It has been suggested that the low status of teacher education is due in part to the low status of teachers. Historically, the status of teachers has improved steadily during the twentieth century.[40] However, the United States lags behind other countries in paying its teachers even though the time demands on American teachers are among the highest in the world. In addition, the average salary of an American teacher falls far short of that of other university graduates in the United States, while in many other countries teachers earn more than other university graduates on average.[41] Thus, U.S. teachers and teacher educators still posess relatively low status, and there is no reason to believe that this will change in the short term.

TECHNOLOGY AND THE FUTURE OF TEACHER EDUCATION

The term "technology" is derived from the ancient Greek word *techne*, meaning art, craft, or skill. For Plato, *techne* and systematic or scientific knowledge were closely related. Aristotle asserted that *techne* was the systematic use of knowledge for intelligent human action. Thus, technology is not simply reducible to things or hardware.[42]

There are three philosophies about the nature of technology:

- Technology is a positive and uplifting force that will, over time, mitigate or eliminate most or all of the ills that afflict humanity. Marshall McLuhan, author of *Understanding Media,* and Alvin Toffler, author of *Future Shock,* are proponents of this philosophy.

- Technology is an inherently evil, dehumanizing force that will inevitably lead to the moral, intellectual, or physical destruction of humankind. Jacques Ellul, author of *The Technological Bluff,* and George Orwell, author of *1984,* are proponents of this philosophy.

- Technology is a tool and can be used for either good or evil, depending upon the intentions of the person employing the tool. James Carey, author of *Communication as Culture,* and Andrew Feenberg, author of *Critical Theory of Technology,* are proponents of this philosophy.

Thus, much of the debate about educational technology is philosophical rather than empirical.

There is no such debate among the general public, however. In 1997, 85 percent of the public believed that schools well equipped with technology have a major advantage over schools that are poorly equipped, and 74 percent believed that technology would have a positive impact on education.[43] Thus, this chapter assumes that educational technology is an important aspect of teacher education.

It is difficult to overestimate the importance of technology in today's society. Our entire culture is being converted into digital form. Technology has changed the way we do business, the way we communicate, the way we play, the way we live. The very definition of what it means to be human is being changed by technology. Thus, it should come as no surprise that technology is also changing the way we teach, the way we learn, and the way we educate teachers.

History of Technology in Education

Educational technology can be traced back to the time when tribal priests systematized bodies of knowledge, and early cultures invented pictographs or sign writing to record and transmit information.[44] We have always used technology in teaching. Pencils, paper, chalk, and chalkboards are examples of technology. Early scholars saw the potential for new technology to change the way we teach and learn. For example, Comenius, a seventeenth-century scholar, saw the printed book as an important means to disseminate knowledge.[45]

In the modern era, the earliest view of educational technology developed in the 1930s and emphasized technology as media. This view grew out of the audiovisual movement, which saw educational technology as ways of delivering information that were alternatives to lectures and books.[46]

An instructional design or instructional systems view of educational technology became popular in the 1960s and 1970s. This view originated in military and industrial training and was based on the belief that both human and nonhuman resources (teachers and media) could be parts of a system for addressing an instructional problem or need.[47]

Once computers began to be used in classrooms in the 1960s, another view of educational technology known as educational computing was prominent. By the 1990s, the Internet and other information technology devices resulted in educational technology being viewed as a process of determining which electronic tools and which methods for implementing them are appropriate for given classroom situations and problems.[48]

Because it engenders change, educators typically do not embrace new technology quickly. The printing press changed the organization and transmission of knowledge in the fifteeenth century, and today computers and the Internet are having the same effect. As a result, new technology inevitably receives a great deal of criticism from the educational establishment. According to the critics, technology (no matter the specific technology or time period) will: lower the quality of education, make education less personal, increase the cost of education, decrease accessibility to education for poor people, and decrease the teacher's control of education. Despite these criticisms new technologies are constantly being integrated into education. In 1997 alone, spending on educational technology exceeded $5 billion.[49]

Current Status of Technology in Teacher Education

Computer-to-student ratios in public schools have declined steadily from 125:1 in 1983 to 5:1 in 1998.[50] In 1999, 95 percent of public schools were connected to the Internet, and 63 percent of instructional rooms had Internet access.[51] In 1997, 76 percent of students in grades 1–12 used a computer at school, and 45 percent used one at home.[52] In 1999, 97 percent of teachers used a computer at home and/or at school for professional activities.[53]

Unfortunately, most teacher education programs are not keeping pace. In 1997, only thirty-two states had technology requirements for teacher licensure, and only 15 percent of teachers had received nine or more hours of technology training.[54] A 1998 study found the following:

- Only 40 percent of teacher education students are required to design and deliver instruction incorporating various technologies during their on-campus program.
- Only 28 percent of teacher education students are required to design and deliver instruction incorporating various technologies during their student teaching.
- Only 45 percent of teacher education faculty regularly use computers, televisions, and VCRs as interactive instructional tools during class periods.
- Only 42 percent of teacher education classrooms were wired for the Internet.
- Only 55 percent of teacher education programs had budgeted a plan to purchase, replace, and upgrade educational technology.[55]

A 1997 Task Force on Technology and Teacher Education found that teacher education faculty: have an insufficient understanding of the demands on classroom teachers to incorporate technology into their teaching; do not fully appreciate the impact technology is having on the way work is accomplished; and undervalue the significance of technology and treat it as merely another topic about which teachers should be informed.[56]

Moreover, educational technology seems to be a blind spot for teacher education leaders. For example, the National Council for the Accreditation of Teacher Education did not bother to include educational technology in its standards until 1995. Even more embarrassing, the report and recommendations of the 1995 National Congress on Teacher Education failed to even mention educational technology.[57] It is no wonder that only 20 percent of teachers feel prepared to integrate educational technology into classroom instruction.[58]

Research on the Effects of Educational Technology

Since 1920, many technologies have been introduced to the classroom (e.g., film, radio, television). Research studies generally did not confirm the expected gains in learning from these technologies. This, in turn, created a great deal of skepticism regarding the efficacy of educational technology in general.[59]

However, a 1995 review of the research on the use of technology in the classroom concluded that technology has a positive affect on student learning, the development of student skills, and student attitudes toward school.[60] Unfortunately, there is relatively little data on the effects of technology on teachers.[61] One of the few studies of this type was a 1990 survey of teachers who were "accomplished" at using technology. This study found that 88 percent felt that computers had changed their teaching; 72 percent felt they expected more of their students; 63 percent felt they could present more complex material; 61 percent felt that computers permitted greater individualization in their teaching; 65 percent felt that computers facilitated more independent student work; 70 percent felt that computers allowed them to give greater attention to individual students; 52 percent reported that they spent less time lecturing to the entire class; and 43 percent reported that they had more time to spend working with small groups or individual students.[62]

Perhaps the most salient point regarding research on educational technology is about the irrelevance of most of it. The Internet is unlike the educationally disappointing technologies of the twentieth century such as film, radio, television, and even the stand-alone computer. The latter are passive technologies whose artifacts are expensive, quickly out dated, and difficult to produce or modify. Thus, they are not well suited to quickly changing instructional environments. The Internet, on the other hand, is an interactive technology that provides access to vast amounts of free, constantly updated information that is easy to produce and modify. Thus, it is much more useful in dynamic environments such as instruction. In addition, the Internet is not just an entertainment media; it is also changing the way we work and live. In short, the Internet is a harbinger of a paradigm shift in society and in education.

Educational Technology and Paradigm Change

Paradigms are mental models or ways of thinking about something. Our current educational system, for example, contains many vestiges of the agrarian paradigm (e.g., summer vacations so that students can be home to help with the farm work) and the industrial paradigm (e.g., a lock-step curriculum and bell schedule so that education can proceed in an assembly-line fashion). It has frequently been observed that information technology is fueling a new information paradigm that is, in turn, changing the nature of education. Thus, the effects of the information paradigm on teacher education will be considerable.

Today most educators are unequivocal in their support of books, but view the Internet with suspicion. Modern educators are blinded by over five centuries of educational domination by the paper/print paradigm. But books, like the Internet, are not all good or all bad. For example:

- Books made oral memory less important. Because we can rely on books and written notes, we have much worse memories than people of more than five hundred years ago. The basic skills have changed from listening and speaking to reading and writing.

- Books increased the pace of change and this, in turn, made contemplation less important. Word of mouth is much slower than a printing press. More information than anyone could possibly assimilate suddenly became available to everyone. This meant that anticontemplation skills such as skimming, speed-reading, and so on became essential.

- Books caused illiteracy. Prior to the printing press, it was not important for most people to be able to read or write. After the printing press, these skills were essential for success.

Every new technology changes what it means to be human and to be educated. These changes disadvantage certain kinds of people who previously were advantaged and advantage other kinds of people who were previously disadvantaged. Today no one advocates outlawing the printing press. It is almost universally agreed that books are good. In fact, the invention of the printing press is often referred to as one of the most important turning points in human history and a major reason that human culture has progressed to its current level.

The reason that the printing press changed society and education so dramatically has nothing to do with the people who were advantaged or disadvantaged. Printed books became so ubiquitous because they were cheaper and better (fewer errors) than the previous technologies (i.e., lectures, papyrus scrolls, and illuminated manuscripts). Books made more information available to more people more quickly and cheaply than anything that had existed previously. Despite their negative consequences, the domination of printed books was inevitable.

Today, the Internet is the most powerful educational environment that has ever existed. It is better than books at conveying information and entertainment via sound and motion. It is also global, interactive, and nonlinear (i.e., you can instantly jump from one website to another via hyperlinks) in ways that books cannot be. But the Internet does have its dark side. For example:

- The Internet makes reading and writing less important. Just as speeches were supplanted by books as the primary method for conveying information, books will yield to websites as the most important information source. Information skills (e.g., information acquisition, analysis, and display) will become the basic skills of the twenty-first century.

- The Internet increases the pace of change and this, in turn, makes ownership of ideas less important. The Internet disseminates information almost instantaneously and that information constantly changes. This means that anti-ownership skills such as downloading, copying, and pasting will become essential.

- The Internet causes illiteracy. Prior to the Internet, it was not important for most people to be able to use computers and navigate through information space. After the Internet, these skills will be essential for success.

Like the printing press, the Internet is good for some people and bad for others. Like the printing press, the Internet makes more information available to more people more quickly and cheaply than anything that has existed previously.

Today, educators fear that the Internet will cause a degeneration in basic skills. What is really happening is the augmentation of the basic skills of the Industrial Age (the 3 Rs—reading, 'riting, and 'rithmetic) by the basic skills of the Information Age (the 3 Is—information analysis, information acquisition, and information display). These Information Age skills are not, as some have claimed, intellectually bereft. Information acquisition includes the ability to navigate, locate, retrieve, solicit, and store information. Information analysis includes the ability to process, evaluate, and synthesize information. Information display includes the ability to organize, visualize, and communicate information.

These changes are occurring despite the fact that there is never enough research to justify a paradigm change. That is because critics insist on judging new paradigms by criteria generated by the old paradigm. For example, educators initially resisted books because they feared a degeneration in the ability to remember oral lectures. Of course, they were quite correct about this, but misguided in their belief that oral memory would forever remain the most significant educational skill. If we judge the success of the Internet as an educational tool by standardized tests meant to measure the basic skills of the old paradigm, we are likely to be disappointed in the outcomes. Teacher educators of the future must throw off the conceptual shackles of industrial paradigm concepts such as mass-produced standardization and develop concepts that are consistent with the information paradigm such as individualized customization.

The Future of Educational Technology in Teacher Education

According to John Naisbitt, internationally renowned business consultant and author of the best-selling book *Megatrends*, there are three stages of technological innovation. In the first stage, we learn about the new technology and get used to the idea of it. In the second stage, we use the new technology to accomplish existing goals more efficiently. In the third stage, we discover uses and possibilities for the new technology that are new and different.[63] For example, the first movie makers placed cameras in the pit of a theater and filmed stage plays. Eventually, they realized that they were allowing the structures of the older art form to limit their use of the new technology. They then, and only then, were able to develop new techniques and an entirely new art form.[64]

Before the use of information technology in teacher education can reach stage three, the very nature of education must be redefined. The concepts, principles, and advantages of the new paradigm must be fully articulated. Currently, 79 percent of U.S. higher education institutions offer virtual courses (courses where teachers and students do not have to reside in the same classroom), mostly via the Internet and TV.[65] Predictably, a review of Internet courses reveals that almost all can be characterized as stage two (using the new technology to accomplish existing goals more efficiently). It is likely that stage three will not be fully realized until the current generation of teacher educators retire and are replaced by teacher educators who are not limited by their knowledge of and experience with the old technology.

Perhaps online educational games will become the first stage three use of the Internet. Educational games are nothing new. A quick search of ERIC online yielded a 1970 handbook that listed over 2,000 educational games. Playing games on computers is also not new; it has now been over twenty years since ATARI claimed its first addicts.

Online gaming is a new and quickly growing phenomena, however. On a recent weekend, over a half million players spent more than two million hours playing a single online game.[66] The video and computer game industry was the fastest growing segment of all entertainment industries in 1998, beating out television and movies for the second consecutive year. Game hardware and software is currently a $6 billion annual market that is projected to grow 25 percent annually for the next five years. A third of Internet users play online games, and it is no longer a male-only activity; females now compose half of online game players.[67]

The advantages of online games include the following:

- multimedia sensory stimulation (e.g., sound, moving images, etc.)
- person-person (multiplayer) and/or person-machine (single player) interaction
- asynchronous (players can play at any time and place) and/or synchronous (i.e., real-time) interaction
- constant availability (players can play anytime of the day or night)
- nearly infinite resources (the entire Internet)
- individualization (players can interact with learning materials at their own pace and in their own style)
- replayability (players can make mistakes and replay poorly understood situations as often as desired)
- instant and automated record-keeping, feedback, and diagnosis
- format familiarity (today's students are inveterate game players)

The evolution of online educational games in teacher education is not easy to predict, but their first incarnation may mimic educational computer games such as *SimCity*. In *SimCity*, the player must build and maintain a city, balancing revenues with expenditures while being subject to the vagaries of nature (e.g., natural catastrophes) and human nature (e.g., population booms and busts). It is easy to visualize the application of these principles to an online teacher education game called *SimSchool* where the player must build and maintain a school. The effects of teacher strikes, student expulsions, parent conflicts, vouchers, low standardized test scores, failed lesson plans, and so on could be illustrated within *SimSchool*.

The second iteration of online teacher education games may model the simulated training environments for pilots and police officers. Pilots, for example, are trained to fly and land airplanes in a flight simulator. The cockpit exactly mirrors a real cockpit, and the pilot must react to whatever is seen on the screen. Pilots can experience different kinds of airplanes and flying environments and when they crash, no one is hurt. It is not hard to envision the development of a school simulator. Different kinds of classroom environments could be simulated so that teachers would have a chance to practice much more efficiently and make errors without inflicting any damage on real students.

Perhaps the third generation of online teacher education games will involve virtual reality environments such as the holodeck illustrated in the TV show *Star Trek: The Next Generation*.[68] The holodeck is an interactive, self-directed, multisensory computer-generated, holographic environment that provides an illusion of participating in a realistic three-dimensional environment. In the holodeck, the player can visit any time or place and play any role. Imagine the advantages to teacher educators of being able to design total immersion learning environments for prospective teachers to experience in a holoschool. Think of the experiential base that prospective teachers could build before ever setting foot in a real school. It has been estimated that this technology, which already exists, will be mature enough to do just that within the next decade or two.[69]

In summary, a new paradigm is in the process of forming. Educators eventually embraced the printing press, and they are on the cusp of embracing the Internet. Today, 94 percent of teachers surf the Internet (99 percent under the age of thirty-five),[70] 61 percent use the Internet for instruction,[71] and 90 percent consider Internet access in their classroom valuable or essential.[72] These technologies fundamentally change society and the very meaning of the word "educated." Even now the digital technologies of the Information Age paradigm are supplanting the paper/print technologies of the industrial paradigm. For example, 13 percent of schools subscribe to online curriculum materials,[73] and more than 90 percent of students who have access to the Internet use it to complete school assignments at home.[74] Thus, in the twenty-first century teacher education will be transformed by the Internet. However, it is only a matter of time until the Internet is challenged by the next paradigm-generating new technology. Such is the nature of humans, technology, and teacher education.

THE LONG-TERM FUTURE OF TEACHER EDUCATION

Two things seem likely regarding teacher education in the twenty-first century. First, there will continue to be teacher education critics, and reform of teacher education will continue to be an important issue. As education continues to increase in importance, so too will teacher education. Conferences such as the 1995 National Congress on Teacher Education are likely to be repeated in 2095.

Second, the long-term future will not simply be an extension of the present. The famous futurist Alvin Toffler warned, "We must do more than identify major trends. Difficult as it may be, we must resist the temptation to be seduced by straight lines."[75] Unpredictable major events will occur, and these will change the very nature of society, education, and teacher education.

For example, at the beginning of the twenty-first century, nearly every school in the United States was connected to the Internet. Although it would have been difficult to predict the Internet in the year 1900, it clearly has great ramifications for the conduct of teacher education. It is likely that the vast amounts of information made accessible by the Internet will result in less emphasis on discipline-based skills and more on information skills (e.g., information acquisition, information analysis, information display). Moreover, the asynchronous (independent of time and place) nature of the Internet may require that teachers be trained to function in both real and virtual time and in both real and virtual places.

In addition to technological changes, social changes can also cause dramatic changes in teacher education. For example, the development of inner cities in the twentieth century caused teacher educators to include urban issues in their curricula. Similarly, the women's movement, the civil rights movement, and the special education movement had dramatic impacts on the content and conduct of teacher education. No doubt social changes will continue to occur in the twenty-first century and cause equally dramatic changes in teacher education. The lengthening of the lifespan, overpopulation, global warming, cloning, the spread of democracy, genetic engineering, nano-technology (i.e., machines that operate at the molecular level) and other yet to occur phenomena have the potential to change social behavior and shift teacher education in ways that are not predictable at this point in time.

Social traditions may also block or delay the application of technological innovations to education and teacher education. For example, the Internet makes telecommuting and home schooling available to vast numbers of parents and children. If current trends continue, the necessity of building and maintaining physical plants for instruction may be diminished in the not-too-distant future. However, current social customs must change before school buildings are abandoned because for many parents schools function as respites from child-rearing. Most parents do not currently wish to spend all day every day with their children, so schools as physical places will not disappear until those attitudes change. (Note that there may also be other reasons to abandon or not abandon school buildings and that not all changes that technology makes possible are necessarily desirable.)

There were dramatic changes in the twentieth century for some professions. For example, a physician trained in 1900 would not have been able to function in the year 2000. However, change in the twentieth century was not so dramatic for teacher education—lectures and chalkboards dominated the entire century. The twenty-first century promises to be different.

By the year 2025, teacher education may emulate the current training of pilots and police by employing computer-generated and evaluated simulations. For example, teachers may be required to log a sufficient number of successful hours on a teacher simulation machine.

By the year 2050, technology may advance to the point where the holodeck becomes the primary mode of both education and teacher education. Teachers may be required to visit a certain number of educational environments and interact with a certain number of holographic personalities.

By the year 2100, biotechnology may evolve to the point where computer chips are implanted into the human brain or nervous system (this is already being done now in an admittedly crude fashion).[76] Education and teacher education may then become mostly a matter of downloading the latest software in a fashion similar to scenes depicted in the popular 1999 movie *The Matrix*. Teachers may be required to update their embedded chip at specified intervals.

Of course, it is entirely possible that the changes described in the preceeding paragraphs will never happen. The predictions in this chapter may look quite silly in a few decades. However, there is no doubt that dramatic, unpredictable social and technological changes will occur during the next one hundredyears just as they did in the preceeding one hundred years (e.g., cars, airplanes, telephones, television, and robots). The idea of a worldwide network of computers would have seemed at least as farfetched one hundred years ago as computer chips embedded into human brains seems today. For teacher education, the twenty-first century will prove the wisdom of Toffler's advice—the future will not be found by simply drawing a straight line from the present.

NOTES

1. Christopher Dede, "Futures Research and Strategic Planning in Teacher Education," in *Handbook of Research on Teacher Education*, ed. W. Robert Houston, Martin Haberman, and John Sikula (New York: Macmillan, 1990), p. 83.

2. *Projections of Education Statistics to 2008* (Washington, D.C.: U.S. Department of Education, National Center for Education Statistics, 1998), chapter 5, <http://nces.ed.gov/pubs98/pj2008/p98c05.html>.

3. Thomas D. Snyder, ed., *120 Years of American Education: A Statistical Portrait* (Washington, D.C.: National Center for Education Statistics, 1993), p. 46.

4. *The Digest of Education Statistics, 1998* (Washington, D.C.: U.S. Department of Education, National Center for Education Statistics, 1999), <http://nces.ed.gov/pubs99/digest98/chapter1.html>.

5. Harold L. Hodgkinson, "Reforms vs. Reality," *Phi Delta Kappan* 73 (January 1991): 8–16.

6. National Coalition of Educational Equity Advocates, *Educate America: A Call for Equity in School Reform* (Washington, D.C.: National Coalition of Educational Equity Advocates, 1994), p. 2.

7. America's Teachers: Profile of a Profession, 1993-94 (Washington, D.C.: U.S. Department of Education, National Center for Education Statistics, 1997), p.10.

8. Nancy L. Zimpfer, "The RATE Project: A Profile of Teacher Education Students," *Journal of Teacher Education* 40 (June 1986): 27–31.

9. Barbara G. Burch, "A Response to Chapter 5, 'The Preparation of Teachers for a Diverse Society,' by Martin Haberman," in *Teachers for the New Millennium*, ed. Leonard Kaplan and Roy A. Edelfelt (Thousand Oaks, Calif.: Corwin Press, 1996), p. 134.

10. Zimpfer, "The RATE Project," 27–31.

11. Ibid.

12. Roy A. Edelfelt, "Agenda for Tomorrow," in *Teachers for the New Millennium*, ed. Leonard Kaplan and Roy A. Edelfelt (Thousand Oaks, Calif.: Corwin Press, 1996), pp. 198–99.

13. Geraldine Jonçich Clifford and James W. Guthrie, *Ed School: A Brief for Professional Education* (Chicago: University of Chicago Press, 1988) p. 39.

14. Edelfelt, "Agenda for Tomorrow," pp. 198–99.

15. John E. Morris, and others, "Standards for Professional Laboratory and Field Experiences: Review and Recommendations," *Action in Teacher Education* 7 (March 1985): 73–78.

16. Harold Judge, "Teachers and Universities: Vive la Difference: The Uncommonalities of Teacher Training in England, France, and the United States," *Education Week,* 14 December 1994, p. 56.

17. Mary Hatwood Futrell, "The Courage to Change" in *Teachers for the New Millennium,* eds. Leonard Kaplan and Roy A. Edelfelt (Thousand Oaks, Calif.: Corwin Press, 1996), pp. 10–11.

18. Edith Guyton and D. John McIntryre, "Student Teaching and School Experiences," in *Handbook of Research on Teacher Education,* ed. W. Robert Houston, Martin Haberman, and John Sikula (New York: Macmillan, 1990), p. 515.

19. Robert A. Roth and Chris Pipho, "Teacher Education Standards," in *Handbook of Research on Teacher Education,* eds. W. Robert Houston, Martin Haberman, and John Sikula (New York: Macmillan, 1990), p. 119.

20. Edelfelt, "Agenda for Tomorrow," pp. 198–199.

21. *Teacher Quality: A Report on the Preparation and Qualifications of Public School Teachers* (Washington D.C.: U.S. Department of Education, National Center for Education Statistics, 1999), <http://nces.ed.gov/pubs99/1999080.htm>.

22. Editors, "Who Should Teach? The States Decide," *Education Week,* 13 January 2000, pp. 8–9.

23. W. Timothy Weaver, *America's Teacher Quality Problem: Alternatives for Reform* (New York: Praeger, 1983).

24. Leslie Huling-Austin, "Teacher Induction Programs and Internships," in *Handbook of Research on Teacher Education,* ed. W. Robert Houston, Martin Haberman, and John Sikula (New York: Macmillan, 1990), pp. 536–537.

25. "The Induction of New Teachers" in *Promising Practices: New Ways to Improve Teacher Quality* (Principal's Office, September 1998), <http://www.schoolhousedoor.com/principal/article-teacherquality6.htm>.

26. *Teacher Quality,* p. v.

27. Linda Darling-Hammond, *The Right to Learn: A Blueprint for Creating Schools that Work* (San Francisco: Jossey-Bass, 1997), p. 317.

28. Phillip Schlecty and Victor Vance, "Recruitment, Selection, and Retention: The Shape of the Teaching Force," *Elementary School Journal* 83 (April 1983): 469–487.

29. Philip J. O'Connell, *Adults in Training: An International Comparison of Continuing Education and Training (1999)* (Paris: Organisation for Economic Co-operation and Development, 1999), <http://www.olis.oecd.org/OLIS/1999DOC.NSF/LINKTO/CERI-WD(99)1>.

30. Dennis Sparks and Susan Loucks-Horsley, "Models of Staff Development," in *Handbook of Research on Teacher Education,* ed. W. Robert Houston, Martin Haberman, and John Sikula (New York: Macmillan, 1990), p. 234.

31. "Training Magazine's 18th Annual Industry Report," *TRAINING Magazine* 36 (1999): 37.

32. *Teachers' Tools for the 21st Century. A Report on Teachers Use of Technology* (Washington, D.C.: U.S. Department of Education, National Center for Education Statistics, 2000), <http://nces.ed.gov/spider/webspider/2000102.shtml>.

33. *Education Budget Alert for Fiscal Year 2000* (Washington, D.C.: Committee for Education Funding, 1999), p. 42.

34. *Teacher Quality*, p. v.

35. Martin J. Haberman, "The Preparation of Teachers for a Diverse, Free Society," in *Teachers for the New Millennium*, ed. Leonard Kaplan and Roy A. Edelfelt (Thousand Oaks, Calif.: Corwin Press, 1996), p. 119.

36. *1998 Amendments to Higher Education Act of 1965 (Public Law 105-244)*, "Title II: Teacher Quality," <http://165.224.220.67/legislation/HEA/sec201.html>.

37. A List of Professionally Accredited Schools, Colleges, and Departments of Education (Washington, D.C.: National Council for Accreditation of Teacher Education, 2000) <http://www.ncate.org/accred/list-institutions/abbrev_listfall2000.pdf>.

38. Walter Doyle, "Themes in Teacher Education Research," in *Handbook of Research on Teacher Education*, ed. W. Robert Houston, Martin Haberman, and John Sikula (New York: Macmillan, 1990), pp. 6–7.

39. National Faculty Salary Survey by Rank and Discipline in Public Four-Year Colleges and Universities (Washington, D.C.: College and University Association for Human Resources, 2000), pp. 6–9.

40. Mark B. Ginsberg and Renee T. Clift, "The Hidden Curriculum of Pre-service Teacher Education," in *Handbook of Research on Teacher Education*, eds. W. Robert Houston, Martin Haberman, and John Sikula (New York: Macmillan, 1990), p. 451.

41. *Education at a Glance: OECD Indicators* (Paris: Organisation for Economic Co-operation and Development, 1998), chapter B.

42. Paul Saettler, *The Evolution of American Educational Technology* (New York: Libraries Unlimited, 1990), chapter 1.

43. *Preparing Our Young People for a Changing World: A Milken Exchange on Education Technology* (Santa Monica, Calif.: Milken Family Foundation, 1997), pp. 6–7.

44. Saettler, *The Evolution of American Educational Technology*, p. 4.

45. Ibid., chapter 1.

46. M. D. Roblyer, Jack Edwards, and Mary Anne Havriluk, *Integrating Educational Technology into Teaching* (Columbus, Ohio: Merrill/Prentice Hall, 1997), chapter 1, <http://www.eiu.edu/~edtech/lesson_06/chap1.htm>.

47. Ibid.

48. Ibid.

49. Andrew Trotter, "Taking Technology's Measure," *Education Week*, 10 November 1997, pp. 6–11.

50. David Moursund and Talbot Bielefeldt, *Will New Teachers Be Prepared to Teach in a Digital Age? A National Survey on Information Technology in Teacher Education* (Santa Monica, Calif.: Milken Exchange on Education Technology, 1999), pp. 14–15, <http://milkenexchange.org/publication.taf?_function=detail&Content_uid1=154>.

51. *Internet Access in U.S. Public Schools and Classrooms: 1994–1999* (Washington, D.C.: U.S. Department of Education, National Center for Education Statistics, 2000), <http://nces.ed.gov/pubsearch/pubsinfo.asp?pubid=2000086>.

52. *The Condition of Education 1999, Section II. Quality of Educational Environments (Elementary/Secondary)* (Washington, D.C.: U.S. Department of Education, Na-

tional Center for Education Statistics, 1999), <http://nces.ed.gov/pubs99/condition99/summary2x.html>.

53. Erik Fatemi, "Building the Digital Curriculum," *Education Week,* 23 September 1999, pp. 13–22.

54. Trotter, "Taking Technology's Measure," pp. 7–8.

55. Judy A. Beck and Harriet C. Wynn, "Technology in Teacher Education: Progress Along the Continuum," (Washington, D.C.: ERIC Clearinghouse on Teaching and Teacher Education, 1998), <http://www.ed.gov/databases/ERIC_Digests/ed424212.html>.

56. *Technology and the New Professional Teacher: Preparing for the 21st Century Classroom* (Washington, D.C.: National Council for Accreditation of Teacher Education, 1997), <http://www.ncate.org/projects/tech/TECH.HTM>.

57. Leonard Kaplan and Roy A. Edelfelt, eds., *Teachers for the New Millennium* (Thousand Oaks, Calif.: Corwin Press, 1996).

58. *Teacher Quality: A Report on the Preparation and Qualifications of Public School Teachers* (Washington D.C.: U.S. Department of Education, National Center for Education Statistics, 1999), <http://nces.ed.gov/pubs99/1999080.htm>.

59. Robert D. Hannafin and Wilhelmina C. Savenye, "Technology in the Classroom: the Teacher's New Role and Resistance to It," *Educational Technology* 33 (1993): 26–31.

60. *Teachers and Technology: Making the Connection* (Washington, D.C.: U.S. Congress, Office of Technology Assessment, 1995), p. 57, <http://www.wws.princeton.edu/~ota/disk1/1995/9541.html>.

61. Ibid., p. 51.

62. Karen Sheingold and Martha Hadley, *Accomplished Teachers: Integrating Computers into Classroom Practice* (New York: NY Center for Technology in Education, Bank Street College of Education, 1990), pp. 5–21.

63. John Naisbitt, *Megatrends: Ten New Directions Transforming Our Lives* (New York: Warner Books Inc., 1982), pp. 27–31.

64. Micahel G. Moore, "Is Teaching Like Flying? A Total Systems View of Distance Education," *The American Journal of Distance Education* 7 (1993): 1–10.

65. Peter J. Dirr, "Distance and Virtual Learning in the United States," in *The Development of Virtual Education: A Global Perspective,* ed. Glen Farrell (Vancouver, Canada: Commonwealth of Learning, 1999), p. 28, <http://www.col.org/virtualed/>.

66. Battle.net, "Blizzard's Battle.net Remains Largest Online Game Service in the World," 4 February 1999, <http://www.blizzard.com/PRESS/990204.shtml>.

67. *1999 State of the Industry Report* (Washington, D.C.: International Digital Software Association, 1999), <http://www.idsa.com/pressroom.html>.

68. *Star Trek,* <http://www.startrek.com/>.

69. Dan Verton and Dan Caterinicchia, "Army Enlists Tinseltown," *Federal Computer Week,* 1 May 2000, <http://www.idg.net/go.cgi?id=42853>.

70. *Annual NEA Today Readership Survey* (Washington, D.C.: National Education Association, 2000), <http://www.nea.org>.

71. Henry Jay Becker, *Internet Use by Teachers* (Irvine, Calif.: Center for Research on Information Technology and Organizations, 12 February 1999), <http://www.crito.uci.edu/TLC/FINDINGS/internet-use/>.

72. Fatemi, "Building the Digital Curriculum, " p. 14.

73. *Technology in Education 1999* (Shelton, Conn.: Market Data Retrieval, 1999), <http://www.schooldata.com/publications.html>.

74. Ipsos-Reid, "Internet Invaluable to Students Worldwide," 11 September 2000, <http://www.angusreid.com/media/content/displaypr.cfm?id_to_view=1073>.

75. Alvin Toffler, *The Third Wave* (New York: Morrow, 1980), p. 145.

76. For example, electrodes have been implanted into human brains in an attempt to remedy blindness and Parkinson's disease. See http://www.discovery.com/area/technology/virtualtech/issue1/manmachine.html for more details. For a description of a more ambitious project see Kevin Warwick, "Cyborg 1.0," *Wired* 8.02 (February 2000), <http://www.wired.com/wired/archive/8.02/warwick.html>.

Epilogue: A Note to Policy Makers

Advice is seldom welcome; and those who want it the most always like it the least.

Lord Chesterfield

Since the Second World War, there has been a steady flow of highly polemic works by a diverse group of educational critics, all of whom exhibit a profound antipathy toward professors of education. Typical of the genre is Richard Mitchell's *The Graves of Academe*, published in 1981.[1] In this book, Mitchell, an English professor, attacks the work and intelligence of professors of education.

Such attacks are typically greeted with rave reviews by everybody except the subject of the attacks. For example, James Kilpatrick, one of the country's most widely read newspaper columnists at that time, praised Mitchell for treating the "educationists of our land with the contempt they so royally deserve" and concluded that the first step in improving teacher education is to abolish all schools of education.[2] A dozen years later, George Stephanopoulos, television pundit and former senior adviser to President Clinton, repeated the same refrain. "The surest way to ruin a good young teacher," Stephanopoulos said, "is to have that person complete teacher training."[3]

As we noted in the prologue, this book is primarily about perspective. Our intent in this epilogue is to provide some perspective for current policy makers who will, no doubt, be faced with making important policy decisions regarding teacher education during their terms of office. We offer this epilogue with a great deal of respect for those who consent to serve and the myriad of forces that they must consider when making decisions. Despite Lord Chesterfield's pessimism, we hope that our advice will be taken in the spirit that it is offered—as an honest attempt to further the debate about one of the most important elements of a democracy, public education.

Coming to grips with complex phenomena such as teacher education requires a sophisticated and sympathetic perspective. It is unfortunate that so many prominent American policy makers and pundits minimize the complexity of the art and craft of teaching and the importance of teacher education. Rather than chastising teacher educators, who over the years have accomplished much with scant resources (and who have, as a group, been most responsible for raising the pedagogical *and* the academic standards of public school teachers), we should publicly recognize that good teacher education is essential for the improvement of public school education. Policy makers should establish policies and programs that encourage teacher education institutions and public schools to create teacher-training programs worthy of a professional teacher—programs that give prospective and practicing teachers a compelling vision of what education at its best should be and the skills, knowledge, and intellectual perspective necessary to make this vision a reality in the schools where they work. Above all, that vision should be grounded in the future, for that is where the lives of their students will be played out.

As we hope is apparent to all who have read the preceding chapters of this book, the proper education of teachers is anything but a simple issue. Thoughtful policy makers will realize the limitations of any single view of education and teacher education and resist simple solutions to complex problems. Moreover, perceptive policy makers will understand that truly effective remedies require greater recognition of systemic forces, entirely outside the field of education, that prevent teacher education from fulfilling its promise. The most critical task of policy makers is to craft policies and marshal public support to address these underlying forces, and it is to that issue that we now turn.

The speed, magnitude, and quality of school and teacher education reform and the enhancement of teaching as a profession are ultimately dependent upon society at large. To have great schools and teachers on a wide scale in the United States is an attainable objective, but only if this objective becomes a national priority. In France, the national newspaper *LeMonde* ranks the country's universities on the basis of the quality of their preparation of secondary school teachers. In Finland, teachers are paid nearly as much as doctors and lawyers, and there is great competition to enter a university and become a teacher. Much the same thing can be said about Japan and some other countries in Europe and Asia. In these countries, the teaching profession has status and prestige because the populace honors—in word and deed—their schools and the teachers in them. Citizens in these countries recognize that their national well-being demands quality schools staffed with quality teachers. America and its citizens can afford nothing less. Our best and final advice to policy makers faced with difficult decisions regarding the future of teacher education is to heed the words of the ancient Greek philosopher Thucydides, "What is honored in a country will be cultivated there."

NOTES

1. Richard Mitchell, *The Graves of Academe* (Boston: Little, Brown and Co., 1981). For other examples, see such books as: Arthur Bestor, *The Restoration of Learning: A Program for Redeeming the Unfulfilled Promise of American Education* (New York: Alfred A. Knopf, 1956); James D. Koerner, *The Miseducation of American Teachers* (Boston: Houghton Mifflin, 1963); Rita Kramer, *Ed School Follies: The Miseducation of America's Teachers* (New York: Free Press, 1991).

2. James Kilpatrick, *The Daily Oklahoman*, 21 December 1981, p. 14.

3. "Educators Disagree over Whether Private Schooling Is Better," *Birmingham Post-Herald*, 7 January 1993, sec. A, p. 6.

Selected Bibliography

Included are only works actually cited in this book that were especially helpful to the authors in the writing of the book.

A Nation Prepared: Teachers for the 21st Century. New York: Carnegie Corporation,
1996.

Barzun, Jacques. *Teacher in America*. Garden City, N.Y.: Doubleday, 1955.

Berliner, David, and Bruce Biddle. *The Manufactured Crisis: Myths, Fraud, and the
Attack on America's Public Schools*. Reading, Mass.: Addison-Wesley, 1995.

Bestor, Arthur. *The Restoration of Learning: A Program for Redeeming the Unfulfilled
Promise of American Education*. New York: Alfred A. Knopf, 1956.

Borrowman, Merle. *Teacher Education in America*. New York: Teachers College
Press, 1965.

Brameld, Theodore. *Education as Power*. New York: Holt, Rinehart and Winston,
1965.

Clifford, Geraldine Joncich, and James W. Guthrie. *Ed School: A Brief for Professional Education*. Chicago: University of Chicago Press, 1988.

Conant, James B. *The Education of American Teachers*. New York: McGraw-Hill,
1970.

Cremin, Lawrence. *The Genius of American Education*. New York: Vintage Books,
1965.

————. *The Transformation of the School: Progressivism in American Education,
1876–1957*. New York: Alfred A. Knopf, 1962.

Darling-Hammond, Linda. *The Right to Learn: A Blueprint for School Reform*. San
Francisco: Jossey-Bass, 1997.

————. *Solving the Dilemmas of Teacher Supply, Demand, and Standards: How We Can
Ensure a Competent, Caring, and Qualified Teacher for Every Child*. Kutztown,
Penn.: National Commission on Teaching and America's Future, 1999.

Darling-Hammond, Linda, and Gary Sykes, eds. *Teaching as the Learning Profession: Handbook of Policy and Practice*. San Francisco: Jossey-Bass, 1999.

Dewey, John. *Democracy and Education*. New York: Macmillan, 1916.

Doing What Matters Most: Investing in Quality Teaching. New York: National Commission on Teaching & America's Future, 1997.

Finn, Chester E., Jr. *We Must Take Charge: Our Schools and Our Future*. New York:
Free Press, 1991.

Goodlad, John. *Teachers for Our Nation's Schools*. San Francisco: Jossey-Bass, 1990.

Griffin, Gary A., ed. *The Education of Teachers*, pt. 1, Ninety-eighth Yearbook of the
National Society for the Study of Education. Chicago: University of Chicago
Press, 1999.

Houston, W. Robert, Martin Haberman, and John Sikula, eds. *Handbook of Research on Teacher Education*. New York: Macmillan, 1990.

Hutchins, Robert. *The Higher Learning in America*. New Haven, Conn.: Yale University Press, 1936.

Illich, Ivan. *Deschooling Society*. New York: Harper and Row, 1972.

Kaplan, Leonard, and Roy A. Edelfelt, eds. *Teachers for the New Millennium*. Thousand Oaks, Calif.: Corwin Press, 1996.

Kerchner, Charles, Julia E. Koppich, and Joseph G. Weeres. *United Mind Workers: Unions and Teaching in the Knowledge Society*. San Francisco: Jossey-Bass, 1997.

Long, Delbert H., and Roberta A. Long. *Education of Teachers in Russia*. Westport, Conn.: Greenwood Press, 1999.

Loveless, Tom, ed. *Conflicting Missions? Teacher Unions and Educational Reform*. Washington, D.C.: Brookings Institution Press, 2000.

Murnane, Richard J., and others. *Who Will Teach? Policies that Matter*. Cambridge: Harvard University Press, 1991.

Pauly, Edward. *The Classroom Crucible: What Really Works, What Doesn't and Why*. New York: Basic Books, 1991.

Powell, Arthur G. *Lessons from Privilege: The American Prep School Tradition*. Cambridge: Harvard University Press, 1996.

Promising Practices: New Ways to Improve Teacher Quality. Washington, D.C.: U.S. Department of Education, National Center for Education Statistics, U.S. Government Printing Office, 1998.

Rohlen, Thomas P., and Gerald K. LeTendre. *Teaching and Learning in Japan*. Cambridge: Cambridge University Press, 1996.

Saettler, Paul. *The Evolution of American Educational Technology*. New York: Libraries Unlimited, 1990.

Silberman, Charles E. *Crisis in the Classroom: The Remaking of American Education*. New York: Random House, 1970.

Stevenson, Harold W., and James W. Stigler. *The Learning Gap: Why Our Schools Are Failing and What We Can Learn from Japanese and Chinese Education*. New York: Summit Books, 1992.

Stigler, James W., and others. *The TIMSS Videotape Classroom Study: Methods and Findings from an Exploratory Research Project on Eighth-Grade Mathematics Instruction in Germany, Japan, and the United States*. Washington, D.C.: U.S. Department of Education, National Center for Education Statistics, U.S. Government Printing Office, 1999.

Tomorrow's Teachers: A Report of the Holmes Group. East Lansing, Mich.: Holmes Group, 1986.

Tyack, David, ed. *Turning Points in American Educational History*. Waltham, Mass.: Blaisdell Publishing, 1967.

Tyack, David, and Larry Cuban. *Tinkering Towards Utopia: A Century of Public School Reform*. Cambridge: Harvard University Press, 1995.

V. Sukhomlinsky on Education. Moscow: Progress Publishers, 1977.

Welsh, Patrick. *Tales Out of School: A Teacher's Candid Account from the Front Lines of the American High School Today*. New York: Penguin Books, 1987.

What Matters Most: Teaching for America's Future. New York: National Commission on Teaching & America's Future, 1996.

Whitehead, Alfred North. *The Aims of Education and Other Essays*. New York: Free Press, 1967.

Wilson, Kenneth G., and Bennett Davis. *Redesigning Education*. New York: Henry Holt and Company, 1994.

Index

About the Authors

DELBERT LONG is Professor Emeritus, School of Education, University of Alabama at Birmingham.

RODNEY RIEGLE is Professor of Education, College of Education, Illinois State University.